Doing E-Business

Upside Books examines events in business and management through the lens of technology. *Upside Magazine* is the preeminent magazine for executives and managers eager to understand the business of high-tech.

Published:

High Tech, High Hope: Turning Your Vision of Technology into Business Success, Paul Franson

Risky Business: Protect Your Business from Being Stalked, Conned, or Blackmailed on the Web, Daniel S. Janal

Web Commerce: Building a Digital Business, Kate Maddox

Managing Telework: Strategies for Managing in Virtual Workforce, Jack M. Nilles

Playing for Profit: How Digital Entertainment Is Making Big Business Out of Child's Play, Alice LaPlante and Rich Seidner

Business Speak: Using Speech Technology to Streamline Your Business, Daniel S. Janal

Doing e-Business: Strategies for Thriving in an Electronic Marketplace, David L. Taylor and Alyse D. Terhune

Doing E-Business

*Strategies for Thriving in an
Electronic Marketplace*

David Taylor, Ph.D.
Alyse D. Terhune

John Wiley & Sons, Inc.

New York • Chichester • Weinheim • Brisbane • Singapore • Toronto

To my wife, Karen, for her loving devotion, constant support, and extreme patience, and for actually reading and reviewing the entire book. To my parents, Dorothy and Edson, for raising me to be independent and make my own choices. And to Karen's family, who encouraged her to stay with me—in spite of everything!

To my husband, George McCathern, for his unending patience and support throughout this project. I love you. And to my parents, Helen and Wayne, who taught me that anything was possible.

Contents

Acknowledgments

This book could not have been completed without the help of our network of friends, colleagues, and clients. Thanks to our many friends who commented on our ideas and our writings. We want to especially thank several current and former Gartner Group colleagues for taking time to help us. These folks include Myron Kerstetter, Mike Schumer, Barbara Reilly, Erik Keller, Chuck Shih, Susan O'Connor, and Carol Rozwell. In addition, Charlie Garland of EBMatch provided a detailed review of several chapters. These critiques kept us from straying too far from our analytical roots.

Thanks to our clients for providing us with some great examples, both named and anonymous, as well as for giving us the opportunity to work with them over the past year. Specific mentions go to Bill Turturro and Jim Worth of Philips Lighting; Joe Davis of Dow Agrosciences; David Surber of AgConnnect (formerly with Dow Agrosciences); Ellen Holladay of Motion Industries; Jo-anne Boyd of Cebra; David O'Toole of Broadlane (formerly of Cebra); Zach Zettler of Sterling Commerce; Todd Ostrander and Mark Foege of Essential Markets; Rob Lerman and Rick Allen of B2BPKG; Dan Ferguson of Faulkner & Gray; Stuart Sawabini of Eventra; Grant Castle, Lynn Rotando, and Erin McAndrew of CMO Group; Peter Watts, Frank Wander and Libby Hamilton of Group Intelligence; and Jay Roccaforte and Barry Crawford of TPS Holdings.

Thanks also to the many people we interviewed during the course of this book. In some cases their companies or associations are mentioned in the book; in other cases not. These folks include Dr. Kimberly Young of the Center for Internet Addiction; Dennis DeAndre of Loopnet; David Kahl of PCQuote.com; Terry Waters of ScreamingMedia;

Calvin Braunstein and Gary MacFadden of the Robert Francis Group; Dave Jastrow of Computer Reseller News; Art Mesher and Beth Enslow of Descartes Systems; Tom Ryan of Esync; Chris Jones of SynQuest; Vinnie Mirchandani and Brian Sommer of IQ4Hire; Bruce Barlag of Crater Valley; Greg Stebbens and Ray Everett-Church of AllAdvantage; Rix Kramlich of i2 (formerly SupplyBase); Dion Buhman of AgWizard; Scott Sexton and Chris Renner of INC2inc; Paula Dunn and Mitch Bishop of Channelpoint; Melissa Joseph of PJM Interconnection; Tery Spitaro of Ogilvy & Mather; Bob Abromsky of Filmstuf.com; Cathy Subatch of IPNet Solutions; Ryan Moran of Carepackages.com; Doug Alexander of E-Campus.com; Don Buhman of Farmchem.com; Bill Bingham, Kurt Franke, and Esteban Gonzales of Nuforia; Pete Rumpel and Joe Ryan of the Hay Group; Paul Fennick and Tim Fay of Oracle; Steve Mott of Priceline.com; Deb Boulanger of Icon-Nicholson; Klaus Kater of Artificiallife.com; Kurt Weitzel of Nordstrom; Jack Ross of CRPG; Bud Mayo of Fibertech; Magnus Gink of Result Ventures; Daniel Hamburger of Grainger .com; and Bruce Guptill of CMGI Solutions.

We should also note that we have interacted with thousands of people involved in e-commerce and e-business in over a decade of consulting on the subject. A great deal of what we have put into this book is drawn from the strategic vision of our mentors and colleagues, juxtaposed against the practical experience and constrained realities of our clients.

Finally, we wish to thank our writing advisor, Claire Green, whose chapter edits often made the difference between relevance and irrelevance along with our editors, Jeanne Glasser at Wiley and Ginny Carroll at North Market Street Graphics, for helping us turn our ideas into a book.

Introduction

For a while, it was very fashionable to talk about the "new economy" as if traditional rules did not apply. Hundreds of profitless dot-coms were rewarded with hot IPOs, infinite praise by Wall Street analysts, and stratospheric valuations by professional, and not-so-professional, investors. Today some of these same Internet stocks are trading at 90 percent below their high points. Many seasoned executives are second-guessing their decision to leave the corner office for the garage, and venture capitalists talk less about B2B and B2C and more about the P2P ("path to profitability") in any startup. Seems like old times.

But while there is little doubt that the capital markets have moved way past the giddy stage, the roller coaster ride is far from over. As we progress from *starting* e-businesses to actually *running* e-businesses, just having an innovative idea or a new technology will not be enough. In fact, those ideas and technologies will need experienced management talent in order to scale and deliver real value—value that is shared throughout the economy.

What the past 3 years of furious technology and economic experimentation have done is form the basis for the next 20 years of business value. The trick will be to recognize and capitalize upon *real* value in the context of extraordinary and often disruptive change.

It is this ongoing *operational* environment for which we have written this book. Throughout the book, we offer both forward-looking e-visions and present-day practical strategies to guide e-business managers. Underlying both our e-visions and our advice are a few "golden rules" that we have garnered from analyzing and participating in e-commerce for the past decade. We believe that, properly applied, these golden rules will form the basis for virtually any long-term successful e-business.

■ THE GOLDEN RULES OF E-BUSINESS

1. *Buyers, not market makers, will drive the growth of e-business.* Much of the current focus has been redirected away from consumer commerce and toward B2B commerce, especially B2B exchanges, marketplaces, and other types of *cybermediaries.* This misses the point of e-business altogether. It presents e-business as a choice between investment opportunities rather than a transition of economic fundamentals brought about by the increase in buyer power. The final cost and, therefore, price of the car, CD, insurance policy, airfare, or research report is ultimately the issue. The shift toward buyer power puts margins throughout the supply chain at risk, regardless of the sales channel. In any value chain with decreasing margins, buyers and sellers will be reluctant to pay out their hard-earned money to any intermediary, whether real or cyber. Cybermediaries are actually more vulnerable than physical distributors, since the aggregation of information about products can easily be shifted to other points in the value chain.

Buyers, whether giant corporations or individual consumers, simply have more choice, more knowledge, and more power—and that power is growing. One of the inevitable results will be the tendency to buy direct where practical, with a corollary being the tendency to negotiate every price based on a real-time, shared knowledge of supply and demand. The more that the first movers are able to employ their early lessons from using the Web channel to constantly change their business model and the nature of the solutions they offer, the greater the degree to which they will be able to demonstrate lasting value in the e-age.

2. *Measuring e-business is much more than just measuring a web site's traffic and usability.* We are about to move into an era in which people will stop talking just about doing e-business and start talking about *how well* they are doing e-business. So far, about the only aspect of e-business

quality that companies measure is their web site design and traffic. But e-business is much more than that. Measuring an e-business is very different from the way businesses have been measured in the past. The keys to measuring the quality and value of an e-business are contained in three principle areas: (1) how well the company handles the integration of the flows of information to and from the online world; (2) how the company manages its relationships with its business partners as it shifts from the isolationist view to the community participant view; and (3) how the company adjusts its internal processes, policies, and practices to take advantage of new online business models. Our point is that new metrics for return on investment and success are needed when measuring an e-business: What we measure is different, how we measure it is different, and the benchmarks by which we judge success are different.

3. *Relationships are everything!* As we demonstrate at a number of points in this book, the ability to capture the hearts and minds of empowered customers is what really matters about e-business as it is practiced today. This usually involves understanding buyers at an emotional level and/or understanding the tasks that they must perform on a daily basis. That is hard to do when a company is just getting started and the management team is spending all its time raising money, hiring staff, and launching products. Hence, customer churn is, and will continue to be, a fact of life for any company that doesn't stop and take the time to really understand its customers. Most dot-coms not only don't do the needed research, but don't even give dissatisfied customers a chance to talk live to a person who can solve their problems. Such relationship-killing strategies will likely be the short-lived refuge of startups that cannot scale up their support staff as fast as their technology.

4. *Cybermediaries are a risky venture.* How many times have you heard or read the phrase, "We bring buyers and

sellers together," on the web site of a would-be market maker? This simple, almost noble, business objective managed to get a lot of e-marketplaces well funded over the last two years. But, given the congestion we've seen lately, a would-be market maker had better be able to figure out why these buyers and sellers haven't met already and, more important, why these buyers and sellers are going to continue paying the market maker once they've met.

Consumers and, particularly, business buyers won't use an intermediary more than once if they have a need to buy repeatedly and can buy directly from the seller for a better price. Entrepreneurs need a lot better sense of how they will add lasting value to these increasingly savvy online buyers and sellers. These come only from research and understanding, not from clever technology or a new twist to an old revenue model.

5. *Real collaboration among enterprises is very rare.* We are not suggesting that all the "collaborative" e-marketplaces announced in early 2000 by same-industry rivals are bogus. But we do believe that they will actually result in an increase in competitiveness among these same companies. That is, despite all of the hype focused on the increased efficiency brought about by buying consortia (e.g., Ford, GM, Daimler-Chrysler, and a hundred others), their overall impact is likely to be much less significant than most press stories would lead one to believe. Why? At the end of the day, these companies still must compete for the same buyer. Assuming they wish to survive as independent enterprises, each aspect of commonality must be balanced against some form of differentiation. Thus, each company will take the opportunity of working together to find new points upon which to compete. As a result, we believe it is unlikely that the vast majority of these collaborative efforts will have much long-term impact on the position of these companies in the market, on overall profitability, or on the cost of goods to the consumer.

But there are some significant implications of these

buyer consortia for the suppliers. Masked in a façade of "frictionless commerce" and corporate camaraderie, these consortia really just mirror a time-honored supply chain practice: dominant buyers dictating business practices and prices to suppliers. A related golden rule to arise from these buyer consortia is that the huge industry players will likely subsume prominent market makers and other intermediaries. In the end, the history of e-commerce suggests that the coalitions and their network of networks will splinter into their respective buyer-dominated supply chains before the companies will sacrifice their competitive advantage.

This book is all about treating the Internet as a fact of life, a pervasive aspect of business, and a strategic tool to improve a variety of aspects of business operations, as well as competitiveness and profitability. This book charges its readers to act responsibly—to avoid adopting technologies, marketing ploys, and belief systems that are valuable only if acted upon quickly because their value decays rapidly. It encourages its readers to spend at least as much money understanding customers as they spend pitching to them. And even though we are skeptical when people use the term "win-win" too often, we encourage you as readers to look for material ways to show suppliers and other partners that they are respected, even though we know that such respect may last only until you can get a better deal!

This book covers both the business-to-business (B2B) and business-to-consumer (B2C) aspects of e-commerce. But like these market segments themselves, our analysis intertwines them. In fact, we believe that the B2B and B2C segmentation will gradually dissolve over the next decade for many companies, as they concern e-business processes and how the Internet is used.

This book is more about the present and future, and less about the past. We make a number of predictions about the near-term future in each chapter, and offer suggestions and recommendations to help our readers capitalize on the trends and opportunities we foresee as having business impact.

Chapter

1

E-Consumers:
Power to the People

Information is power, or so the saying goes. If true, then Internet-enabled consumers should be some of the most powerful people in the world. But the reality is that the Internet only offers people the potential to use its information to become more powerful. Few consumers realize this potential. In fact, many of the consumers we talked with felt more overwhelmed than powerful, because of the glut of information available online. What most consumers want is the power to get the information they want and, more important, avoid the information they don't want. Of course, a big part of the information consumers don't want is the advertising that pays for the information they do want. Can you say "catch-22"? Consumers don't want to pay for information either, as we'll discuss later in this chapter.

One empowering aspect of the Internet, beyond simple access to information, comes from a reduced dependency on others. Take, for example, individual investors. No longer dependent on brokers, who get their information from analysts, who get their information from the press releases and the management of the companies they recommend, individual investors are now able to get those same press releases, marketing hype, and other information directly from the web sites of the companies in which they are considering investing. Better than that, there are over 20,000 infomediary web sites aimed at individual investors, all trying to empower them with information (that is closely intermingled with advertising). There are sites that rate the other sites, and even metamediary sites that offer a list of the best rating sites. The mere description of the market is overwhelming!

Savvy Internet users are those who figure out a method for integrating the dozens or hundreds of information and advisory sources to reach better conclusions than they might have reached by depending on a single source, such as a stockbroker. Less savvy Internet users are those who wind up accepting the advice of someone pointing to an investor bulletin board, because they *appear* not to have a hidden agenda. This strategy for using the Internet for investment (or other types of) advice looks particularly questionable when one considers the case of Jonathon Lebed, a 15-year-old boy who made $273,000 by buying stocks and then hyping them using aliases on Yahoo! Finance. His case illustrates the hidden agenda of many who give advice online.

Many consumers seem to have traded trust for power. Instead of blindly trusting their doctors, bankers, and brokers to be experts, an increasing percentage of consumers has chosen to second-guess these professionals by spending their days, nights, and weekends doing the research that they used to entrust to others. This process can be used to reduce transaction costs (e.g., stock trading commissions, banking fees, number of doctor visits) and may keep people from blindly accepting advice. On the downside, empowering consumers is also creating an air of what we would call global skepticism—a general mistrust of the ability of others to do their job and to act responsibly. Thus, Internet-empowered consumers also tend to be distrustful, skeptical, and even downright cynical. This is important for the management of corporations to understand, as they must develop new types of messages and new delivery vehicles designed to respond to these empowered, distrustful consumers.

■ TURN INTERNET INFORMATION INTO POWER

While it is easy to say that the Internet has caused a major shift in the balance of power to the consumer, we found that most of the Internet-using consumers we talked to are really not doing much to actually use the information they find online. Even though customers now have better information than customer service representatives or the average salesperson, most people are not using this information to negotiate a better deal.

> **E-Vision:** The quality and potential negotiation value of information available on the Internet will greatly outstrip the ability of average citizens to use this information to their advantage over the next two to three years, giving rise to a variety of analytical tools and third-party negotiation services that will help consumers exercise their market power.

One of the informal tests we conducted for this book was to go to corporate web sites of shipping companies, car dealers, banks, brokerage houses, phone companies, and other companies where price information, account status, and other transaction information is available online. The purpose of our test was to see whether we, as moderately sophisticated, nontechnical Internet users, could use the power of Internet information to get a better deal or special treatment, or just to overwhelm salespeople and customer service representatives with our superior information. Our results were not scientific, as there was no sampling procedure. But we found that in over half of the 20 or so situations where we tested our power, we were

able to get some sort of concession from companies—
mainly because we were able to impress the representatives with the information we had obtained from the
Internet. We also asked these corporate representatives
how often folks were using Internet information in negotiation. In most cases, the answer was: rarely (with the exception being the car dealers). The known flexibility of the
pricing of cars, combined with the easy availability of
dealer invoice data is causing over 40 percent of new car
buyers in the United States to walk into the showroom
armed with a printout of a direct car seller's Web page or
the dealer's invoice. We expect this trend will continue, as
shown in Figure 1.1, with the Web providing even better
tools for negotiating even more critical services up to and
including legal and surgical fees.

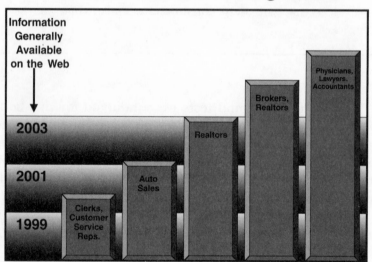

Figure 1.1 Better information offers the tools needed to
negotiate with a broader range of merchants and service
providers.

■ REFUSE TO PAY FOR CONTENT

When the commercialization of the Internet began in earnest in the period from 1994 to 1996, many entrepreneurs we spoke with were convinced that content was king and that consumers would pay to access a wide range of content. Forrester Research introduced a business model called Transactive Content (see Figure 1.2) that was embraced by many firms that wanted to sell content online. A variety of micropayment technologies were developed to enable consumers to pay for content in very small units (e.g., single-page documents), and dozens of companies were launched to market these technologies. What these companies didn't count on was the growing value of consumers—and that gathering a crowd online would enable an online advertising model that supported giving away almost all forms of content. The result was the failure of the transactive content model in almost every case where it was applied. That is, people are generally unwilling to pay for information

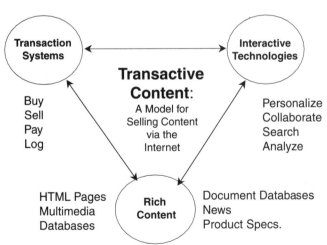

Figure 1.2 Transactive content. *Source:* Forrester Research.

online unless it meets a very specific and quantifiable need, is not available anywhere else, or has a near-term return on investment (e.g., financial advice from brokerages). Another reason selling content has, so far, failed is that there are so many advertising-sponsored, free content sites. (See Figure 1.2.)

■ GET PAID TO SHOP ONLINE

We have reached the point where there is so much content available online, for virtually every area of interest, that companies that really want to draw visitors (eyeballs) are paying consumers to view their messages. Since many consumers feel overwhelmed by the array of content available, it seems reasonable to offer payment for consumer awareness and attention. Presently, most companies have employed relatively simplistic pay-per-view models, where the consumer is paid for viewing web sites or reading e-mail messages. From the sweepstakes sites (iWon, TreeLoot) to the "we pay you to surf the Web" sites (AllAdvantage, Gotoworld, UtopiAd, Spedia, ClickDough), the growing power of consumers can be directly measured by the amount that companies are willing to pay for their time, attention, and contributions. But where is this headed? Are companies going to have to start bribing empowered consumers to evaluate their products, pay their shipping charges, and give them a stipend every time they use the customer service web site? The answer is yes and no. We doubt that the proliferation of general-purpose payout sites will continue much longer (as advertisers begin evaluating the quality of leads received and the conversion rate into sales). But the value of quality consumers (e.g., those with money, who are willing to spend it online, and are hard to reach via other media) will make some functionally and demographically specialized payout sites worth funding by advertisers.

■ START MULTIPLE WEB BUSINESSES

One of the most significant factors driving the growth of consumer power is the Internet's ability to turn all humans into e-business entrepreneurs. The ability to start a Web-based e-business for virtually nothing has been well documented, as has the fact that most such businesses are more recreational than anything else—that is, don't expect to get rich. It would seem from the media hype that the Internet economy has made it possible for a person to turn a business idea into a commerce-enabled web site before breakfast, launch a Web publicity campaign of 100,000 e-mails and get the business listed on 100 search engines before lunch, rack up 5,000 visitors and $50,000 in sales before dinner, and do the same thing all over again the next day. Getting $5 million in venture capital (VC) funding should only take another 48 hours! Of course, statistically, it's extremely likely that a Web business will fail, but the odds are still better than the lottery. What the Internet has done is empower entrepreneurs at a greater rate than ever before, and that is compelling to anyone with a vision. We believe that as more micromarkets are defined online (see Chapter 3), helping consumers be entrepreneurs will continue to be a winning strategy, but the growing number of companies pursuing the incubator opportunity will create a highly regionalized and vertically specialized marketplace for such services.

The bottom line is that having the vision and tools to start an e-business isn't enough. After all, the potential customers of these businesses are also powerful, skeptical consumers, who are no longer impressed with simple e-stores that are not clearly differentiated. People who want to be successful Web entrepreneurs must have real talent or skill or possess goods that have unique value. If so, these entrepreneurs can prosper by accessing the global market, assuming they know how to promote their efforts in a cost-effective manner and understand the needs of empowered consumers. (See Chapter 4 for more information on the tools.)

■ BAND TOGETHER: DEMAND AGGREGATION

Demand aggregation unites buyers and presents them as a buying group to interested sellers. Examples of demand aggregation sites include Accompany.com, Mercata.com, Buytogether.com (Germany), and dozens of others. Their aim is essentially the same: Use the power of the Web to pull together consumers from all over who are interested in specific products and services, and give them direct contact with sellers or even manufacturers who wish to sell direct.

There are variations on how these e-businesses implement the demand aggregation model. Some, like Accompany and Mercata, bring together a group of buyers to push down prices on products. Respond.com, on the other hand, puts buyers in touch with sellers to track down hard-to-find goods and services. NexTag helps an individual negotiate with a group of sellers.

The bottom line is that demand aggregation does save money for consumers, but it does not always produce the lowest price, as shown in Table 1.1. For example, not so long ago, Mercata offered a Ryobi drill via a Dutch auction, at a starting price of $40. As more visitors bid, the price dropped. When the so-called power buy was finished four days later, 500 people had bought the drill for $34—well below the suggested retail price of $89. Even those who had bid higher got the $34 price, while those who had made lower offers clicked away empty-handed. Accompany, which sells high-technology goods, uses a similar descending auction method. For example, Accompany listed a Palm V organizer on its site for $350, a price comparable with those of lower-price online retailers. Once Accompany had more than 20 bids at that amount, the price dropped to $325, where it stayed until the bidding was closed two days later, with 75 buyers. In a standard descending auction, not all buyers get the same price. Of course, prices drop only to a level that has been prenegotiated with the manufacturers.

TABLE 1.1   The Value of Buyer Aggregation

Web Retailer	Type	Method	Initial Price	Final Price
Amazon	Discounter	Price stays flat	$149.99	$149.99
eBay*	Auctioneer	Price rises	90.00	142.50
Mercata	Aggregator	Price falls as more buyers place orders	159.99	144.86[†]

*Used.
[†]Free shipping.

■ AGENTS AND BOTS AMPLIFY CONSUMER POWER

As we said up front, consumers have long since passed the point where more information equals more power, because they cannot absorb and understand all the information available to them. But over the next few years, consumers will be able to use powerful software agents that can visit, synthesize, and summarize nearly infinite numbers of web sites and pages of content. As this agent technology becomes more widely accepted, agents will be able to search more sites, compare more prices, and find closer matches for the things consumers want. (For a more detailed explanation of agents, readers should see Chapter 8, for their impact on pricing, or Chapter 12, for a discussion of the technology.)

But it is a mistake to believe that agents are focused primarily on empowering the consumer. In fact, agent technology shifts the power structure within an industry toward the more technologically sophisticated players—those that know how to manipulate software agents.

For a corporation, the key is to provide access to agents, while at the same time optimizing web site content to ensure unique or differentiated content is presented to the

> **E-Vision:** The opportunities for software agent technologies will increase significantly in the 2003–2004 time frame, thanks to the technology as well as the globalization of online markets.

consumer. Since agents will not be standardized anytime soon, and since the number of agents will multiply as they become more specialized beyond commodity product and price comparisons (e.g., by industry and by function), extensive testing of the interoperability of agents and agent technologies will have to be implemented before the broad proliferation of shopping agents will be possible.

■ CONSUMER POWER DRIVES COMMODITIZATION

We recently sat in on a series of focus groups where the attendees were CEOs of small B2B companies ($20 to $200 million annual revenue). The subject was the effect of Web business on customer relations. One of the biggest concerns expressed by these CEOs was that their customers might find out that they charged some customers more than twice as much for the same products as they charged other customers. The differences were not just due to volume discounts, but were in many cases the result of the fact that some customers were simply better negotiators than others. The issues are: (1) Will the availability of pricing information on the Internet force both B2B and B2C businesses to charge all their customers the exact same price?, or (2) will personalized pricing, based on loyalty or region or negotiating skills, lead to more price variability over time?

One common complaint is that the Internet leads people to be overly sensitive to price, which will tend to drive out companies differentiated by higher-quality products and superior service. We disagree with this contention. Virtually every day, we talk to people who are disappointed with things they purchased via the Internet, usually because of poor service and sometimes because of poor quality. The comparison sites and shopping bots may be programmed to find the lowest prices right now, but there is absolutely no reason to believe that consumers care any less about quality and service just because they are buying online. In fact, one of the most significant changes we expect over the next two years is that consumer power will be further manifested in the form of a variety of product and service guarantees, particularly by trusted third parties, such as credit card companies and other financial institutions. We also expect that a variety of tools will emerge to measure and compare such factors as product quality, total cost of ownership, and other variables, which will help shift attention away from price comparisons.

■ PRACTICAL STRATEGIES FOR COPING WITH POWERFUL CONSUMERS

1. Improve online sales and service guarantees. With e-business fraud and business failures gaining increasing attention, guarantees—particularly by known and trusted third parties—will be in heavy demand by both buyers and sellers. Such guarantees can help differentiate Web vendors, and they can help protect small start-ups from unscrupulous customers. Mainly, guarantees help give customers trust and a greater sense of control. When a consumer feels wronged by a company, sending an e-mail message to a customer support organization just doesn't cut it. Wronged customers want to speak live to someone and complain. They want positive assurance as to exactly how and when their problem will be handled, and they want this in real time.

Credit card companies in the United States, such as Visa and MasterCard, already protect consumers from fraud, thanks to the U.S. government's Uniform Commercial Code (UCC) Regulation E, the act that sets a $50 consumer liability limit on credit card transactions. But exercising this protection is still a hassle. Therefore, merchant guarantees will definitely separate the wheat from the chaff and create an opportunity for financial institutions to offer third-party guarantee services.

By 2002, one of the major factors used to rate Web businesses will be the strength of their guarantee and whether the guarantee is offered in conjunction with a third party. For example, eBay, Amazon, Go Networks, Yahoo! Auctions, and other e-tailers use a service from Iescrow, which charges from 1 percent to 4 percent for its service and holds payments until goods are received and the customer is satisfied. But with the growing amount of fraud, e-tailing failures, and the subsequent consumer distrust, the market for escrow services, performance guarantee services, and other third-party services will see significant growth over the next few years.

2. Place a clear value on consumer input. Another type of power exhibited on the Internet is the ability to express one's opinion. The Internet is chock-full of people with opinions. Of course, in the early days of the Internet it was reward enough simply to be able to rant and rave in the vain hope that someone else would read it. Nowdays, that's not enough. Empowered consumers want to get *paid* for expressing their opinions. That's where consumer review sites come in. Amazon, CNET, CDNow, iVillage, and thousands of others have encouraged consumers to write reviews and provide content to their sites without paying them, by catering to the human need for a sense of context or community.

But a new group of web sites has focused on just the opinions and reviews segment of the online community. By combining a review site with an online marketplace of related products, these businesses seek to turn the sense of empowerment that comes with writing reviews into transaction revenue, while also getting ad revenue from merchants who wish to reach these enthusiasts. Sites such as ePinions, Deja.com, Productopia, and ConsumerReview .com have formalized and structured (somewhat) the free-for-all that was (and is) the Usenet newsgroups. (See Table 1.2.) While both ConsumerReview.com and Deja.com generate content from existing Usenet communities with shared interests in audio equipment, fly-fishing, photography, and so on, ePinions.com pays reviewers from 10 to 30 cents each time someone reads their review and RateItAll uses a sweepstakes strategy to attract content.

In general, we believe that providing a high-quality, well-organized experience will prove more important than payments or sweepstakes. Empowered consumers don't want to waste their opinions on a community that is not as smart or savvy as they are. We expect that the winners in this market will concentrate on creating a focused, well-managed set of enthusiast sites and eliminate the name-calling and bickering that has characterized Usenet newsgroups.

TABLE 1.2   How Consumers Add Value to E-Businesses

Site	# Products	Reviews
ConsumerReview.com	30,000	125,000
Deja.com	39,000	900,000
ePinions.com	60,000	100,000
Productopia	2,000	3,000
RateItAll.com	10,000	150,000

Source: San Francisco Chronicle research, January 2000.

3. Offer a premium for the truth and for personal data. Have you ever considered auctioning off your birthday? Not the party itself—you'd still get to keep that—but auctioning off your date of birth and other pertinent information about yourself. Already companies such as AllAdvantage.com (and 20 to 30 others) are paying people to fill out forms and surf the Web. Other companies, such as Money for Mail, are paying consumers to enter information about themselves on the site and read e-mail advertisements from companies that want to reach their demographic. Consumers are paid when they read the e-mails.

Of course, any e-business that bases its revenue model solely on fees from personalized advertising is taking a big risk. Outrage over consumer privacy violations is likely to continue, causing companies that gather personal information to face increasing regulation, which will probably require them to use only aggregate data, shielding individual identities from the advertisers.

4. Exploit consumers' sense of power and their jaded attitudes. For example, iExchange.com has created a marketplace where amateur stock pickers can make money (usually $1 to $3 each) by selling reports they have written on their favorite stocks. iExchange tracks the stock picks and rates the "analysts" based on their track record. Thus, the "analysts" with the best track records are most likely to make money selling their reports. The business makes both advertising and transaction revenue, while further empowering consumers by offering them recognition—even though the names chosen are pseudonyms.

Some Web consumers are also becoming jaded. They have seen it all. They've checked out the price comparisons, they've read all the information they care to read about products, they've seen all they eye-catching video and graphics, they've read objective referrals in newsgroups and chat rooms, and, of course, they get lots of notifications of special promotions via e-mail. Companies that understand this attitude and know how to appeal to it will prosper more than companies that offer only a standard marketing pitch to these jaded consumers. For example, the web site for Slim Jims—the stick-of-meat product—reflects the aggressive, cynical attitude of its youthful target audience very well.

5. Show you are loyal to your customers. Customers have too much power, thanks to the Internet, to remain loyal to any company. In fact, the issue isn't about measuring customer loyalty, but rather measuring merchant loyalty. Nor is the issue just one-to-one marketing. Certainly personalizing content to expressed interests and remembering what someone bought last time are good things. But consumers have come to expect this from Web merchants. The question is: What can companies do to demonstrate their loyalty to customers beyond personalization? We believe the answer is: Make the target clear. Tell web site visitors that you don't want every consumer on your site. This, again, reflects the trend toward more focused micromarkets over the next several years. It is also important to make it clear that for each customer there will be a guaranteed, consistent level of support, including human contact.

■ CONCLUSION

Consumers have gained substantial amounts of informational power via the Internet. But in many cases their power is underutilized. Sometimes, consumer power is manifested through new demand aggregation marketplaces that make list prices and suggested retail prices little more than a faint memory. Whatever the manifestation, the key to understanding what will happen to Internet-enabled consumer power is to be found in the phrase *balance of power.* E-businesses will have to not only recognize the power the Internet gives consumers (e.g., by moving away from fixed pricing), but also further empower consumers with additional information.

Empowered consumers want more services and tools to help them avoid the clutter of marketing messages, most of which are irrelevant. It is important to understand just what consumers need and demand from an e-business. It is also important to understand that as consumers become more powerful, they become increasingly distrustful of those who provide content. They have learned that, all too often, content providers are motivated by some hidden relationship between themselves and their partners or affiliates.

The bottom line is that there is an opportunity to charge for content, but only if the quality can be guaranteed and only if the charges are discrete (e.g., a small membership fee). Empowered consumers are looking for more control over their environments, and control over media is one important aspect of this. To see the future of Internet interfaces, take at look at the personal TV systems (e.g., from Philips and Panasonic) that give viewers a set of tools and services to control what they watch and when. We believe these systems are leading-edge indicators of the type of Internet content controls that consumers will be willing to pay for. The period from 2001 to 2003 will see a greater emphasis on the separation of the high-end (i.e., nonsponsored, high-speed, agent-driven) Internet experience from the low-end (or sponsored, low-speed, find-it-yourself) experience.

Building E-Motionally Involving E-Businesses

We are involved with the Internet in many ways every day. It brings us information about the weather, what to wear, what to buy, what to do, what is happening. Even when we learn about such things from other sources, the Internet may be behind it all (e.g., the writer of a TV newscast who uses an Internet newsfeed as the source of a story). Whether we are conscious of it or not, the Internet intrudes on every aspect of our work and our personal life. It is a force that pulls us and pushes us in different directions. Its information causes us to make different decisions, and its communities cause us to have new global, yet impersonal, reference points in judging ourselves and the things around us. But even as it pushes us, pulls us, and shapes our lives, the Internet is gradually becoming just another part of life. The more pervasive it becomes, the more invisible its influence.

The Internet is both good and bad at the same time. It may be critical to doing a job, but it can also waste time and resources. Sometimes the Internet becomes a surrogate family or community that steals time and attention from one's actual family and community.

> **E-Vision:** Over the next few years, more than 30 percent of the content development and Web marketing expenditures will go toward adding personality, attitude, and humanity to web sites, in order to generate loyalty and increase profit margins by shifting the buyer focus away from price shopping.

■ WHAT PEOPLE DO ON THE INTERNET

In behavioral studies published in early 2000 by Georgia Tech University's Graphics, Visualization and Usability Center, 86 percent of respondents stated that they go on the Web to find specific information or to accomplish a task. Consumers are increasingly task oriented as the Web becomes a routine part of their everyday lives. This helps account for the relatively low reported weekly usage of the Internet: an average of 5 to 10 hours per week, depending on the study. A 1999 study by Forrester Research suggests that more than 30 percent of Internet users shop while online, even if that may not be their initial reason for getting on the Internet. This is up from 19 percent in 1997. Also, people spend fewer than 10 minutes on even the most popular sites.

The bottom line is that most e-businesses have not been able to get people to spend more than a few minutes on their site, and most of that time is not spent shopping. If these companies are going to continue to justify their advertising rates, they need to take action to increase the time the consumers and business customers spend on their site. We believe the solution is to understand and increase the factors that generate emotional involvement. (See Figures 2.1 and 2.2.)

■ HOW PEOPLE FEEL ABOUT THE INTERNET

Studies by the University of Texas, Georgia State University, and the Kellogg Graduate School at the University of Michi-

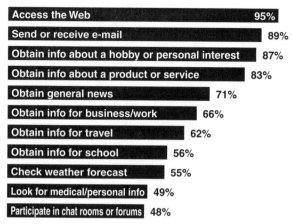

Figure 2.1 What people are doing online. Multiple answers were possible. *Source:* Intelliquest, 10 1998.

gan all indicate that people are developing specific patterns in their use of the Internet. In some cases, the Internet is a facilitator of communication among far-flung individuals regarding the most mundane and the most bizarre personal interests, hobbies, and lifestyles. In other cases, the Internet is a global soapbox from which to make impassioned pronouncements on all conceivable topics. The Internet is emotionally involving when the content placed there by individuals and groups was produced with emotion or the content was specifically designed to produce emotion. Beyond such political and personal content, those sites that facilitate interpersonal interaction are also emotionally involving. Sites that feature chat, clubs, gaming, and auctions are emotionally involving, since real people are being

Figure 2.2 Time online per week. *Source:* eStats, 1999.

connected by the Internet. These types of web sites have the most stickiness (in terms of both time spent on the site and the number of return visits by a person), according to Nielsen//NetRatings.

Over the last few years, best-of-breed e-business web sites have been creating a sense of involvement on the part of their customers—for example, auction sites such as eBay, gaming sites such as Snap, and shopping sites such as Price-line. However, we argue that the vast majority of efforts to create emotional involvement have been ineffective. Most e-businesses are doing a poor job of involving their visitors emotionally because they are too focused on loading up their sites with as much stuff as possible, in an effort to offer something for everyone. The goal is to generate more visits, which leads to more advertisers. But, ultimately, the number of Web hits will not ensure success. Web e-businesses will never be able to compete with TV because they haven't bothered to understand what it takes to really involve people emotionally. The purpose of this chapter is to analyze emotional involvement and offer suggestions to e-businesses on how to make their web sites more compelling for the audience that they are targeting.

> **E-Vision:** Because most people who shop online are not getting on the Web with that as their primary task, adding shopping to other, emotionally involving, content will be more profitable than creating sites that are focused solely on shopping.

■ HOW PEOPLE FEEL ABOUT E-BUSINESSES

The businesspeople and consumers we interviewed reported feeling few if any emotions when they are buying, selling, or otherwise interacting with e-businesses via the Internet, even though other media and other types of Web content are able to produce a wide range of types and degrees of emotional involvement. To improve the emotional involvement of visitors with e-business web sites, we present an analysis of some of the most important emotions that can be (and are) generated by the Internet and we suggest how e-businesses can work to generate and manage each of the emotions. To succeed as Internet markets mature, e-businesses must understand how visitors experience the many possible electronic interfaces to their organization (e.g., computer, personal digital assistant, Webphone). Differentiation via affect, or emotional experience, will prove to be a major step forward in the refinement and reorganization of e-businesses over the next few years.

➤ Euphoric

Almost 86 percent of Web users report that they are trying to find something or accomplish some task. While finding just the right site may not feel like finding the pot of gold at the end of the rainbow, designers should recognize this characteristic and put it to use. However, less than 20 percent of the e-businesses whose sites we surveyed had a search engine. For those sites that did, the engine was generally very basic with few options. Since the goal is to involve users and make them feel euphoric about the site, it is important to let users know about all the different things that are on the site: Count the elements of information, count the documents, and so on. Let visitors know what other people have searched for and what they have found. Track and post the most frequent searches, along with the FAQs (frequently asked questions), so people can understand what searches are likely to be successful and get a sense of what others are looking for and expect from your site. To avoid creating negative emotions (such as frustration) from searching, it is important to test and improve the search engines regularly. Providing examples of how the engine works also can cut down on negative emotional responses.

➤ Delighted

The literature on creating customer delight is extensive. John and Sheryl Paul, in their book, *Achieving Customer Delight in Your Organization* (Association Works, 1999), found that customer delight occurs when a company clearly goes above and beyond expectations. For a web site to accomplish this, a company must understand what customers expect from the site. It must know exactly what other, similar sites offer and how the experiences of the different sites compare. This is the only way to ensure that customer expectations are overfulfilled. Initially, Web electronic commerce (EC) companies such as Amazon did this by offering a larger selection than local stores and shipping orders within a few days. Now, as customer expectations have heightened, achieving customer delight is more difficult. The best way is to do the necessary research to determine what about your business or industry is particularly frustrating to customers and to focus on improving that interaction. We suggest e-businesses focus on something other than time savings, because there are limits to how much this can be improved. For most companies, service, human interaction, product quality, and consistency are more likely to generate customer delight.

➤ Self-Satisfied

All businesses want their customers to be satisfied: with their products or services, with their interactions, with service levels, and with the company itself. In their desire to satisfy the customer, they can sometimes miss the customer's need to feel that he or she accomplished something independently. Think about how you feel if you negotiate a great deal on a new car or when you complete a project on time and under budget. Focus on ways to make customers feel that same sense of accomplishment. One of the best tools for doing this is adding auction or gaming functionality, or providing people with the opportunity to negotiate with others or even with bots. This type of functionality gives people a chance to put themselves on the line, take a risk, and make a decision. This sense of risk, of course, is one of the key reasons that auction sites (such as eBay, uBid, and OnSale) retain their visitors so well. Another way to create self-satisfaction is to enable people to do good things while online. For example, the shopping service GreaterGood.com has managed to become a highly rated site in a short time by donating a portion of every transaction to the charity of the user's choice. The company also finds out an above-average amount of information about its visitors in the process.

➤ Powerful

Consumers have gained a lot of power through the use of the Internet (see Chapter 1). Customers feel like smart shoppers when they can find better bargains or be better negotiators. But e-businesses could help customers feel powerful in other ways, too. For example, more e-businesses could follow the lead of the portals and offer "My" versions, which enable customers to make specific decisions about how a site appears to them, what products they want to see, and, most important, what they don't want to see. Generally, e-businesses are so focused on creating opportunities to generate impulse buying of ancillary items that they try to put as broad a selection as possible on the screen. Few e-businesses have taken the step of allowing shoppers to see only a small subset of available products, as that would probably reduce advertising revenues. Because enabling this editing would create a sense of power and control for the customer, we believe the benefits of this type of personalization would be well worth the loss of advertising or impulse purchase revenue.

➤ Confident

Confidence arises from a strong sense of self, based on years of family life and socialization, and from being knowledgeable. Of course, joining a Web community or participating in a chat room will not have a major impact on a person's self-confidence. But just as crisis counselors help people in difficult situations, the Internet and the people who use it may make a difference to another person's life, as has been documented in Howard Rheingold's *Virtual Community* (MIT Press, 1992) and elsewhere. People also feel confident when they are well informed, and the Internet is spectacularly good at providing information. With this global trivia machine at one's command, a person can always be confident of having up-to-date information on subjects from the mundane to the bizarre. Beyond having news and trivia contests on one's web site, one example of helping visitors feel confident might be to offer a moderated business advice service that is personalized to each member or to each job title.

➤ Amused

Companies that develop a strong sense of humor about their sites and their offerings will be able to improve loyalty. A quick comparison of the Web with TV indicates that touching the audience's sense of humor seems much more important to television networks and producers than to corporate Web masters. The Web is a medium that offers multiple channels—from home shopping, to sex and gambling, to the highest levels of academic insight. Every conceivable type of humor could be accommodated. But although there are thousands of sites with humorous content, most e-business sites do not integrate humor well with e-commerce. We believe developing sites with a humorous "personality" is one of the best ways to generate emotional loyalty and the type of involvement that makes TV sitcoms the subject of workplace conversations. All companies would benefit from that kind of word of mouth.

➤ Bored

The cardinal sin of web sites is to be boring. Although there are many ways to bore the visitors to a web site, one of the most critical problems is a boring appearance, since this can keep visitors from even reading about your company or clicking any button. One problem with turnkey web site packages is that they leave little or no room for the company's personality. The only options are button positions, labels, and colors. Of course, a site that looks interesting won't necessarily attract and retain visitors. But when a company chooses a web-site-in-a-box, visitors are that much more likely to be bored by the home page and never to read the content the company has so painstakingly developed. In general, we would recommend not using any of the web-site-in-a-box template products if the company has an interest in developing the emotional involvement of visitors to the site.

➤ Shy

For the painfully shy, the Internet is a great way to find, buy, and sell things while avoiding human contact. Many people like the impersonality of the Internet (until they have a problem—then they want to talk to a human). When they don't have a relationship with a company, it's incredibly easy to switch from one provider to another without guilt or confrontations. Clearly, some people like the personal touch, but it is important not to force a relationship on people who don't want one. For example, companies that use follow-up e-mails with marketing appeals should implement them with the opt-in feature (where the visitor must actively choose to receive the message) rather than either an opt-out or a no-choice implementation. Studies by Forrester (released March 6, 2000, and quoted in Ecommercetimes.com) have found that people do not like to be intruded upon, and opt-in e-mail gives consumers the power over the relationship. Thus, they are somewhat less hostile to marketing messages, and various studies have found they are two to four times more likely to act upon them. We expect continued growth of opt-in messaging and other tools that don't try to force a relationship on customers and make them work to get "uninvolved" or unsubscribed.

➤ Anonymous

Over the last decade, chat systems have grown steadily in popularity. This is due, at least in part, to the anonymity that users enjoy. Chatters get to create a persona that many people use to enhance their actual personality. About 30 percent of Web users lie when filling out online forms—even about demographic characteristics such as age, nationality, appearance, income, residence, race, weight, and, of course, gender. Corporations trying to capitalize on Internet psychology should develop psychographic segmentation strategies that take advantage of this need for anonymity and arm's-length interactions. Companies should also assume that any databases built from forms filled out by consumers are highly questionable, unless they have been independently verified. Thus, we believe there will be a growing opportunity for service companies that will independently verify the information that people supply via online forms.

➤ Overwhelmed

Back in 1996 and 1997 when the Internet was just taking off, there was a lot of research into the idea that people were feeling overwhelmed by all the information available online. Even as recently as 1998, a study by Reuters (a news service and major purveyor of information) found that 61 percent of managers believe information overload is present in their own workplace, and 80 percent believe the situation will get worse before it gets better. Among American managers, 48 percent said that this sense of overload led to decreased job satisfaction; 47 percent of both U.S. and U.K. respondents said this puts a strain on their personal relationships. As a result, people are looking for ways to simplify the Internet, while still giving them a feeling for the breadth of information and services it provides. Consumer portals and the industry-focused business-to-business portals can play this role. One of the most helpful things an e-business can do is to develop a clear image or brand, so customers can stereotype its site. The easier it is to mentally pigeonhole an e-business, the less overwhelmed people will be. In both the business-to-business (B2B) and business-to-consumer (B2C) markets, there is a real danger of people being overwhelmed by the multitude of similar sites. The shakeout in B2C and B2B is already beginning to force the also-rans in each segment to develop more of a niche focus.

> **E-Vision:** Ninety percent of would-be portal sites that contain lots of content (shopping, clubs, auctions, news, chat, advice, polls, sweepstakes, horoscopes, jokes, gift registries, buying guides, research, etc.), in the hope that something will be sticky, will find they are wasting their money, as visitors seek out more focused sites that better match their interests and needs.

➤ Frustrated

Frustration is at the opposite end of the emotional spectrum from delight. Frustration results when a person can't find what he or she is looking for, even though the person knows it's out there somewhere or when a frustrated customer can't reach a live human when he or she needs to. E-businesses must understand directly from their customers what are the most frustrating aspects of their relationships with the company, from hard-to-use Web pages to customer service representatives who cannot answer questions. In addition to solving such problems, companies must make it clear to customers that the customers' comments, complaints, and ideas helped solve real problems. This gives customers more reason to air their frustrations in the future.

➤ Suspicious

Relationships, as well as information, are overloading customers these days. Too many business executives who have read Peppers and Rogers' *The One-to-One Future* (Currency/Doubleday, 1993) have oversimplified its message to the point where they feel that they must reach out and touch customers as often as possible. Many companies are implementing customer relationship management (CRM) and interactive marketing applications, which often call for gathering lots of customer data to present customers with just the right products or services. As a result, more and more customers are suspicious about how companies will use their data, so they provide incorrect information whenever possible. Many companies feel they have addressed this issue by putting their privacy statement on their web site and putting the TRUSTe logo next to it. But we believe the suspicion about data collection goes far deeper, and customers will begin demanding more restrictions on what is done with their information. Privacy management (the process of controlling how a person's information can be used) will be a growing market for the next several years.

➤ Addicted

Addiction is the ultimate form of involvement, and Internet addiction is growing. About 6 percent of the 17,251 persons surveyed by Dr. David Greenfield of the Center for Internet Studies meet his criteria for Internet addiction, and more than 30 percent report using the Internet to escape from negative feelings. Certainly one of the most addictive features of the Internet is the ability to interact with other people and observe events (for example, auctions or the stock market) in real time.

Somewhat shy of addiction, but still very important to e-businesses, is obsession with information. A study by Dr. Kimberly Young, in her book, *Caught in the Net* (Wiley, 1998), found that 72 percent of respondents to a survey felt that Internet use was beginning to lead to obsessive information gathering. For e-businesses, it is important to offer information of real value to go along with all the marketing hype and catalogs. Developing comparatively objective white papers, which offer an analysis of what is going on in your market and explain why your business is different, without giving away any trade secrets is an excellent way to add value and is growing in use. Licensing or referencing any reports by Wall Street analysts or other objective research firms will also give the obsessed persons something valuable to consider. This is particularly important to purely Web-based e-businesses, which, we have found, rarely offer enough detail about their company and their industry on their sites.

■ PRACTICAL STRATEGIES FOR CREATING EMOTIONAL INVOLVEMENT

1. Appeal to specific interests. In the old days, whoever owned the relationship with the customer owned the future. The goal was to build a relationship with customers that would bridge the life cycles of particular products or services. In the world of the Internet, customers gain more and more power through information about price, quality, and selection, so customers own their relationships. This growing power carries fundamentally significant implications for all businesses. Empowered customers will force changes in corporate strategies and tactics. Appealing to one or more of the emotions discussed in this chapter is certainly one of the ways to involve customers and turn their power into an advantage. Appealing to their interests is another. While general shopping e-businesses are doing fairly well, the interest-branded sites have been very successful in adding shopping to their list of services (e.g., Eonline.com, web site for the entertainment-focused TV network, has successfully added shopping, while maintaining its demeanor and focus).

2. Get business partners to care. A decade ago, the dominant business model for e-commerce was large retailers forcing suppliers to do business electronically. Today, the Internet has opened up alternative channels for suppliers. Both manufacturers and distributors are bypassing retailers. Global markets are creating new outlets for finished products, components, and services. In light of these changes, all companies, whether real or dot-com, need to figure out how to involve their suppliers in critical business decisions on a real-time basis. For example, we recommend that readers consider implementing a variety of collaborative applications, which we discuss in detail in Chapter 11. The type of ongoing contact that collaborative planning and other applications require is more likely to create caring and understanding on the part of management throughout the value chain. As executives understand the importance of the shared fate of the companies, it makes it less likely that companies will seek to break off long-standing business relationships in favor of short-term financial gain.

3. Get employees emotionally involved. In their haste to improve customer service and relationships with trading partners, some fast-growth e-businesses have wound up sacrificing employee satisfaction and loyalty. Despite all the talk of Internet billionaires and millionaires, many rank-and-file employees have shared the largesse marginally or not at all. And many of these potentially disgruntled employees are in customer-facing jobs such as those in contact centers, marketing, and sales, where they can damage a start-up's reputation for service at the very time that e-businesses must differentiate on something more long-lasting than price or selection. Efforts to placate these employees with traditional team-building rhetoric are falling on cynical ears. Those who are mobile find it easy to switch jobs, raising costs and hurting service quality. Those who are less mobile are considering unionizing, among other things. Some of the most visible efforts are under way in Seattle, where the WashTech union (washtech.org) is attempting to organize Microsoft's and Amazon's frontline employees. The lesson for e-businesses is simple: Make genuine efforts to understand the pressure being felt by frontline employees. It may be necessary to overinvest in these folks, since lack of motivation can be devastating to customer delight and other relationships.

4. Add personality, attitude, and character. Everyone loves a bargain, or so they say. But everyone isn't *in love* with bargains. Just because a business offers competitive prices, great selection, and an e-mail notification service doesn't mean that visiting the company's web site will produce the emotional response necessary to make visitors addicted. You need to add personality and character to a Web business. One simple way to do it is to hire a spokesperson with a personality that matches the message. Flooz, for example, hired Whoopi Goldberg to convey its message to the mass market, and many other dot-coms have followed suit. Another way to do this is demonstrated by Send.com, creator of The Giver, an unseen gift-giving bumbler, in the company's TV commercials. This character's personality is cleverly and humorously reinforced in the text of the Send.com web site. Volvo wanted to enhance the youth appeal of its cars in the United States, so it developed a fictional character called Lars. Lars was a young Swedish guy with a decidedly American attitude. He traveled around the United States, writing about his exploits on a site called SwedenRules. The campaign was successful in drawing in young viewers (via other media cross-promotion) and it demonstrates that character and personality—even if they're not real—can do more to involve people than just facts.

> **E-Vision:** E-businesses that spend the money and effort needed to build characters, stories, and situations on their web sites will be more effective at generating emotional involvement than those that compete on price, convenience, or selection. This emotional involvement will, in turn, generate greater loyalty and word-of-mouth advertising, and greater market value.

5. Add just enough community, but not too much. Some of the most emotionally involving and attitude-conveying web sites are run by and targeted at women and girls—for example, iVillage.com and Oxygen.com. In addition to sites that target every woman, many sites are targeting subsegments of this population. ChickClick, a network of independent, female-powered web sites, produces intelligent, sassy women's content aimed at younger women (65 percent of viewers are between 18 and 35). And the site sells a lot of advertising. ChickClick uses a classic Web business model, but because it conveys attitude it achieves above-average stickiness for its target demographic.

6. Connect the company's site with entrenched emotional experiences. Sites related to movies and TV shows are good at creating stickiness because they are able to transfer the emotional experience from the other medium onto the web site. This is not to suggest that we believe e-commerce web sites should present soap operas, but it does mean that you can profit from understanding what else people want from their lives and try to add some of that into the experience on your site.

7. Learn what people care about and what they don't care about. A site that is visually interesting and presents simulated dialogs with software robots won't succeed unless it fills a need. Understand what people want and expect from your company and your site. Stop focusing only on what is visually interesting and focus more on what is emotionally involving. There are several methods for doing this. One is to design a study of customers, noncustomers, and prospects to examine what makes the company, product, or service unique. Some companies may wish to conduct a series of focus groups with a sample of the web site's visitors (and nonvisitors with comparable characteristics). Another is to observe site visitors one at a time and have them talk about what they are thinking and feeling as they interact with the company via phone or the Web. Still another methodology involves visiting chat rooms and inviting (via e-mail) the most vocal advocates and detractors of a company's products or services to Web-based discussion forums. Bring them together (online or in person) for a frank discussion of why they like, love, hate, or don't care about particular companies, brands, products, or services. By combining multiple methodologies it is possible to understand what generates emotional involvement and how it can be nurtured, managed, or extinguished.

8. Assume that people lie when filling out online questionnaires. It is very important to supplement the online data collection efforts with psychographic profiles compiled with the observational research methodology. For example, Jack Katz, in his recent book *How Emotions Work* (University of Chicago Press, 1999), used real-world observational research to understand what causes emotional behavior. This type of methodology is particularly important to understand why and how web sites generate (or don't generate) emotional involvement and under what circumstances this leads to repeat visits, purchase behavior, discussions of the web site with other people, and so forth. We expect there will be substantial new research using these methodologies from the academic community and many market research companies. The growing pervasiveness of webcams as a PC accessory will enable real-time observation of users' Web behavior and emotional reactions—as inferred from facial expressions—on a massive scale.

■ CONCLUSION

Most of the companies we talked with in the course of researching this book had never really thought about the type of emotional involvement they wanted to produce in their target user community. We believe this is one of the biggest mistakes companies make when defining their online strategy. Until that far-off day that software agents are the dominant type of life form wandering around the landscape of the Web, the target audience will continue to be human beings. One of the best investments a company can make is to bring in 100 or so humans (preferably a representative cross section of the target audience), have them try out the site with no instructions, and ask them to verbally express what they are feeling while they use it. Then supplement this research by having this same group of people talk—with little direction—about what they like and don't like about using the Internet and their favorite and least favorite web sites and other business experiences. This can reveal a great deal about how to produce emotional involvement. In general, this type of observational research can be much more valuable than either focus groups in controlled settings or questionnaire research in getting at the true feelings of the target audience.

From E-Tailing to Consumer Automation

If you blink, you'll miss the market. In just the last year, e-tailing went from being the hot e-commerce segment to being almost a dirty word. Both the venture capital community and the stock markets have turned their backs on virtually any business idea that even smells like an Internet retail store. While Internet shoppers will spend over $20 billion in 2000 (and nearly $2,000 per U.S. household) on retail goods such as books, groceries, computers, and clothing, e-tailing still equals less than 1 percent of total U.S. retail sales, according to the National Retail Federation. According to the U.S. Commerce Department's first report on e-commerce, issued in February 2000, online retail sales represented only 0.6 percent of the $821.2 billion in total U.S. retail sales for the period from October through December 1999. However, if online consumer retail spending in North America is going to hit $124 billion by 2004, as predicted by the Gartner Group, e-tailing is going to have to move to a next-generation model. We call this model *consumer automation*.

■ PROFIT WARNING

One of the reasons that e-tailing has fallen out of favor with venture capitalists and the stock markets is that so many folks actually believed the hype that e-tailers would be much more profitable than brick-and-mortar retailers because they didn't have physical stores to build and maintain. This, of course, was never more than a marketing pitch on the part of e-tailing entrepreneurs. In reality, e-tailers may well be less profitable than established brick-and-mortar stores because they have to build warehouses and infrastructures, just like traditional stores. They also have to hire and train people to deal with returns, and they have to spend like crazy to establish brand amid the tremendous noise of the Internet. For example, think about all the dot-com ad spending on television, even during the Super Bowl, where a 30-second ad costs $2 to $3 million. At this point, except for Amazon, eBay, and Priceline.com, there are very few strong e-tail brands. Lacking brand, many e-tailers are trying to attract customers by slashing margins to razor-thin or nonexistent levels. Does that sound like a long-term strategy?

So is e-tailing dying? We think not. We believe e-tailing has reached its first dip in a "hype cycle" that will see the trashed expectations of investors, customers, and employees recover slowly over two to three years. Cookie-cutter online storefronts are boring, and the number of new shoppers, while still increasing, is growing at a slower rate than in the last two years. The easy explanation is that the thrill is gone. The somewhat cynical truth is that people can no longer impress their friends at cocktail parties by talking about what they bought online. Nevertheless, it is not unreasonable to expect a pause while e-tailing reinvents itself, changing from a novelty act to a slice of life—a necessary task or perhaps even an integral part of every person's life over the next decade.

Key to the reinvention of e-tailing is moving the shopping process beyond simply mimicking the physical world. Today's online process requires that consumers sort through a thousand e-tailing sites that sell the items they want, browse through an interactive catalog, put the items they want in an electronic shopping cart, and pay using their credit card. While it was absolutely necessary that first-generation e-tailing sites used real-world analogies in order to capitalize on existing experiences and help consumers cope with this new technology, future e-tailing success will go to those who figure out the next step.

■ E-TAILING IS ABOUT EFFICIENCY

Where do e-tailers go from here? We believe that growing consumer power and the introduction of microprocessors into a wide variety of home devices and appliances will result in a second generation of e-tailing applications that automate the unpleasant tasks of the shopping process. We use the term *consumer automation* to describe the future of e-tailing because a key reason consumers shop online is the inherent efficiency of the experience. They can have a better social experience or get a better sense of an item in a physical store than on the Web. People go online to buy because it takes less time, saves them money, and gives them access to an almost infinite variety of items. Given the shifting view of shopping from being a source of entertainment to being a tool to maximize efficiency, it makes no sense for consumers to engage in many fruitless online searches for household items, gifts, groceries, and so forth. We believe this will create a new type of software/service we call *household management*.

■ HOUSEHOLD MANAGEMENT APPLICATIONS

One of the e-business opportunities over the next few years will be the development of new types of household management applications. These applications will be a step beyond the bill payment and home inventory programs that already exist today to help consumers keep track of their bills, collections, consumables, and the like. We expect that the next generation of household management applications will offer replenishment agents that will search the Web, find goods or services from a series of merchants, and integrate the results into the household management application. The household management applications will be similar to the range of small-business B2B Web purchasing applications that are coming to market. Their role will be to assist high-end home owners (not every home owner will need or want these services) in managing the process of buying goods and services.

Examples of the type of value we expect household management applications will provide by 2003 include (1) online monitoring of the price of telephone, cable, electric, and other digitally switchable services, and shifting providers to optimize savings and/or service; (2) online monitoring of special deals at a preset group of merchants for a preset list of products, and automatically placing orders for preset quantities; (3) online monitoring of the household's inventory of consumables (e.g., via bar-code scanners in microwaves and/or refrigerators), and placing replenishment orders; and (4) online monitoring of bank and other account balances, shifting money based on pre-set criteria, and, of course, automatically paying bills.

■ AS E-TAILERS DIE, IS THERE LIFE BELOW THE TOP TIER?

In 1999, everybody wanted to be the next Amazon, or Yahoo!, or eBay. And they spent unbelievable amounts of money on advertising and promotion in order to achieve it (see Table 3.1). Most, of course, didn't make it. So, if 1999 was the year of e-tailing excess, then 2000 was the year of

TABLE 3.1   Retail Categories with Largest Increase in
Share of Online Ad Impressions

Rank	Category	Week of 7/5/99	Week of 11/8/99	Increase
1	Drug and toiletry	2.0%	8.9%	6.9%
2	Toys and collectibles	1.6%	7.9%	6.3%
3	Auction houses	11.4%	16.3%	4.8%
4	Office supply	0.7%	4.7%	3.9%
5	Jewelry and accessory	0.0%	1.6%	1.6%
6	Grocers	0.0%	1.6%	1.5%
7	Pet supply	0.1%	1.5%	1.3%
8	Home and garden	1.3%	2.3%	1.0%
9	Apparel	0.5%	1.4%	0.9%
10	Event and ticket*	0.0%	0.7%	0.7%

*Advertising began week of July 19.
Source: AdRelevance.

e-tailing redress. Many of the e-tailers, with their go-for-broke ad campaigns, got just what they were going for. But many Internet e-tailers are still spending more than 60 percent of their annual revenues on sales and marketing (their SMR ratio), according to a study by the *Industry Standard* in June 2000 (see Figure 3.1). With e-tailing layoffs for 2000 already reaching tens of thousands of workers, it's time for e-tailers to cut back even further on these expenditures and to work on alternative strategies to being the next big brand.

We believe the answer for most of the second- and third-tier e-tailers is that they will have to join one of the micromarket malls, which are being launched under the umbrella brands of the major portals and top-tier e-tailers. But will these lower-echelon e-tailers be able to find their audiences without the massive advertising blitzes? The

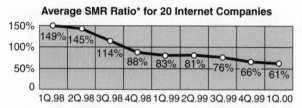

Average SMR Ratio* for 20 Internet Companies

*Sales and marketing expenditures expressed as percentage of revenue.

Figure 3.1 Net firms bring down marketing spending. *Source:* "Dot Coms Cut Ad Spending," *Industry Standard,* 6/12/2000.

short answer is: yes. The long answer is: It depends on how homogeneous their audience is, how well they are defined by their interests, and how well tied in they are to branding networks (see Chapter 4) or whether they are part of a micromarket mall.

Micromarket malls have already been launched by Yahoo! and Amazon (see Amazon's zShops and Yahoo!'s shopping mall). We also expect that such brick-and-mortar category killers as Wal-Mart and Kmart will enter the space by leveraging their physical presence and offering an e-market platform to specialty e-tailers, along with access to their e-fulfillment services. This will provide the micromarkets built on top of their platforms with a degree of integration and simplicity not possible from independent e-tailers. As a result, we believe the microsegmentation of the e-tailing industry will make it possible for e-tailers to serve the smallest conceivable demographic and psychographic segments, while still taking advantage of the brand equity and fulfillment capabilities of their partners. While we do not believe that all (or even most) independent e-tailers will go away over the next few years, we do expect that the requirements of powerful consumers, who increasingly view shopping online as efficient rather than fun, will force companies looking for micromarket opportunities to seek out one of a few dozen common platforms on which to build their store. Our recommendation is to focus the energies of the company on defining a unique space, a plan for continuous evolution of strategy, and a compelling marketing message.

> **E-Vision:** By 2002, over 25 percent of all niche-focused e-tailers will be part of one or more micromarket malls, which will provide a common set of branding, hosting, rewards, sourcing, and fulfillment services to those e-tailers.

IMPORTANT E-TAILING TRENDS TO WATCH

We predict the following trends will be important in the evolution of e-tailing.

➤ Auctions

Over the last several years, eBay and thousands of second-tier and specialty auction sites have transformed the auction industry by creating a global consumer-to-consumer marketplace. More recently, we have seen a trend away from specialized auction sites and the incorporation of the auction model into all forms of Web-based businesses. In other cases, e-tailers such as uBid and OnSale sell new products with broad availability and use an auction as a marketing tool. Case in point: Just as the auction for a particular model of digital camera ends, another auction for the same item begins with the same parameters. The marketing purpose behind this type of model is to lend the immediacy of an auction to the transactions. For consumers in real need of excitement, this model may offer advantages, but other options, such as shopping agents or demand aggregation sites will produce lower prices and offer a greater selection of comparable products. Nevertheless, we expect that the proliferation of auctions is all part of a move to flexible pricing, which we cover in detail in Chapter 8.

➤ Reverse Auctions

Also called *name your own price* after Priceline's implementation of the model, reverse auctions work very well for
sellers (such as airlines and hotels) that adjust pricing
based on yield management models. Yield management
refers to the fact, known to all who fly, that an airline seat's
price varies directly and continuously based on customer
demand and supply. But Priceline and others are proving
that a reverse auction is an ideal way to dispose of unwanted
or hard-to-sell inventory. For grocery stores, gas stations,
health clubs, and other retailers, the reverse auction is a
way to create store traffic by discounting items that are relatively high margin or that can serve as loss leaders for
other items in the product line or simply draw customers
into a store.

In the retail implementation of reverse auctions, such as
Priceline's Webhouse, consumers pay for goods in advance
online and then print out their list of prepaid items and
take it to the store. While this works to some extent like
couponing, it has the additional advantage to the store (and
Priceline) that some consumers simply forget to pick up
certain prepaid items, which increases the margin on this
type of business model. Retailers like the business model
because they get full retail price for all Webhouse purchases.
But the big issue clouding the success of Priceline's Webhouse is that, unlike airline seats and hotel rooms, most
groceries and gasoline do not lose their value (or cease to
exist) if not used by a particular date. (Technically, the yield
management models that govern airline seats and hotel
rooms do not work very well for goods that have a long shelf
life.) This is one of the main reasons that Webhouse has not
been able to convince most large manufacturers and oil
companies to absorb the discounts that Webhouse offers in
return for the increased loyalty they promise. We suspect
the major differences in the governing revenue models will
make it difficult for Priceline's Webhouse to generalize to
many categories of goods and services.

➤ Buyer Aggregation

Buyer aggregation, or demand aggregation, is based on the idea of creating a database of what people want or need and letting merchants bid to get that business (for example, the mortgage company eLoan and general-purpose aggregators such as iWant.com and eWanted.com). The value of these marketplaces to sellers depends on the size and quality of the group of people the market maker is able to pull together. In general, the more focused, the better for the sellers, who are able to target their marketing efforts and gain access to a relevant, homogeneous group of prospects. A variation on this model is the group buying model (for example, Accompany, Mercata, and LetsBuyit, which is a European implementation of the model), which pulls together a group of people who want the same thing and uses their combined clout to get volume pricing from sellers. While it sounds as though the buyer aggregation businesses will get customers the best price, there are two limitations: The level of discount has been predetermined between the market maker and the sellers, and these buying groups are often much smaller and less powerful than high-clout warehouse clubs like Sam's Club and Costco.

➤ Shopping Agents

Shopping agents (such as Bottomdollar.com) aim to give consumers access to comparison tools while still offering enough value (and price protection) to the sellers to make them willing to participate. This point is important since sellers must agree to have their sites shopped by these online agents. These agents present a difficult dilemma to the nonprice competitor: If you list your store, you never come out on top of the search results; if you don't list your store, no one who uses the bots or comparison engines sees your name at all.

Shopping bots or agents are presented as consumer empowerment tools. In reality, many agents are working on behalf of merchants. Up-and-coming e-tailers pay for these tools because they help customers find their sites. The most powerful e-tailers, of course, protect their brands and their pricing by blocking the agents. In fact, some agents are not very powerful because few merchants will cooperate with them. For example, Healthstore.com offers a shopping agent that searches 11 different drug, health food, and nutrition web sites for items, out of the thousands of sites in this category.

E-Vision: By 2004, shopping agents will be significantly enhanced, with particular emphasis on quality, service, and other nonprice considerations, as standards for such considerations are developed to minimize pricing pressure on e-tailers by price-focused agents.

➤ Rating Services

Rating services compare online stores, which is useful to consumers. However, e-tailers value ratings based on user feedback. Their experiences and opinions are solicited, rewarded, analyzed, and fed back to participating merchants. Companies such as BizRate, Gomez, and ePinions are not merchants. Rather, they are like *Consumer Reports,* but with a different business model. They derive revenue from selling aggregated marketing research based on feedback from consumers at the point of sale and on choices consumers make on their sites (for example, men prefer on-time delivery over lower prices). The merchant members pay fees based on traffic driven to their sites. Consumer-focused e-businesses can build visibility by participating in these rating services. But to participate, merchants must be competitive in service quality, usability, responsiveness, and price, or the resulting ratings may prove embarrassing. For consumers, these sites make it possible to find smaller merchants of high quality that they might otherwise overlook.

■ PRACTICAL STRATEGIES FOR E-TAILING SUCCESS

1. Focus on a well-defined micromarket. We have worked with dozens of companies (both brick and click) that point to a successful dot-com and, in essence, say: We want to be like them. Our answer is often: That company is already in that space, and they spent time and money getting there. Better define a micromarket within theirs and split it off. From Nets, Inc., to Value America, to Toysmart to Boo.com, two of the most consistent reasons that e-tailers have failed are lack of focus and differentiation. Those companies didn't have a well-defined micromarket and a homogeneous target customer in mind. Considering that this problem is straight out of Marketing 101, it is hard to feel too sorry for such e-tailing failures.

We are already beginning to see the next generation of e-tailing entrepreneurs. These are the folks who are starting micromarkets. Personal and microbusiness web sites already generate more than 75 percent of the Web's aggregate page views (according to Forrester Research), so it is not surprising that some of the fastest e-tailing growth is among the entrepreneurs that are establishing micromarkets to focus on a single buyer, a single seller, or a narrow segment with multiple buyers and sellers. Some of these are affiliated with malls, or affinity groups, such as Affinia.com, Amazon's zShops, or Yahoo!'s eShops; others are stand-alone stores that do their own promotion.

The names of most of these micromarket e-tailers are very revealing. They have to be, as most do not have tens of millions of dollars for marketing. Fridgedoor.com prides itself on its selection of refrigerator-door magnets.

Comparable selection-based strategies can be found at Justsocks.com, Justballs.com, Raremaps.com, and Mustardstore.com. The owners of Mustardstore recently opened Vinegarstore.com and GourmetOilStore.com, suggesting that a collection of micromarkets, with enough promotional funding, could at some point challenge the online mall approach of Amazon, Yahoo!, and others.

2. Focus on e-fulfillment. Having a clear micromarket strategy has the ancillary benefit of making an e-fulfillment infrastructure easier to develop or outsource. The more homogeneous the customer base and the product set, the more logistically efficient the company's operations can be. For instance, Drugstore.com focuses on prescription drugs that are cost effective to ship. And EthnicGrocer.com specializes in nonperishable and high-margin ethnic products that are hard to find at local groceries. FurnitureFind.com, an online furniture retailer, offers a kid-glove delivery experience for furniture that involves unpacking, assembly, minor repairs, and an extended warranty. Because micromarkets are really online specialty stores and not exchanges, they do not require a new fulfillment infrastructure. However, micromarkets are not able to optimize the infrastructure for specific categories or end-use applications, so there are no major process improvements.

3. Reduce abandon rates. Concerns over shopping cart abandon rates of 40 to 60 percent—and the associated loss of $14 to $15 billion in revenue it represents—are leading companies to spend lots of money on usability improvements and customer service tools that provide live agents to dialog with customers and walk them through the buying process. Forrester has also found that typical e-tailers have conversion rates that range from under 1 percent to 2 percent. However, best-of-breed e-tailers like Amazon have conversion rates of 5 percent or so. How is this achieved? They draw task-oriented individuals—people who are there to shop. Of course, they are also a trusted Internet brand (see Chapter 4). Portals and community sites get folks to stay longer, but they are less likely to buy. Converting browsers into buyers is the biggest problem for the B2C and B2B portals. We expect that the portals will be largely unsuccessful in dominating their shopping segments through 2003.

4. Maximize local knowledge.   Retailers that target a local market should do their best to capitalize on their local knowledge to compete effectively against distant virtual stores. Local merchants will know local customs, tastes, and product preferences of which virtual sellers may be unaware. Endorsements from local citizens, references to local landmarks, awareness of important local events that may influence purchase patterns, and other local content strategies should help make a merchant's web site more meaningful and appealing to the local target market. While it is difficult for globally oriented Web businesses to capture the same degree of local relevance at this time, they will address that challenge over the next two to three years. A new generation of databases with extensive local content and local merchant participation (e.g., Switchboard.com) will make this possible.

5. Be a concerned merchant.   Because most e-tailers are not identified with particular communities or causes, they should undertake a specific effort to demonstrate that they care about the issues that concern their customers. For example, KBKids.com has instituted a Parents Advisory Council to gain understanding of the needs and concerns of the parents who act as shopping agents for their kids. The goal is to build community discussions and generate word of mouth among parents that KBKids is a concerned e-tailer. Of course, parents who participate are compensated with discounts and merchandise from KBKids.

6. Don't drive the last mile. While consumers like the potential convenience of having their purchases delivered to their home, in reality the solution doesn't scale very well. That is, consumers are not at all pleased at the prospect of having delivery trucks show up at their house four or five times a day, bringing them all the stuff they would have bought in one or two trips to a shopping center. On the other hand, the new crop of home delivery companies has yet to figure out an acceptable model or system for reconciling the handling of all the different products destined for the same home or street. We believe that if home delivery is going to be successful, it will require the reaggregation of deliveries across many categories of e-tailers to realize economies of scale—that is, it will require filling up the trucks with many different types of merchandise bound for nearby destinations.

Companies such as Streamline.com, Kozmo, PinkDot, and HomeRuns are attempting to carve out regional and industry micromarkets that will allow them to coexist with the likes of UPS or FedEx. If these last-mile e-fulfillment companies are to succeed, they must figure out how to profitably deliver goods with different purchase cycles and different fulfillment characteristics at the same time. One of the ways to do this is to use complex route management tools to optimize the home delivery process. For example, some home delivery companies today constrain delivery timing in order to make home delivery more cost effective. Grocery industry home delivery specialists, such as Peapod and Webvan, in an attempt to achieve profitability, have adapted yield management and route optimization algorithms from the airline and trucking industries. But despite this advanced technology, these companies have either failed or performed poorly in almost every case due to the high cost of the infrastructure and the low consumer demand for the services they offer. The practical strategy for the near term should be to leave the driving (to the local grocery store) to the consumer.

7. Retailers must fight back. Physical retailers must work to capitalize on their investments in human capital, infrastructure, and brand awareness in order to generate customer loyalty and emotional involvement. Part of this strategy is based on using every opportunity to get customers to care about being in the physical store. This could include getting clerks to engage customers in eye contact or dialog, or developing displays or signs designed to provoke an emotional response or provide a "community" atmosphere, such as the poetry readings and musical performances many bookstores are holding to compete with Amazon and other online booksellers. Those retailers that are unwilling to do this will have to compete on price, service, and fulfillment directly with the e-tailers. Another strategy for retailers is to optimize their business processes to maximize efficiency and reduce costs. For example, Nordstrom is moving, department by department, to implement an intelligent sourcing strategy; thus it is providing suppliers, beginning with the shoe industry, with direct visibility to SKU (stock-keeping unit) sales, by store, so suppliers can automate replenishment and drop-ship directly to retail establishments the specific items that have been sold, thereby speeding up, simplifying, and reducing the cost of Nordstrom's distribution process.

> **E-Vision:** Retailers will, by and large, not be able to beat e-tailers on price alone. Instead, leading retailers will buy leading e-tailers, and vice versa, creating numerous click-and-mortar brands.

8. Retail groceries must adapt to survive. Forrester Research found that online sales of grocery products will be about $500 million in 1999, representing only a small portion of the more than $400 billion grocery business in the United States. While supermarkets are unlikely to disappear anytime soon, they must adapt—in some cases, radically—and evolve. Supermarkets and pharmacies can compete effectively with online retailers by providing online ordering and drive-through pickups of groceries and prescriptions. Supermarkets can also cater to time-starved customers by creating stores within a store focused on speed and service. They can carve out an area of the store that replicates a convenience store environment: limited selection, quick checkout, convenient parking, and higher prices. If they guarantee a 15-minute end-to-end shopping trip, supermarkets can gain an edge over online grocers. By acting swiftly to create click-and-mortar hybrid models, supermarkets and pharmacies can defend their franchises quite effectively from online players that lack a physical point of presence.

9. Know when it's too late. Both entrepreneurs and mom-and-pop retailers hoping to make it big on the Web may be too late, depending on their chosen industry. For example, consider travel agencies, already one of the most mature of the online industries. This industry is already heavily consolidated, with the big three—Expedia, Travelocity, and Preview Travel—controlling nearly 50 percent of the online travel market. Why did this consolidation happen so quickly? Because the product (i.e., tickets) could easily be digitized and because there were no dominant corporate players in the brick-and-mortar travel industry, it was easier for the online players to take over the market and drive out the mom-and-pop travel agencies. Thus, a key to success is knowing enough about industry structure and trends to stay out of segments that are in an advanced state of consolidation. Of course, this does not mean there are no e-business opportunities left in travel or other consolidated segments. It just means you should plan to work *with* the major players, rather than compete with them.

10. Push e-tailing into new sales venues. The lack of physical stores continues to create a branding problem for e-tailers. As a result, e-tailers must look for new venues and new segments to keep consumers coming back. One of the more interesting new opportunities is to bring e-tailing into entertainment venues such as movie theaters and amusement parks. The opportunity is to strengthen the association between entertainment and e-tailing. The most obvious examples are AOL/Time Warner/EMI, SONY, and especially Disney.com, which has done a better job than almost any other company (in the real or the dot-com world) of blurring the line between entertaining and selling.

11. Define a global strategy. Europe, especially the ever growing European Union, presents an amazing opportunity for U.S. investors. With the introduction of the new currency, the Euro, Europe has established one of the most important infrastructures for e-commerce. For the first time in history, a U.S. company can serve hundreds of millions of customers outside the United States with only one physical location. In addition, because Europe still has not produced many global brand-name e-tailers, there are substantial opportunities for developing global e-tailing brands. In some cases this will be very expensive, but in other cases global brands can be established less expensively through marketing and fulfillment partnerships.

12. Develop an agent-handling strategy. As software agents or bots get more powerful, the question for e-tailers is whether they should block agents (e.g., those that search for the lowest price) or allow them to search the site, since blocking them could mean missed sales. Powerful retailers, such as Amazon and eBay, have consistently blocked most agents and comparison services (for example, Auctionwatch.com), which is the approach one would expect of any market leader. In general, we believe that it is impossible to develop a single policy or software solution for handling all types of shopping agents or bots. As this technology evolves, a technical differentiator among e-tailers will be found in how intelligently they handle shopping and other types of agents. We argue that this should be an important component of any e-tailer's technical strategy.

13. Implement a multicentric business architecture. Most of the e-tailers we spoke with in the course of researching this book had as their objective the development of a single online storefront. While this is perhaps a necessary place to start, we believe it is not a sufficient strategy for most companies going forward. Rather, we believe the market will move to what we call a multicentric content architecture. This is really just a geeky way of saying that in the age of the Internet, there is absolutely no reason that a company cannot have 2 or 4 or 10 different types of e-tailing storefronts selling exactly the same product. Rather than complicate a site with a traditional catalog, plus an auction, plus a comparison shopping site, plus a multimerchant shopping mall (e.g., Amazon, Yahoo!, Lycos, and the other general-purpose portals), a company can easily develop a series of related sites that share all or part of a URL (uniform resource locator), while still providing unique shopping experiences and business models. A few such e-tailers already exist today. Some are the results of mergers or acquisitions, others are the result of having the same VC or incubator parentage, but some were deliberately designed to offer different e-tail views of the same content. For example, uBid and eCost are different front ends on highly similar content, as both are owned by the same company, Creative Computers. See Figure 3.2.

14. Execute better than the next e-tailer. E-tailing (and e-business in general) is and has always been about execution. Sites that are not accessible, pages that don't work, and fulfillment that doesn't happen are no longer acceptable because e-tailing is no longer new in the eyes of consumers. The back end of e-tailing is still the critical differentiator, according to consumer behavior researchers.

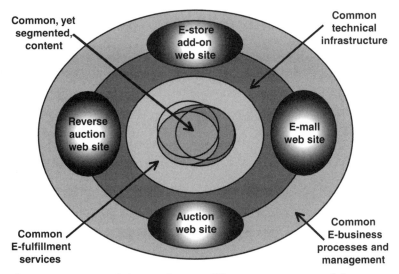

Figure 3.2 Multicentric e-tailing content architecture. *Source:* eMarket Holdings.

Customer service, inventory, shipping, and return handling are the major factors that determine whether consumers will return to the same e-tailer the next time.

■ CONCLUSION

The e-tailers that survive and thrive will be those that build from a few clearly focused marketplaces rather than try to offer a broad range of services to a broad base of Internet users. Successful e-tailers will build on an integrated business process that includes fulfillment, as opposed to trying to maximize traffic at the expense of back-end processes and operations. They will build a multicentric, multielement business model, with more than one type of business front end to the same or similar sets of content and a shifting mix of revenue sources.

Chapter

4

Building and Managing Microbrands

Despite the $3 billion that dot-com companies spent on advertising in 1999, and over $4 billion in 2000, virtually everyone we have spoken with in the past year is having a tough time understanding who's promising what or why they should shop at one e-store over another. Sure, everybody knows Amazon sells books, Dell sells computers, and Priceline sells airline tickets, but most e-stores and all of the e-malls are pretty vaguely positioned in the minds of the many folks. This should not be surprising. After nearly five years of the Internet phenomenon, the messages of e-businesses, particularly B2B e-businesses, can be reduced to, "Hey! We're on the Internet and we can do anything for everyone." Regardless of the medium, we believe the single-minded focus on simple awareness has been a huge waste of money for most of the pure dot-coms. Why? Because most dot-com companies, in their race to build awareness, haven't bothered to establish the other components that make up a brand—something that many of their brick-and-mortar counterparts have had generations to do.

■ THE COMPONENTS OF BRAND

A brand is composed of a number of factors, including awareness or recognition, customer loyalty, image or brand traits, name and logo design, personal benefits, positioning in relation to competitors, media presence, pricing relative to value, perceived quality, reported satisfaction via word of mouth, reputation, and perceived popularity. Some components of brand are very subtle. Jean-Marie Dru, in his book *Disruption* (Wiley, 1996), argued that brands have personalities, opinions, and attitudes; Apple expresses liberty regained; Pepsi, youthfulness; Oil of Olay, timeless beauty; Saturn, the American competitive spirit; and AT&T, the promises of the future. A successful branding campaign must establish what the brand represents relative to both the obvious and the most subtle of these factors.

To adapt their branding strategies for the Internet, companies must move beyond simplistic approaches to branding. The next step in building Internet brands is to define brands that appeal to specific psychographic segments. Companies need to establish brand traits, reputation, popularity, and personality. This is particularly important, since "brand zealots," as defined in an article in *Strategy and Business* magazine (Fourth Quarter, 1999) by Rozanski, Baum, and Wolfsen, can function as a fan club for certain brands and become major drivers of revenue and recognition if understood and nurtured. (This issue is covered in more detail in Chapter 2.)

E-Vision: Microbrands and microbranding strategies will first supplement and then replace corporate branding strategies being used today to promote Internet businesses.

■ THE EMERGENCE OF MICROBRANDS

The Internet, combined with collaborative design technologies and mass-customization manufacturing, is enabling the production of unique products in segments as diverse as health and beauty care, apparel, and even automotive manufacturing. For example, Procter & Gamble spun off a stand-alone Internet company called Reflect.com to develop a line of personalized beauty products to be sold only via the Internet. The personalization built into this line of beauty products was based on over 50,000 possible product and packaging combinations.

Just as it is becoming possible to create these relatively unique, personalized products, the Internet also makes it feasible to define narrow brand concepts for small groups of users, down to the point of developing what Tom Peters has called *microbrands*. For Peters, the final evolutionary step in microbranding is a one-to-one relationship between the traits of a product or service and the traits of the individual who buys and uses that product or service. (See Figure 4.1.) Building on the pioneering work on one-to-one marketing by Peppers and Rogers microbranding

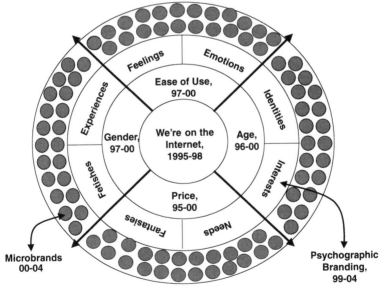

Micromarkets and Microbrands Emerge

Figure 4.1 Micromarkets, online specialty stores, will be segmented along a variety of demographics and psychographic factors.

involves more than product customization and personalization; it requires message customization based on both
demographics and psychographics (the measurement of
psychological reactions, particularly to visual stimuli). We
don't all laugh at the same jokes, we don't all like the same
music and food or have the same feelings about our fax
machines.

■ WHEN DOES A WEB SITE BECOME A BRAND?

Many marketing executives of dot-com start-ups refer to
their web sites as brands—but this is an optimistic mis-
nomer. While simple awareness of a company or product
can be created comparatively quickly thanks to the Internet (though it helps if you've got the $50 million advertis-
ing budget of, say, Amazon.com), we believe that *brand* is
much more than simple awareness. Brand is in the eye and
mind of the beholder. Brand is bestowed on a company or
its products by the marketplace. Brand is measured by
whether customers and prospects have a sense of the image
or distinguishing traits or the personality of the company
and its products or services. While most dot-com companies have ignored the hard-to-quantify aspects of brand, a
few have made significant efforts to define and reinforce
an image for their virtual enterprise. For example, in early
2000, Bargainbid launched a campaign advertising "auctions with respect" and hired comedian Rodney Danger-
field (Mr. "No Respect") as a spokesperson. After shopping
on the site, we could not determine exactly how this respect
was delivered. About a month later the campaign was over
and all references to respect were gone from the site. A few
months after that, Bargainbid's web site was gone. Our
point is that the personality of an e-business or a web site
or a microbrand must be more enduring than a single mar-

keting campaign. It must be clearly conveyed in the content of the site and the operation of the business. If not, there is not much point in spending the money to develop microbrands in the first place.

➤ Keep Customers Happy and Involved

The success of a microbranding initiative cannot be measured by simple awareness or brand recognition. Since microbrands are unique to each individual, there is nothing to recognize. Rather, the success or failure of a microbranding program is tied up in two metrics:

1. **Personal experience**—did each customer (business customer or consumer) get out of the business what he or she expected and what he or she wanted?
2. **Emotional involvement**—did the customer develop a positive sentiment or at least some sort of feeling relative to that experience?

Virtually all Web businesses have so far failed to generate much emotional involvement, as we discuss in Chapter 2. In addition, most Web businesses are also rated poorly when it comes to more straightforward metrics, such as customer satisfaction. For example, a Forrester Research study found that shopping cart abandonment rate was 66 percent. Other studies (e.g., by CreativeGood, a customer satisfaction consulting firm) have pegged the cart abandonment rate as high as 75 percent. In our own research, for every comment we heard or read from someone who raved about online shopping, there were four or five other stories about hard-to-navigate sites, the inability to interpret search results, and the inability to reach a human when needed. In spite of the billions being spent trying to build brand and name recognition, all of it can be lost with the click of a mouse. One bad experience, and customers are gone like a shot.

► The Context of Satisfaction and Involvement

Surprisingly, most companies spend very little time actually interviewing their customers about their experiences, even though they have phone numbers or other contact information. They rely on third parties and Web forms, which produce quick statistical reports that offer usable aggregate data but little insight into the all-important factor of context. That is, for a microbranding effort to succeed, the brand must fit into the context of the customer's work and/or home life.

We argue that every person in an e-business, from designers to executives, needs to do a better job of understanding the personal and corporate goals of their customers and the specific tasks the company's products or services enable each customer to accomplish. While most people don't think of impulse buyers as task oriented, making a purchase does accomplish something for the buyer. It is up to e-business managers to understand the personal and emotional context of each purchase and develop a campaign that effectively targets the most common contexts for buyers.

Localize Brands. One aspect of microbranding that the Internet makes possible is brand localization. This refers to the ability to tailor a message and to promote an interpretation of the value and image of a company and its products that varies by location. Today the number of national and global businesses that have localized content and fulfillment capabilities is still very small. Even e-tailers that have local fulfillment capabilities, such as Toys "R" Us, Sears, and Barnes & Noble, have centralized messages on their web sites. However, we believe this will change over the next two to three years, as the availability and integration of local content improves, along with the richness of geographic targeting data. We believe that localization of content and branding, along with the need to create a more personal and involving experience for Internet users, will be a critical driver of brand localization. This trend will be paid for by both local and national advertisers frustrated with the lack of consumer clickthrough on the generic portals and the general-purpose e-malls.

Develop Vortals or Vertical Portals. Two years ago, there was a struggle to win the portal wars by establishing the most broadly functional—yet personalizable—consumer portal. The brand equity of owning the consumer's entry point is obvious. But now it's time to declare a few winners, such as AOL, Yahoo!, and maybe a couple of others, and move on to a more interesting area: *vortals,* or segment-specific portals. The recipe for success is the same: Combine the three C's—content, community, and commerce. Some of these are focused on ethnicity, such as Terra.com (Hispanic) and Korealink.com (Korean). Others are interest focused, such as Horsenet.com (horse lovers) and Mountainnet.com (outdoor sports). In each case, the revenue model is primarily advertising based, with some transaction revenue from online sales. Going forward, we believe that these vortals are simply an intermediary step toward the micro-ization of Internet entry points and that portals will become even more personalized.

Develop a Cobranding Strategy. Cobranding is a trend that we expect to become even more refined in both B2C and B2B. The idea of having multiple companies sponsor or brand products or services that are at the intersection of their interests is decades old. Companies from Disney and McDonald's to Microsoft and IBM to Amazon and Yahoo! have found activities, items, and web sites where there is significant opportunity to work together. These cobranding efforts are becoming much more popular in e-business because of the ease with which content that attracts a common set of customers can be defined and created. Actually, we believe cobranding is the tip of the iceberg in terms of the Internet creating opportunities for companies to work together to jointly establish and reinforce their brands.

Sponsor Personal Portals. One of the implications of the move to personalization and microbranding is that all but a very few of today's portals will decline in importance until they fade away or, more likely, are reinvented. Data from Nielsen//NetRatings show that portals account for 54 percent of referrals to e-commerce sites. As surfers gain experience, however, they are more likely to bypass portals and head directly to e-commerce sites. It is likely that, over the next two years, marketers will rely less on the major portals and more on personally defined, cobranded (or multibranded) home pages to drive traffic and establish brand. Instead of focusing so much on giving people access to information, we believe that personal portals will help people accomplish tasks. Instead of monitoring streams of data (like stock tickers and message boards), personal portals will feature negotiation agents that understand my to-do list (from my personal assistant), my risk tolerance (from my broker), my emotional attachments, and my interests (from my club memberships, even if they are dispersed across the Internet), among many other things. From this information, not only can companies build personal portals, they can also build personal brands.

Define Personal Brands. The ultimate example of cobranding or microbranding is the branding of individuals. As practiced by C2C (consumer-to-consumer) auction sites, personal branding enables individuals to cash in on their reputations as merchants and the trust placed in them by other buyers and sellers. A form of personal branding is already built into the rating systems of most online auctions. Customers can assign sellers points, based on their satisfaction with their purchase and the treatment they received from the seller. Beyond assigning these points, users can also provide extensive comments and they may rate a seller multiple times. In most auction sites, restrictions prevent a person from inflating his or her own rating while also preventing disgruntled customers from completely destroying another person's reputation or brand.

The technology is just coming to market from companies such as Engage that will enable companies to gather data on individuals and on very small aggregations of less than 10 individuals (for those persons who wish to be individually anonymous) from across the many sites where they have registered for services, are members of clubs, have electronic wallets, and so on. This information can and will be used to assemble personal brands. As an analogy, think about sports and games. Tennis players, golfers, and chess players who play in tournaments are rated—in computer databases—so they can be set up for more even matches with one another. Personal brands will be like having a global rating for your interests: Persons will have a score for the importance of gardening, furniture refinishing, TV watching (by type of channel), and, of course, golf and other sports. This information will, in essence, become a key part of a person's representation in cyberspace over the next five years.

Sponsor Episodic Content. Sponsoring content that relates to the interests of the targeted audience is another way to build brand image. But rather than sponsoring text pages or other static content, we recommend sponsoring episodic content. One of the concepts from television that has so far been underutilized on the Internet is the episode. We expect that will change dramatically in the next two years. Movie and TV production companies such as Warner Bros. and Disney, talent agencies such as William Morris and Creative Artists Agency, software companies such as Pulse Network and MacroMedia, and animators such as Tim Burton (*The Nightmare Before Christmas*) and Matt Stone and Trey Parker (*South Park*) have signed up to play significant roles in building episodic content that they will either use themselves or syndicate to many web sites. A particular target is the youth market, which wants the attitude these animations offer and has either broadband access or plenty of patience. Examples of sites that already offer such episodic content include Broadband Interactive Group, Icebox.com, Entertaindom (owned by Warner Bros.), as well as independents like Jibjab and Crater Valley, which aim to give readers direct input into the outcome of an episode.

The opportunity that all of these companies are pursuing is to create a series of episodes that will be posted to the Web in much the same way that TV shows air now, but the length of the shows will be only a few minutes and they will not be particularly involving. The hope is that visitors will return each week (or every day) for the new episode, then shop, search, and generally engage in other activities, including visiting the web sites of the sponsors of this content. So far, however, bandwidth limitations prevent any real character development and force very short episodes, so the focus is on a single punch line. Over the next several years, as broadband reaches more homes, episodic content will mature to the point where sponsorship will be valuable for reaching a more general audience.

Join Branding Networks. Most people don't pay much attention to details—they don't read instruction manuals, they don't read warning labels, and they certainly don't read the text in advertisements. It's not always true, but it's a good rule of thumb to use when trying to build an online brand. In the online world, successful microbranding will not be aimed at trying to get people to recall thousands of uniquely customized tag lines, images, and benefits statements. Microbranding will be about using networks of web sites that will collectively reinforce the experiences of users. In contrast to the portal sites of today, which want to be the single point of departure from which a person's Web adventure starts, the branding networks of the early twenty-first century will be focused on creating a multi-sponsor access point that the individual controls, but which gives slight preferential treatment to the sponsors' e-businesses.

The next-generation branding network is exemplified by companies like CMGI and Adsmart, one of CMGI's portfolio of companies. Another branding network, Engage's AudienceNet, allows advertisers to develop microbrand messages targeted at very specific consumers. Unlike models that require advertisers to buy space on a media channel, AudienceNet lets them reach individual consumers across a spectrum of web sites. These companies, and dozens of others that believe in this model, are collecting tens of thousands of online and offline brands from different companies, grouping them into related categories (or affiliate groups), and developing a branding network to support these companies.

■ OBSTACLES TO BUILDING MICROBRANDS

There are a number of existing obstacles to building microbrands.

➤ Data Integration Problems

Companies have been collecting data on individuals for decades, but never have they had the potential tools for information collection that the Internet makes available. Yet most companies are unable to integrate and analyze the data that they have on their customers, let alone use it to drive a customized microbranding campaign. Part of the problem is that there are few standards relative to the semantics (or the meaning) of the data elements, and these will be required before widespread integration of the data needed to implement microbranding will be possible. However, we expect these problems to be addressed by a new generation of data mining technology that will emerge over the next three years.

➤ Notification Overload Problems

Sometimes the concept is better than the reality. Take the concept of notification. It makes logical sense that people would like to be notified of an upcoming sale by their favorite retailer, or when the airfare for a trip they have been considering drops to a level they can afford. In theory, the web site that knows enough about you to notify you about those events that are important to you is valuable. The brand value goes up because you associate the site with your interests and because you have given the company information about yourself. Logically, these notifications will keep you as a subscriber much longer and will get you to revisit that web site. But let's say that this is the 12th e-mail notification you've gotten today. How do you feel about the web site now? More and more people, overwhelmed by too much e-mail, are establishing secondary free e-mail boxes from Hotmail, Excite, Yahoo!, or many others, just for receiving their junk mail and notifications. Generally, people check these messages only periodically and mainly to delete the accumulated marketing messages. This is a downside of too much personalization.

➤ Banner Advertising Problems

Even though banners are widely used today to generate initial visits, they should not be considered a major part of a branding strategy. Recently, the size of the average advertising banner has actually decreased, according to a study by AdRelevance, a division of Media Metrix. More companies are using microbuttons and other small-size online ads because of their lower price and the simplicity of the message being conveyed. According to Nielsen//NetRatings Inc., the average Web user clicks on fewer than one of the 89 banners he or she sees per week—a click rate of 1.1 percent. Only 7 percent of consumers surveyed last year by Forrester said they used banner ads to find URLs. More than half of online consumers have never clicked on a banner advertisement. Of those who have, 69 percent do not remember the last banner ad they clicked on. We believe that building brands requires more space than banners provide in order to get across the complex messages or images that companies need to convey. As banners become buttons, they will become even less useful as brand-building tools.

➤ Brand Control Problems

Beyond building their online brand, both real and dot-com companies are beginning to experience problems controlling and managing the way their brand name and image are used by others on the Internet. Individuals now have the potential to cheaply and easily spread negative information about a company and its products or services. The issue isn't stifling freedom of expression by individuals. The issue is the unauthorized use of a company's brand and image by third parties. This problem has become rampant in recent years, as Internet companies are involved in so many deals to buy, sell, and lease content from one another. However, we have talked to a number of companies that found their products being sold and their logos and brand names used on sites (e.g., shopping sites) in a way they felt was harmful to their pricing policies, their warranty programs, and their overall corporate reputations. Anyone who establishes a web site related to a company or its products should be seen as a threat to the company's control of its message and should be dealt with accordingly. For example, Porsche filed legal claims against 130 web sites that it believed were using or trading, or related to the use of, its brand and product names without authorization. Some of these claims have been settled, but others are still pending.

➤ Word-of-Web Problems

Beyond monitoring the newsgroups and chat rooms, as already noted, companies should undertake concerted efforts to understand all Web activity that is directly or indirectly related to the company and its brands. This is because brands can be severely damaged by the strong word-of-mouth capability that is built into the Internet. All sorts of companies in a broad range of industries have been trashed by a variety of mechanisms. This phenomenon extends far beyond a few disgruntled individuals complaining in chat rooms or on message boards. For example, fuckedcompany.com has emerged as a popular online newsletter and chat site dedicated to spreading the word (both rumors and published reports) about dot-com failures. It even includes a contest, in which those who submit rumors or reports about companies are awarded points (and potentially prizes) based on the degree to which the company mentioned is likely to go out of business. This type of web site can be both insightful and damaging to the company in question, and it is important that company representatives monitor such sites to ensure that their brand and image are accurately represented.

Another type of brand-eroding site is the parody site. For example, HomeDepotSucks.com parodies the real Home Depot site's look, but is really a site dedicated to presenting the negative aspects of Home Depot's environmental record. There is a comparable WalMartSucks.com site, which publishes articles critical of Wal-Mart's policies and practices. In fact most major corporate URLs with "sucks" added have been taken. Some companies, like General Electric, Bell Atlantic, and Macy's, thought ahead and bought their own "sucks" URLs a while ago. There are also hundreds of protest or parody web sites that have been developed by companies and individuals that have had unpleasant experiences with corporations. For examples (which change too regularly to put in a book), try searching on words and phrases such as "dishonest" and "don't buy from." These sites also come up when searching for

> **E-Vision:** By 2003, the development of microbrands and branding networks will dramatically change how companies measure their brand equity, as well as the techniques they use for building brand equity.

the business in question, which is another good reason to monitor one's detractors.

■ PRACTICAL STRATEGIES FOR BUILDING MICROBRANDS

1. Monitor active newsgroups concerning your company. Newsgroups can be either very beneficial or very detrimental. There are many people who may have problems with a company's product, customer service, price, or what have you. In the past they could write the Better Business Bureau or call the company's complaint department. If they were really angry and could afford it, they could pay for a negative advertisement. Today customers can go to newsgroups or chat rooms and say wonderful things or terrible things about you. If you have an unhappy customer, you want to be able to solve that problem as quickly as possible. But finding active newsgroups or chat rooms is not always easy. People who want to trash a company seek as large an audience as possible. Certainly, Yahoo!, AOL, Excite, and the other portals manage to bring together many people. In addition, check all the financial web sites that actively follow the company for negative content. Depending on the nature of the content, legal action may be appropriate.

2. Employ consent-based (opt-in) e-mail marketing. In a belated recognition of consumer anger over marketing e-mail messages, most companies are switching their strategies to the point where customers on a web site have to consciously choose to receive marketing messages from a company. In fact, consent-based e-mail marketing is emerging as a new product category. For example, DoubleClick has developed a new opt-in e-mail marketing product line called DARTmail, a suite of online consent-based e-mail marketing solutions for advertisers and the media to help develop more personal messages while offering more sophisticated campaign management solutions. DARTmail aggregates e-mail newsletter content into affinity categories. The key thing to keep in mind when sending messages to customers and prospects is that if a company sends entertaining and/or useful e-mails, then recipients will keep opening them. As long as e-mail is consent-based, personalized, and relevant, companies shouldn't expect a consumer backlash.

3. Implement an e-mail relationship management (ERM) program. ERM is essentially the addition of customer profile and buying pattern data to programs that generate customized mailings. The idea is to build a set of business rules from behavioral history data and data on the characteristics of the product line (i.e., what types of products sell to what types of people, under what conditions, and relative to what other products). These business rules can then be used to personalize e-mail campaigns, resulting in product recommendations, promotions, and up-sell/cross-sell opportunities that are more relevant to the individuals whose behavioral data have been used to generate the rules. ClickAction and a number of other companies offer ERM products.

4. Define a strategy for continuous marketing. Continuous marketing on the Internet is already in use by the "get paid to surf the Web" companies, such as AllAdvantage (see Chapter 1). But it will become much more widely employed over the next few years. By 2003, most consumers in developed regions of the world will be almost continuously connected to the Internet, through computers at work and home, televisions, PDAs, wireless phones, and even smart appliances and monitoring devices. The e-business opportunity is to develop a set of messages designed to be delivered on a continuous, but less obtrusive, basis. Today we think of the world as being broken into programs versus commercials, or articles versus advertisements, and content versus banner ads. We see these things as separate. Consumers try to mentally screen out the commercials, advertisements, and banners, while attending to the programs, articles, and content. The world of e-business is all about continuous, almost sub-liminal messages, scrolling across our environment like a stock ticker or news bulletin. Already we have seen the first signs of continuous marketing, with the sponsored browsers and sponsored Internet access. As access and intelligence in the form of microprocessors connected to the Internet become pervasive, the continuity of commer-cialization will spread beyond browsers to all aspects of the lives of consumers.

5. Develop a viral marketing application. Twenty-eight percent of consumers surveyed last year by Forrester said that they find out about the best web sites by word of mouth. *Viral marketing*—also called *organic marketing* and *contagion marketing*—refers to the ability of the Internet to build self-propagating visitor streams. It is a more sophis-ticated version of e-mail marketing, because it is built around an application or service that the recipients of the campaign actually want. The concept adapts the offline word-of-mouth campaign, but with the Internet as a turbo-boost. Viral marketing effectively compounds the benefits of first-mover advantage. Hotmail was one of the first viral-marketed products. When Hotmail users send e-mails, they "infect" the recipients with the tag line at the bottom of their messages (see box). A more recent example of a com-pany using viral marketing is Evite.com, a free Web e-mail service that invites people with e-mail addresses to events. Evite.com tracks the RSVPs and shows the accep-tances and excuses to the inviter on a private, personalized group event Web page. More important, with each e-mail the recipients are encouraged to schedule their own event through Evite. The issue with these services is that the user has to give up a lot of information in order to take advan-tage of the service—in this case, the addresses of his or her friends or business associates, the type of event, the loca-tion, and so forth. We expect that viral marketing will prove to be very adaptable to the demands of microbranding and will prove valuable in personalizing brand messages and building communities.

GET YOUR FREE E-MAIL AT HOTMAIL

That sentence, at the bottom of every outbound Hotmail message, enabled Hotmail to become the fastest start-up in history, signing up 12 million subscribers in its first 1.5 years. The idea was very contentious at the time. Some investors and members of management feared that users would resent having an advertisement and its implied endorsement attached to their personal messages. But it worked, and every Hotmail user became a sort of salesperson for Hotmail.

6. Adopt new brand equity metrics.   Traditional measures of brand equity and the effectiveness of advertising campaigns need to adapt to the new brand-building techniques of the online world. For example, the emergence of viral marketing and continuous marketing breaks down the concept of the advertising campaign. While it is easy to determine which ad placements and which messages did the most to generate traffic to a web site and convert visitors into buyers, such factors will prove less important in determining the overall value of a brand's equity. It is more important to determine whether a person understands and identifies with the sense of brand that the company is trying to convey, and this cannot be determined from clickstream analysis. Our point is that as companies develop and promote microbrands for the highly personalized world of the Internet, they must redefine brand equity in terms that reflect the personalization of the brand message, not simply on the basis of whether users clicked on an ad or visited a site. The reason is that a series of tests of understanding and emotional involvement with personalized content will prove to be the best predictors of whether the campaign will generate word of mouth, brand loyalty, and repeat purchase behavior in the long term.

■ CONCLUSION

From the broad emotional identification that we have with global brands like Coca Cola, Rolls Royce, and Sony, the Internet enables us to evolve to a set of personal brands, which mirror our desires, activities, and emotional states at a given moment in time. We see first-generation personalization efforts such as "My Yahoo!" and "My AOL" as precursors to the creation of a new generation of microbrands—interactive experiences that are crafted in real time from databases that have captured all that we will allow others to know about who we are, what we do, and what we want. We agree with those who consider brand to be a property of the viewer, rather than of the product. Given that branding is a psychological response to a marketing message, we see brands in the age of the Internet becoming not only more personal, but also changing more rapidly. The bottom line is that as we know more about who people are, we can use the power of the Internet to create thousands of combinations of product, service, and packaging characteristics, to craft a message that is as flexible and multifaceted as the human experience itself.

Chapter

Can Customer Loyalty Survive the Web?

My father went to the same gas station for 30 years. It wasn't the closest, and it wasn't the cheapest. Even when he could get a better price closer to home, my dad still went to the same station. It wasn't because of the brand. He had all the gasoline credit cards, and on vacations he stopped at whatever station was handy. But at home, gasoline was personal. He liked the people, and they were nice to him. I, on the other hand, always went for the low price. I didn't want or need a relationship with my gas station attendant.

These differing priorities—in the same family, no less—show that there are different degrees of loyalty and different reasons people are loyal. Companies have always used a wide array of strategies and tactics to tap into the many dimensions of customer loyalty. With the Internet, they have even more possibilities—as well as greater challenges.

The convenience of online shopping has created a commitment crisis for merchants. All businesses that market, sell, service, and support via the Internet must come to grips with the loss of relationship, commitment, and involvement that comes with the awareness of alternatives. Once a consumer drives to the store, he or she is likely to buy something. But at a web site, another store or a chat room or a quick game of poker is just a click away.

Companies in the business-to-business market find the new environment particularly disorienting. Consumer companies have long been challenged to create customer loyalty. But in the business-to-business market, many companies had been able to rely on long-term contracts to keep customers loyal. Now, however, the Internet has greatly increased the volume and dollar value of off-contract buying. As a result, loyalty is a big issue in both business-to-consumer and business-to-business markets. That's why traditional and dot-com companies are spending billions trying to create a sense of relationship, commitment, and involvement via technology. Fortunately, the Internet has also driven the creation of many new tools and techniques to build customer loyalty. This chapter will discuss loyalty in the Internet age and describe some ways to make your customers come back time and again.

WHY IS LOYALTY IMPORTANT?

➤ Loyal customers cost as much as 30 percent less in marketing, advertising, and customer support overhead than do first-time customers.

➤ Loyal customers are better than your sales force at converting prospects into clients, because they are trusted to be objective and because your prospects identify with them.

➤ Loyal customers are the first ones to spot a negative trend in your products, sales, or service. They are an excellent source of advice on how to run your company.

Competing solely on price will commoditize any market and eventually doom all competitors save the one or two with the lowest costs. Yet many companies that would prefer not to emphasize price are being forced to do so, in order to compete on the Web with the wealth of comparison shopping services. But there are many more effective ways to gain customer loyalty: quality (of product and services), selection (Amazon's "The Earth's Largest Bookstore"), convenience and speed (one-click shopping), confidence, brand (image, reputation), entertainment value, and customer service. The relative importance of these elements is different for the Internet than for the physical shopping world. For example, an Internet customer may value confidence more than convenience, since e-tailers, by definition, provide convenience. Customer assistance on the Internet—before and after a sale—may be the most important factor in building customer loyalty in Internet stores. Great service can be the differentiator in Web shopping that even the finest real-world store owner will envy.

But what can companies do to better understand and improve the loyalty of business customers and consumers, even as the Internet enables competitors to be a mouse click away? The following are the factors that we believe will continue to be important for improving customer loyalty on the Internet for years to come.

■ PROVIDE A QUALITY PRODUCT OR SERVICE

Free, perfect, and now—that's what Robert Rodin, the CEO of Marshall Industries, argues people want from businesses, now that the Internet has reset expectations to the highest point in history. When we ask attendees at our conferences and workshops why they bought from one Web merchant over another, price is their first answer more than 50 percent of the time, when it comes to branded or commodity items. However, when we ask these folks why they continue to buy from a particular Web merchant, the quality of service or the quality of the products sold is mentioned more than 70 percent of the time, as either the first or the second response. The message is simple: To keep customers, you need to have both low-price and high-quality product and service. Of course, to avoid total commoditization of all products and services, one of the objectives of companies should be to shift the emphasis away from price as a drawing card for first-time, as well as repeat, buyers.

This effort is being helped by the growing number of third-party comparison services, such as BizRate and Gomez in the consumer products markets. While these services do compare prices, they place most of their emphasis on product/service quality, reliability, and the total experience with the company. This, of course, is because these sites are supported by the merchants that, although they don't formally pay for the referrals, do subscribe to the research services, purchase research reports, and buy advertising space. We're not suggesting that these services are biased. Far from it. We're merely suggesting that it is in the interest of the merchants to deemphasize price as a basis for comparison. In fact, we would suggest that participating in one or more of these rating services is one of the best ways to demonstrate the type of quality that Web-based enterprises need to prove in order to draw and keep customers.

■ PERSONALIZE AND HUMANIZE INTERACTIONS

According to a 1998 survey by Jupiter Communications, 40 percent of all respondents would be more comfortable with online purchasing if there were more human contact. Thousands of e-business leaders must have read that report, because it seems like every Web merchant in the world is asking consumers to fill out forms, with personal information in order to mimic the close, warm, personal experience of chatting with a clerk, a salesperson, or a telephone marketing professional.

While today's personalization is largely the result of human input, the personalization of 2002 and beyond will be driven by closer electronic monitoring of behavior. From the cookies that are being set by thousands of sites, to monitoring tools used by Internet service providers (ISPs), to a click-monitoring chip installed (but supposedly not turned on) by Intel in all Pentium III and up personal computers, we believe that companies that want to truly personalize presentation will have many opportunities to do so, provided concerns about privacy can be effectively addressed. While it is too early to predict whether all these personalization tools will be allowed by governments faced with the outcries of the privacy lobby, we believe that reliance on self-administered surveys to drive personalization will significantly diminish by the end of 2002, in favor of more sophisticated automated alternatives.

■ LOYALTY AND EMOTIONS

According to the results of a survey of 1,600 adults in the United States and Canada by Bristol Group, conducted in early 2000, whether customers return to an online business is often determined by the way visiting the site makes them feel. We strongly agree. For both B2B and, particularly, B2C businesses, online strategy and the physical presence on the Web must reflect a commitment to establishing genuine relationships with customers, rather than to technology-driven transactional encounters. According to the report, customers need to feel that the retailer understands their needs and will provide a human touch when necessary. But this raises the issue of how a company can understand needs unless it gathers this—often very sensitive—personal information. Certainly, this cannot be done by getting people to fill out forms. We believe that labor-intensive research methods such as personal interviews, focus groups, and observation of users will make a resurgence as data collection tools for companies that want to really understand what makes people loyal to one business as opposed to another.

■ BE HONEST AND TRUSTWORTHY, AND PROTECT PRIVACY

Another important factor in generating return visits to an e-commerce (EC) web site is whether customers feel that their information is secure, according to recent research by CyberDialogue. (See Figure 5.1.) The research firm polled 1,000 intensive Internet users in early 2000 and found that transaction security was even more important than price discounts. Factors related to web site ease of use, such as the ability to easily find items and pay for them, are much less important now than they were in the early days of e-tailing, when there was much more variation in web site quality.

Beyond protecting the privacy of their business and consumer customers, many companies have also developed tools and services to create and facilitate trust. Probably the most well known of the trust-building mechanisms

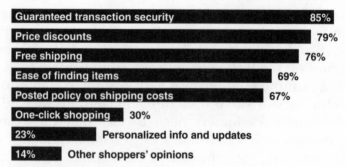

Figure 5.1 What prompts return visits to e-commerce web sites? *Source:* CyberDialogue, 2000.

is the TRUSTe logo, which more than 1,200 B2C and B2B merchants have put on their sites. But it is not hard to become a TRUSTe-approved merchant. The folks at TRUSTe .org must approve your privacy statement and receive a signed license agreement, self-assessment form, and payment of your annual license fee before they will let you put their bug or logo on your site.

Other privacy seal programs include offerings from the Better Business Bureau, which is similar to the TRUSTe program in its review of privacy policies and data safeguards. The WebTrust program of the American Institute of Certified Public Accountants (AICPA) requires a thorough, hands-on review by an accountant of the business practices for handling e-commerce (EC) transactions and business process controls relative to EC transaction data. At this point, the TRUSTe seal is what most consumers are looking for. However, as customers realize how easy this seal is to get (a simple policy and web site review, but no on-site inspection or review of data management procedures), we believe there will be a demand for greater rigor. As a result, we believe that industry trade association endorsement seals, along with financial and accounting seals, will begin appearing on web sites of all descriptions, causing sites to take on the look of a race car driver's uniform. For the near term, we recommend investigating your customers' awareness and concern about this issue before investing in any of these seals. They may not be worth the money.

■ VIOLATING CUSTOMER TRUST: AN EXAMPLE

Personalization engenders customer loyalty—people will come back to a site that they have invested in by providing the company with personal information, because this allows the company to use that information to ensure that the content better matches the customer's needs. Personalization also yields greater profits for the Web merchant that sells advertising space, since banner and other types of online ads sell for 5 to 10 times more if they are driven by customer data. As a result, marketers and Web merchants have strong incentives to gather as much data as they can about customers—particularly online customers. Thus, DoubleClick's acquisition of Abacus—a collector of offline customer data—seemed to be a good fit, as it would give the firm the most comprehensive set of customer data anywhere.

Unfortunately, DoubleClick totally misjudged the privacy concerns of consumers, and the resulting lawsuits and impending regulation caused DoubleClick to back off from its plans to integrate online behavior with offline consumer data. Customer trust in merchants, privacy statements, and online shopping in general suffered a major setback thanks to the overzealous efforts of market researchers to target advertising at narrow audience segments.

> **E-Vision:** As the shakeout among overly generic Web merchants continues, concern about merchant trustworthiness will grow. Business customers and consumers will demand greater rigor in the investigation of Web business viability. Many new third-party assurance programs, from banks, brokers, insurance companies, and trade associations, will blossom in 2001 and 2002. One of the most healthy growth segments during this period will be companies that insure international online transactions, for both completion and fulfillment.

Trust is also a big issue in the consumer-to-consumer area of EC, which is growing in popularity as eBay, Amazon, Yahoo!, and other portals attempt to take over the yard sale market. Not content to let caveat emptor rule in this market, these companies are establishing trust-building tools, such as eBay's Feedback Profile service, which makes it simple to develop a sense of the relative honesty of the person or company selling goods and services via eBay. While it is possible to use multiple e-mail IDs to put in lots of positive ratings, eBay has mechanisms in place to catch those who would falsify their rating.

Another trust-building mechanism in the consumer-to-consumer space is the Web-of-Trust tool developed by ePinions (see Figure 5.2) as a way to collectively determine the quality and trustworthiness of the ideas and writings of other members of the ePinions communities. As the consumer-to-consumer e-business market heats up over the next few years, we expect to see new e-businesses aimed at trust aggregation—that is, companies that buy, sell, aggregate, and give away trustworthiness data collected across a variety of sources. We do not expect to see any broadly recognized standards for trustworthiness of consumer Web sellers through 2002, other than the exist-

The "Web of Trust" Concept

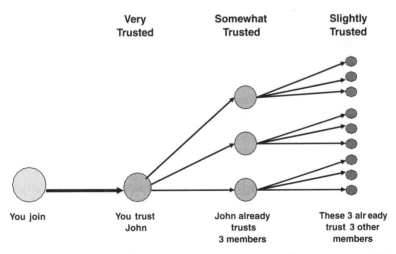

Figure 5.2   Who do you trust? Do I trust who you trust? It depends on how much I trust you. *Source:* ePinions.

ing de facto standards of TRUSTe, the Better Business Bureau, and the AICPA, cited previously.

■ PRACTICAL STRATEGIES FOR IMPROVING ONLINE LOYALTY

1. Increase rewards for creativity. Most online loyalty efforts are variations on incentive programs that have been around for decades, but they are most similar to frequent flyer programs. Building loyalty by consistently entertaining people is a goal of many B2C web sites, but it is really more typical of television. Millions of viewers, faced with 20 to 200 viewing choices at any one time, are loyal to their favorite TV programs because of creative writing, personality, or overall entertainment value. These programs make them laugh, cry, think, dream, and identify with the characters. As Chapter 2 emphasizes, the Internet (and specific web sites) needs to be a lot more entertaining if it is going to build the kind of loyalty and devotion evidenced by television. Consider this example from the gaming industry.

One type of television program that is being nicely adapted to the Internet is game shows. For example, Uproar.com produces and syndicates, among other types of entertainment, a number of online game shows. More like a TV network than a Web-based e-business, Uproar operates web sites tailored for the United States (Uproar .com), United Kingdom (Uproar.co.uk), and Germany (Uproar.de), as well as Prizepoint.com, Amused.com, Mentalstate.com, and Gamescene.com, which collectively draw several million registered users. More than 25,000 web sites run syndicated versions of Uproar's game show formats. In what we expect will be a growing trend, Uproar has licensed game show formats (including *Family Feud*) from Pearson Television, which has an equity investment in Uproar. Like hundreds of other gaming sites, Uproar also offers bingo, trivia, games of chance, puzzles, casino games, and arcade games. The message from entertainment and gaming sites is that it is important to enable visitors to put themselves on the line, so to speak. They don't have to formally gamble with their own money to feel at risk. But they do want fun, they do want a challenge, and even if they lose, they'll keep coming back if the game is interesting enough. After all, most of us are rarely satisfied after playing a round of golf, yet we keep coming back.

> **E-Vision:** As Web-based competitive pressure commoditizes prices and incentive programs begin to standardize over the next two years, the drivers of both business and consumer loyalty will shift from web site content to the quality of business execution and particularly e-fulfillment.

2. Use a third-party loyalty program. Loyalty programs on the Internet have become very creative, going well beyond their roots in the airline industry. Some programs are aimed at keeping users loyal to a particular e-business, such as the AOL Rewards program, which compensates its active members with AOL points for online purchases and participation in AOL tutorials and surveys.

In general, well-executed loyalty programs can be very effective in keeping consumers coming back to clearly branded, well-advertised, high-traffic sites. However, those consumer- or business-focused sites just starting out would be well advised to license their loyalty programs from third parties or to join a loyalty program that has a reputation of its own. Most third-party loyalty programs allow members to accumulate points in a single account, even though they visit a wide range of sites or engage in a wide range of activities. There are dozens of these third-party programs to choose from. Vendors of private-label rewards programs include Netcentives, which offers a program called SecureRewards, as well as Ecentives. There are also dozens of independent loyalty programs that merchants may join, including Flooz, Beenz, and Cybergold. These programs offer credits that can be spent only by going to participating sites, generating repeat traffic and a community of active users, which is attractive to the advertisers who pay to have their promotions included in the incentive programs.

We strongly recommend that all businesses, large and small, implement some type of incentive-based loyalty program, given their effectiveness. In general, features to look for in a Web incentive program include the following:

➤ Complete program management and the ability to handle special promotions
➤ The ability to target industry-focused business customers and consumers
➤ A well-financed company that will not go out of business in the next year
➤ A proven track record, complete with references in your industry
➤ An opt-in marketing program and event-triggered communications
➤ Corporate security handling and personal privacy management

3. Join a site cluster. Along with the emergence of micromarkets, we expect to see more companies building site clusters of hundreds and thousands of sites. The emergence of these Web networks will have significant implications for how loyalty will be measured. While there will certainly continue to be programs aimed at getting individual buyers to return to specific sites, we believe the future of loyalty measurement and analysis will be based on the percentage of an individual's time and revenue that is spent within the site network versus outside the site network. While joint ventures, affiliate programs, licensing agreements, and branding programs will span multiple site clusters, loyalty will be measured only across sites with common financial ties.

Mimicking the portals and their successful use of clubs and communities, many shopping sites have created their own clubs and communities in order to build loyalty, recognizing that people are more likely to be loyal to other people than they are to any business (see Chapter 2). Beyond the type of structured clubs that are formed under the auspices of the parent site, the most popular e-stores have spawned a number of service businesses, independent of the parent site. Users of eBay, for example, have created independent web sites that offer advice on trading strategy and other supporting information. eBay has encouraged these communities by providing message boards so users can interact. Core groups of traders in each category area come to know each other.

Our point is that instead of trying to start yet another Web shop selling the same old consumer products offered by other sites, a new generation of e-businesses will be those that spring up around a relatively small number of e-business clusters or Web networks. Most of these relationships will start out as affiliate relationships, but we expect

---

E-Vision: As Web clutter continues to grow, e-businesses will increasingly establish or join *site clusters* or *Web networks*—groups of hundreds or thousands of sites that do extensive cross-promotion and effectively pass business and consumer customers among these sites. Loyalty will be measured at the network level rather than at the web site level in the next one to two years. By the end of 2002, we predict that over 70 percent of e-business sites will be a member of one or more web site clusters or Web networks.

that more Web-preneurs will see the opportunities to franchise these hub-supporting e-businesses. (See Figure 5.3.)

4. Integrate online and offline customer service. One of the problems faced by brick-and-mortar companies that rushed to go online is that they created (or outsourced) online customer service functions. As a result, customers contacting the company via telephone may hear a different set of information and experience different service levels than customers contacting the company via the Internet. Poor service levels and inconsistent customer data are some of the concerns that were expressed by respondents in a study conducted in early 2000 by Socratic Technologies. The study substantiates the hypothesis that poor customer service leads to reduced customer loyalty and lost revenues. The study found that 87 percent of heavy users of online

E-Business Opportunities: Site Clusters

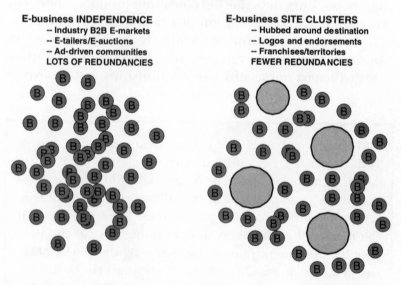

E-business INDEPENDENCE
-- Industry B2B E-markets
-- E-tailers/E-auctions
-- Ad-driven communities
LOTS OF REDUNDANCIES

E-business SITE CLUSTERS
-- Hubbed around destination
-- Logos and endorsements
-- Franchises/territories
FEWER REDUNDANCIES

Figure 5.3 Site clusters are groups of sites that share a financial relationship and a mutual referral relationship.

contact centers, or those spending more than $2,000 online over the last six months, said they were moved to competitive sites by poor service on another site. Another relevant finding was that e-mail appears to be the preferred customer contact method of choice for online purchasers, rather than an online chat session or a live phone call with a human—unless there is a problem! Once a customer encounters a problem with a company's web site, he or she wants to complain to a live person. The customer does not want to send e-mail messages to a software agent.

5. Implement customer self-service. For companies in the business-to-business markets or those with technically sophisticated consumers as customers, Web-based customer self-service is one of the most popular and cost-effective e-business applications for handling the mushrooming volume of inquiries, orders, messages, and so forth. Customers report that it is preferable to waiting in a call center queue and it provides better tracking of transactions, complaints, and the like. Approaches to self-help range from putting manual pages and do-it-yourself diagrams on the web site to creating sophisticated applications that enable customers to diagnose and solve problems that would otherwise require assistance from an experienced help desk associate or technician.

Companies (large and small) that need to handle Web transactions and inquiries and are just getting started should consider problem-solving agents. These applications assist customers in narrow but complex domains. After the customer answers a series of questions, the problem resolution system can provide a short list of documents or pages that could help the customer, and the customer can then choose which best fits the immediate need. There are a number of vendors that offer products in this area, including iContact, LivePerson, and HearMe.

6. Avoid customer care robots. At the automated end of the customer self-service spectrum are customer care robots (CCRs), a tool that is growing in popularity in the customer self-service market. CCRs attempt to simulate human interaction, while providing some level of assistance at any time of day or night, and at a fraction of the cost of using real people. CCRs can understand and answer a predetermined set of context-specific questions typed by the customer. CCRs can perform an ordered set of tasks such as completing commercial transactions, accessing databases or other web sites, and suggesting products based on buying patterns and reported preferences.

However, if you're the typical user, you'll be lucky if CCRs can decipher your grammar and spelling. Most CCRs do a poor job of clarifying what the person wants, and they can be very frustrating at times. Also, CCRs cannot monitor the customer's frustration, and they depend on a possibly angry person to enter data truthfully, which, unfortunately, is happening less and less frequently these days. The bottom line on CCRs is that they're going through that awkward age when they're annoying even as they're trying to be helpful. Readers would be well advised to sample the reactions of their customers to the existing technical alternatives before investing in something that that could hurt loyalty more than it helps.

7. Implement collaborative filtering. For companies that already have contact centers in place but want to gather more information about customers as part of their loyalty program, there is a more sophisticated set of tools that implement collaborative filtering. Collaborative filtering requires users to continually provide feedback about their likes and dislikes by rating (or ranking) the content they are offered. Collaborative filtering does not maintain a user profile per se. In particular, the user interests are not described in terms of content, but rather in terms of content ratings. This methodology allows companies like eToys to track what types of toys children like (e.g., children who like Toy A, also like Toy B), without gathering the type of personal data that has caused significant consumer outrage against DoubleClick, Amazon, and others that associate consumer preferences with personal characteristics.

On the downside, collaborative filtering is sensitive to inaccurate user feedback. That is, when people lie, as they often do, it messes up the process, and significantly reduces the value of this tool. But this is certainly leading-edge (i.e., risky) technology, and B2C companies with an interest in using personalization to drive loyalty should consider Net Perceptions' Recommendation Engine, one of the market leaders in this segment.

8. Offer customized, constantly changing content. One of the major lessons to be learned from the financial services, gaming, chat, and community sites is the importance of constantly changing information—and the more personal the information is, the better. Flashing ads don't count. They're regarded as annoying by most people, and hurt retention rather than help it. News feeds are also generally useless additions to most sites in terms of building loyalty. There are already too many sites that offer news. Adding it to your community site is not going to create any more loyalty, at least not if it comes from one of the major news feeds (i.e., the wire services). Creating interesting and involving chat is not so easy when you're trying to sell someone a blender or spare parts for a nuclear reactor. Generally, there's not a lot to chat about. However, the introduction of B2B and B2C auctions, industry monitors that are not simple generic feeds, and customizable stock tickers have made it easy to introduce constantly changing content to virtually every site at a relatively reasonable cost.

9. Focus on execution, not on marketing. Saying that "companies that sell on the Web need to execute better if they are going to keep customers satisfied" is way too obvious to be worthwhile as a recommendation. So let's be specific. I bought a half dozen music CDs from an e-store in Yahoo!'s e-mall. I searched the Web and they were the ones that had the lowest price. (Remember the story at the beginning of this chapter about how cheap I am?) I wound up waiting over a week. The last time I bought CDs from Amazon, they arrived in three days. I also got regular notification of order status from Amazon.

But do such differences in execution really make a difference in customer loyalty? Generally, about something simple and unnecessary like these CDs, the answer is no. But as business managers and consumers build up dependencies on Web-based e-businesses for necessities like aircraft components and groceries, we will care less and less about incentive programs, human-appearing clones, and whether the site features news and chat. True dependency on a company means no screw-ups, period. Companies that screw up (like eBay, or eTrade, or any of the e-businesses whose sites have crashed under duress) may be forgiven by the market as a whole, but specific customers who feel wronged may never return. This is the downside of moving from mere loyalty to dependency. (See Figure 5.4.)

Quick Analysis of Web Loyalty Factors

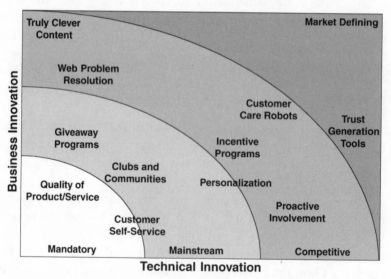

Figure 5.4 There is a spectrum of factors that affect online customer loyalty. *Source:* eMarket Holdings.

■ CONCLUSION

One of the biggest allies that online merchants have as they try to generate customer loyalty is the fact that most folks are more overwhelmed than thrilled at the range of alternatives that are available to them. Whether one is selling to businesses or consumers, the fact that one's competitors are a mouse click away doesn't matter as long as customers are satisfied with selection, price, timeliness of delivery, and the service they receive. In order to continually improve customer loyalty, online merchants should pick out a few leading-edge companies in other industries to watch, particularly in the entertainment industry. The reason is that keeping customers loyal and even involved requires that a company develop its sense of habit relative to online purchasing behavior, much like the habit of watching a particular TV show at a particular time. Web event–oriented programming and the use of episodic content (like an online soap opera) can help generate such habits.

For businesses, this will be driven by budget cycles and replenishment requirements, but it is still necessary to understand the economic, logistical, or emotional factors (e.g., friendship with a salesperson) that drive loyalty and to capitalize on them through the online experience.

Chapter

6

How to Compete
with the Unknown

From the cover stories on the founders of Priceline, Amazon, Napster, and others, it's clear that the typical Internet hero has much in common with Orson Welles's young protagonist in the movie *Citizen Kane*. Charles Foster Kane defied convention to build his newspaper empire—no matter that it wasn't profitable. He had his seemingly inexhaustible Colorado gold mine to support his unprofitable journalistic excursions. Similarly, today's Internet entrepreneur still has access to venture capital and IPO monies, even though the market has tightened dramatically. Like Citizen Kane, he can afford to be adventurous . . . at least until the "mother lode" runs out.

In the meantime, these upstarts can wreak havoc on traditional business models and make strategic planning even more of an educated guessing game than it already is. Can you successfully counter wave after wave of lossleader strategies played out in your industry? Can you anticipate the impact of business models that change as rapidly—and as inexplicably—as teenage romance? Even the realization that virtual companies must have physical infrastructure and generate profits—eventually—has not brought much comfort to the boardroom.

Is strategic planning still important in the fast-changing world of e-business? Yes! A creative and flexible strategic plan is more important than ever in building a successful e-business. Of course, experience, industry knowledge, and leadership still play a primary role in business strategy—but only if today's boardroom warriors realign their thinking to grasp the tremendous impact of Internet technology.

■ DECONSTRUCTION AND RECONSTRUCTION: THE TACTICAL QUAGMIRE

Because of the disruptive nature of Internet-enabled change, the leaders of many companies have taken a "just-do-something-before-we-get-Amazoned" attitude toward strategic planning. Even as Amazon.com struggles with its transition to a click-and-mortar enterprise, its impact on the corner bookstore and the giants of the book industry—remains a fear-inducing lesson. Since it appears that competitive forces, technological innovation, and customer expectations cannot be anticipated very far into the future, many companies simply overlay technology on current busi-ness processes, as shown in Figure 6.1. This leads them through ever more progressive implementations of *tactical* e-commerce initiatives.

There is nothing inherently wrong with implementing e-business strategy along this path. Indeed, great benefits can accrue in the form of satisfied customers, more efficient business processes, lower-cost sales channels, significant operational cost reductions, and, eventually, competitive advantage (or, at least survival). But reactive strategy in a world that is being transformed around you will not ensure market leadership. Rather, reactive strategies work best for companies that have always had a consumer–direct sales model, for example. They can add ever greater levels of e-commerce interactivity directly with their customers without disrupting their other sales

E-Business Strategy Evolution

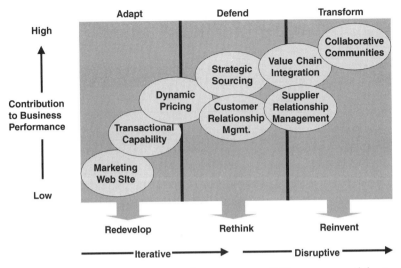

Figure 6.1 Many companies are unwilling or unable to plan for and embrace disruptive change. They take an iterative approach and "experiment" with e-business as an adjunct to their existing business.

channels, since they have none. Dell Computers, e-retailers, and catalog merchants are perfect examples of implementing the stepped approach to e-business. Most companies follow this path and lots of outstanding books have been written describing the tactical progression along this framework, in addition to offering excellent advice on how to proceed.

But this reactive path prescribes *iterative* change. It doesn't give business leaders a framework for anticipating *disruptive* change. Without that, they cannot create a fundamental vision of future e-commerce landscapes within which they must compete. They cannot set the stage for true innovative change. And that is what is necessary to lead rather than follow in the e-age.

> **E-Vision:** Over the next two years at least 50 percent of traditional brick-and-mortar companies with annual revenue of over \$1 billion will try to achieve e-business transformation via an external strategy: They will form dot-com spin-offs, acquire or merge with Internet companies, or invest in independent cybermediaries within their industries.

■ STRATEGIC PLANNING AND CONTEXT

The effect of the Internet on commerce will be as great as the effect of the industrial revolution on population centers and electricity on manufacturing. What those times had in common were waves of great, discontinuous change brought about by technological innovation. Established businesses failed because their leaders either refused to acknowledge change or could not quickly respond to the new economic and competitive environment.

The Internet has unleashed a similar discontinuous change—none greater than buyers' expectations of how commerce should work. Competitive strategies that are based on a pre-Internet view of buyers' perceptions and expectations will no longer work. How, then, to structure strategy in the e-age?

Understanding the concept of discontinuous, disruptive change and its consequences—getting Amazoned—is one thing. Planning for it is another. We think it will help to consider the e-age within three fundamental shifts in context: the merging of B2B and B2C, thoughtful competitive analysis, and the shift away from human-to-computer interaction.

THE CONTEXT OF E-BUSINESS

B2C and B2B as separate business paradigms will disappear. Therefore, business leaders must pay close attention to consumer interaction on the Web. Innovative strategic vision must unite business and consumer strategy as one.

Even during times of great ambiguity and technological innovation, strategic visioning scenarios must be based on a framework of traditional competitive analysis.

Over time, human-to-Web commerce will diminish as the transparency of data throughout the value chain allows for greater use of intelligent software agents acting on behalf of buyers. Therefore, any strategic visioning exercise must include scenarios that progressively rely on nonhuman interaction with information.

■ FEAR OF AMAZON IN THE E-AGE: COMPETITIVE STRATEGY FOR DISCONTINUOUS CHANGE

During times of uncertainty, the future need not be a mystery. Leaders can predict how Internet commerce will change the competitive landscape if they know what to look for within a framework of change. Like chess, strategic visioning exercises can be used to plot likely moves and countermoves in an unstable environment.

Michael Porter developed an excellent framework to analyze the forces that drive industry competition. He defined five competitive forces: (1) the threat of new entrants, (2) the threat of substitution, (3) the bargaining power of suppliers, (4) the bargaining power of buyers, and (5) the intensity of rivalry among competitors. We would add two others: (6) the acceleration of market subsegmentation and (7) the ease of information dissemination.

The e-business visionary must take into account the combination of technology and information availability as it affects these seven factors, as shown in Figure 6.2.

Competitive Context in the E-Age

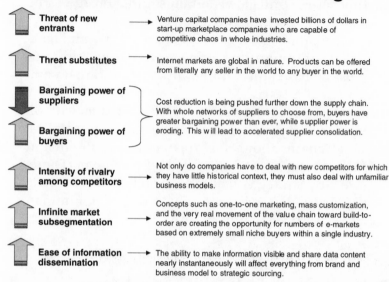

Figure 6.2 The confluence of these seven factors—accelerated and in some cases made possible by Internet technology—make strategic planning even more imperative in the e-age.

Enveloping strategy and tactics within the context of information acceleration and transparency is the key to understanding the ultimate shape of entire industries. This competitive reshaping is evidenced by the efficiencies of Dell's make-to-order supply chain, the influence of Web-based information gathering on the sales process within the car industry, and the rise of B2B procurement consortia.

■ PORTER'S FRAMEWORK IN CONTEXT

Performing analysis within the competitive framework outlined in Figure 6.2 can help anticipate where competition will come from, how market segmentation will occur, whether a company's power within the supply chain is waxing or waning, and the potential risk to margins. Each provides a unique view of the competitive landscape.

➤ New Entrant Juggernaut

The competitive pressure fostered by the Internet is staggering, much of it seeming to come out of left field. The private money that continues to be invested in the technology sector—especially focused on B2B Internet technologies—is creating a whole new generation of independent companies.

MONEY TREES DO EXIST

U.S. venture capital funding hit $35.6 billion in 1999, 150 percent greater than in 1998, according to PricewaterhouseCooper's Money Tree survey.

And the money is still flowing. Even with the market corrections during the first quarter of 2000, U.S. private investment was up. PricewaterhouseCooper's first-quarter 2000 Money Tree Survey reported $17.22 billion was invested in start-up companies—93 percent of the private money going to the technology sector. This was up 17 percent from the last quarter of 1999 and quadrupled the $4.31 billion invested in the first quarter of 1999.

A strong U.S. economy (spurred by the technology sector), enormous amounts of investment capital, and—last but not least—the tremendously high market caps of many high-profile IPOs was partially responsible for the frenzy throughout 1998 and 1999. Two examples were UPS, which completed a $5.5 billion IPO based primarily on its positioning as an e-commerce logistics provider, and Commerce One, an e-procurement metamediary whose per-share stock price went from $23 to over $700 in *less than six months.*

As risky as a clean slate can be, it does allow new entrants to move into industries unencumbered by traditional channels, corporate infrastructure, and old-line organizational structures. They can truly think outside the box and in doing so create new ways of interacting with customers. Therefore the key competitive factor that Porter identifies, the "threat of new entrants," has never been greater than it is today.

Strategic planning for the e-business must take into account the possibility of a massive influx of new players: known, unknown, and unexpected.

➤ Substitution Gets Easier

With the Internet, you never have to say, I can't find it. Because the Internet is global, buyers can choose from among local suppliers and search worldwide for substitutes. This is a scary scenario for manufacturers who fear competition from sources outside their geographic area—unfamiliar challengers who may have very different cost structures.

For example, nowhere has the threat of substitution been more exploited than in computer products. Consider these points from the replacement and substitution policy of Directron.com:

> Should one item be out of stock, we reserve the right to replace it with an equal or better product. We also reserve the right to substitute items with different brands of products of equal or better quality with the same or higher prices without additional cost to the customers. Substitution will be done with items that are of equal specification, quality, brand and price whenever possible.

Directron.com is selling products as diverse as HP printers, Cyrix computers, Mitsubishi digital cameras, and PC monitors from Sony. As these types of discount stores proliferate on the Web, the threat of substitution—replacing branded components with less expensive items that are of equal specification, quality, and so on—will become more commonplace.

➤ Buyers Gain Negotiating Power, Suppliers Lose Negotiating Power

With whole networks of suppliers to choose from, neatly collected by aggregators or dominant distributors into e-markets, buyers have greater bargaining power than ever. Conversely, this same environment weakens suppliers. Aggregated e-markets will lead to less supplier differentiation, more emphasis on price, and will likely accelerate supplier consolidation among commodity goods.

Take the example of OrderZone, an e-market developed by W. W. Grainger and later merged with Works.com. Order-Zone allows corporate buyers to select industrial goods from among seven distributors plus Grainger. These distributors represent a number of manufacturers of maintenance, repair, and operating (MRO) supplies, including uniforms and apparel, office supplies and equipment, safety supplies, electronic components, production supplies, and laboratory and equipment supplies. By allowing a search across multiple MRO distributors, Grainger is trending toward the B2C one-stop shopping model popularized by physical malls, superstores, discount retailers, and their virtual counterparts. The shopping mall paradigm is further underscored by the merger with Works.com—an Internet purchasing service for small and medium-size companies. That is, this merger of a sell-side aggregator with a buy-side aggregator results in broader selection for the buyers and greater commoditization for the sellers.

E-Vision: The online e-market trend will accelerate and further weaken suppliers' power and profitability positions within a value chain. By late 2002, the combination of lower margins, the content management resources required to participate in multiple e-markets, and buyer-initiated procurement extranets will cause suppliers to pull out of low-volume e-commerce activities.

➤ Competitive Rivalries Intensify

Not only do companies have to deal with competitors they know and understand, they also must deal with competitors for which they have no historical context. Rivalry between traditional businesses and their virtual competitors will escalate contention at all points within the buy/sell cycle. For example, not only must car manufacturers deal with competitors who allow cars to be purchased online and even deliver the car to your door, they must do so while minimizing channel conflict.

One response is to focus on the traditional supply chain. General Motors, Ford, and others hope to use a common Internet infrastructure for supplier integration, thus providing more efficient supplier management and lower manufacturing costs. The Automotive Network Exchange (ANX) was an early attempt to create a common Web infrastructure for the exchange of documents between America's big three automakers and their suppliers. The industry expected to reduce the manufacturing costs by $71 per car, equating to billions in savings. Later variations on the "let's collaborate to reduce costs" theme can be seen in the formation of Covisint, an online procurement consortium launched by GM, Ford, Chrysler, Renault, and Nissan. While on the surface these industry initiatives look like collaboration, we believe that they will more likely be implemented at a very high level—among the top-tier suppliers only—and will just be a more efficient way to manage existing business processes and squeeze suppliers harder.

New intermediaries also increase rivalry within an industry by introducing new competitive pricing mechanisms such as auction, exchange, and bid/response, and by creating secondary markets online. Intermediaries such as XSChem in the agricultural chemicals industry provide buyers with a new source for competitive products. Independent intermediaries of this type have a great deal of flexibility. They can offer products outside of the normal distribution channels and are unencumbered by traditional manufacturer/supplier cost structures. They are free to respond to customer demand and even to aggregate demand, as is possible with Vickery auction models, discussed in Chapter 11.

All of these initiatives—e-markets, supply chain extranets, and industry consortia—will intensify rivalry between individual companies. Dealing with them will require a sophisticated and long-term view of competitive pressures.

➤ Micromarkets Emerge

Micromarket segmentation is empowered by the Internet and its ability to easily connect small groups of buyers with niche market suppliers. Where else can you find a virtual market for buying and selling used forklifts or a site that lets you buy personalized underwear? Concepts such as one-to-one marketing, mass customization, and the reversal of the value chain from build-to-buy to buy-to-build are affecting the supremacy of least-cost manufacturing as a competitive advantage. Instead, the ease of segmenting markets creates new opportunities for a virtual explosion of highly targeted suppliers and products. This ability to reach smaller and smaller buyer niches provides the silver lining for suppliers facing intensified competition and the specters of easy product substitution, eroding buyer loyalty, falling margins, and product commoditization, which are the result of Internet commerce.

But how does the strategic planning process take advantage of micromarkets that are formed independently by buyers themselves? For example, SHOP2gether's business model enables individual buyers to form in groups for the express purpose of creating enough specific product demand to attract bids from suppliers. As more buyers join the group, suppliers are encouraged to sweeten the deal. While specific online exchanges like SHOP2gether may not survive, the ad hoc aggregation of demand will likely be one of the most pervasive competitive challenges (and opportunities) faced by companies.

So we have three competitive forces driving micromarketplace segmentation of an industry: manufacturers like Procter & Gamble that create branded personalized product sites such as Reflect.com, infomediaries that create electronic markets targeted to specific niche markets, and buyers that aggregate to buy specific products and services.

➤ The Ease of Information Dissemination

No effect of the Internet has been more profound than the ability it provides for individuals and companies to easily share and distribute information—nearly instantaneously. We already see the effects of B2C commerce on industries such as travel, retail brokerage, and music—from tightening of margins to fundamental threats to industry business models. And as cybermediaries take up prominent residence in the B2B space, we will begin to see similar effects there.

How do you anticipate the potential impact of information sharing in your industry and how much time do you have to react? As shown in Figure 6.3, two excellent measures of the level to which an industry could be restructured due to electronic commerce are (1) the relative ease of substituting one product for another and (2) the degree to which a product itself can be digitized, such as music or movies, or the ease of describing the significant attributes of a product. These two factors are interrelated

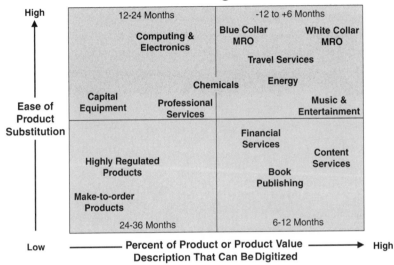

Figure 6.3 Restructuring has already started in industries such as music and entertainment and maintenance, repair, and operations (MRO) procurement. It has not yet begun in the make-to-order (customized manufacturing) industry because of the highly specialized nature and difficulty of the process itself.

on the content side because, while any product description can be digitized as information about the product, that attribute affects commodity products more than highly specialized products. In other words, the level of product information required to make a decision relative to parts used in the manufacture of a satellite is much greater than the level of product information needed to make a decision about which laptop computer to buy.

Two other significant metrics are the amount of legal protection a product has, such as copyrighted material, and the degree to which a product is regulated, such as pharmaceuticals.

■ THE HUMAN FACTOR IN THE AGE OF TECHNOLOGY

People work as a sort of deceleration system for the adoption of anything new . . . especially new technology. Many technically well-conceived software applications fail simply because people refuse to use them. The Web has been phenomenal in that respect—its adoption rate has been much faster than anything we have ever seen in the past. But even the Web has its limitations, and many believe that only after the passage of a generation or two will the Internet reach its full potential.

While there is much truth in that view, we believe that human interaction with machines sets its own natural limits regardless of the passage of generations. When developing long-term business strategy, then, it is important to first consider the Internet's natural limits in the broader context of human interaction, and then consider by what means those limits can be exceeded.

➤ People and Technology: Putting on the Brakes . . . Temporarily

At the beginning of the e-age, some believed that the Web would make it possible for us to have perfect a priori knowledge about the products we buy. Not only would we know all, we would also have access to information without the constraints of time and space. But the proliferation of technological innovation is always tempered by humanity's innate ability, or the lack thereof, to deal with change. Technology disengaged from its human context is just an exercise in science fiction.

A more practical way to view the Web's impact on people is to view it from the perspective of four distinctly human concepts: time, distance, communication, and memory. When time and distance approach zero and communication and memory escalate toward perfection, one of two things happens: People find a balance between the speed of technological change and the rate at which they can absorb and constructively use it. Or technological change so out-distances the ability to adjust that paralysis occurs.

➤ Barriers in Time and Distance

While it is difficult for all interested parties to share data, understand it, and act on it instantaneously, the Internet broadens the concept of "zero latency" beyond processes like just-in-time manufacturing and vendor-managed inventory replenishment. Web-based collaboration can happen simultaneously across time zones with partici-pants viewing information in real time. Employees telecommute. Executives broadcast their messages to all points within the organization at once via an intranet. External business partners communicate via extranet connections. While the barriers of time and distance are surmountable, the cost was often considered prohibitive. Now the Internet, the World Wide Web, and the technolo-gies they spawned are reducing the cost of reaching near instantaneous information exchange.

Geographic convergence and the potential for fluid groups to form, disintegrate, re-form, and so on, is break-ing down market barriers for those who can develop busi-ness models as fluid as the cybercommunities they serve. Viral marketing is possible on a scale not dreamed of before the Internet. The first generation of cybermediaries, whether they are drawn from the banks of VCs or spun off from our best-known business entities, will be successful if they can become virtual transaction brokers—facilitators that see to it that a stream of data is delivered from any point to any other point. Business managers must con-struct strategy that is agile enough to take advantage of the Internet's ability to facilitate instant commerce.

➤ Communication and Memory

With the breakdown of time and distance, the ability to communicate has increased exponentially. Typically, any important innovation in information handling took at least two decades to be adopted in significant numbers. For example, it was 26 years before the telegraph was used extensively in the scheduling of trains, yet until the telegraph was widely used, it was not possible to safely operate the railroad system on an efficient schedule. Typewriting was not commonly used until 29 years after its introduction.* The telephone was last century's most successful two-way communication invention, taking 35 years to reach 50 million people. By contrast, it took only four years for the Web to reach the same number of people, helped to a large extent by the fact that the underlying infrastructure was already in place.

This lag illustrates that it is not only technology that must be taken into account when creating an e-business, but also the rate of its adoption and the learned experience of users. In this, the Web has been truly miraculous. But individual technology usage does not automatically portend broader contextual change. In other words, people individually can deal with change at a greater rate than groups, organizations, companies, and cultures. That's why the Internet has not yet had a greater impact on traditional business process, despite the huge number of people using browsers to surf the Web, as shown in Figure 6.4.

---

* Rob Kling, ed., *Computerization and Controversy,* 2nd ed. (San Diego, CA: Academic Press), 1996, p. 280.

E-Vision: Over the next 12 to 18 months, most Internet challenges will only *seem* disruptive. If examined objectively, 90 percent will fall into a much less threatening category: the Internet enabling of existing business-as-usual models, creating little, if any, fundamental *process* change. Operational efficiency will be gained, but client/supplier relationships will remain stable.

Human Factors in Technology Adoption

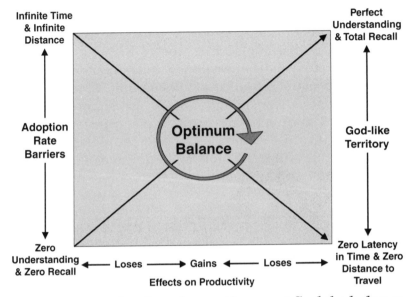

Figure 6.4 Technology innovation must find the balance between what provides productivity gains and losses. As information flow moves toward the right side of the chart it becomes increasingly difficult for humans to deal with. At that point productivity gains will require technology solutions that do not depend on human interaction.

E-business managers must not allow the technology to dictate the strategy. Rather, business process, which is the interaction of people first and foremost, must always be at the heart of technological innovation.

■ BUSINESS AVATARS: CLOSING THE GAP

The aforementioned human-imposed limitations are significant but—to some extent—temporary. Internet commerce is an information and data revolution, enabled by a technology revolution. True discontinuous change will occur when pure technology, in the form of intelligent software agents, is able to act on data in a human-like way. We call these agents *business avatars* because they will incorporate attribute-based decision-making processes into their functionality. Just as robotics on the modern assembly line has replaced scores of humans, software agents will replace the browser-enabled human for gathering and acting upon mundane information. To search out the lowest price, consumers already use shopping bots. These intelligent software agents will transform commerce significantly as businesses, eager to sell goods and services to the widest possible audience, make more and more internal data available to them.

> **E-Vision:** Within the next five years, purchasing agents, business buyers, shop floor managers, and consumers will expand their use of *personal* software agents in cyberspace. By early 2004, sophisticated business avatars representing individual buyers will be used in over 20 percent of business procurement.

Business avatars will transact many forms of commerce over the next five years, freeing us from the drudgery of interactive communication with a software application or stream of data. As the sophistication of these avatars grows, they will do more than just search sites and bring back the lowest-cost items for purchase decisions. They will act within a framework of knowledge about our preferences, shopping patterns, preferred product attributes, and so on. They will also dynamically augment this knowledge as they execute transactions on our behalf.

WHAT IS AN AGENT OR AVATAR?

A *software agent* is a software package that carries out tasks for others, autonomously, without direct intervention by its master once the tasks have been delegated. The others may be human users, business processes, work flows, or applications. A basic software agent has three essential properties: autonomy, reactivity, and communication ability. The notion of *autonomy* means that an agent exercises exclusive control over its own actions and state without control of some external software entity. *Reactivity* means sensing or perceiving change in their environment and responding through effectors. And even the most basic software agents have the ability to communicate with other entities (human users, other software agents, or objects), giving them various forms of social ability.

Information made easily available to software agents will be especially beneficial in B2B transactions. Avatars (representing individuals, companies, and/or cybermediaries) will interact with each other to find appropriate products and negotiate price, availability, and delivery on behalf of their human counterparts. The purchasing manager's avatar may very well store information related to inventory levels that must be maintained for certain items, which suppliers are used to replenish those items, what level of quality is required for each item, acceptable price ranges, and shipping instructions. That avatar will be able to interact with compatible software agents that reside in e-markets, which track hundreds or even thousands of suppliers that have been screened relative to quality, price, availability of products, and so forth. Like the electronic data interchange (EDI) application-to-application transactions of the past, avatars will be capable of conducting human-free commerce in ever more sophisticated ways.

B2B exchanges like those being enabled by Commerce One, Ariba, and I2 are attempting to become gatekeepers for a vast wealth of product data. So they won't be left

behind in the e-commerce revolution, individual companies will provide their product data to these brokers, even
though these data often represent their single greatest
source of differentiation and competitive knowledge.
Eventually, to attract greater numbers of buyers to their
cybermarkets, intermediaries will normalize data and
make it relatively easy to search across multiple suppliers—at least within their own market site. Once data are
accessible by more sophisticated browser search engines,
it is only a matter of time before the human behind the
engine is replaced by a software avatar.

Sound far-fetched? XML (Extensible Markup Language) is rapidly becoming the de facto standard for
defining product data used on the Web. We are already
seeing coalitions such as RosettaNet, an organization of
independent companies, setting XML standards for the
exchange of product information and promoting common e-commerce processes. The most recent example of
this is the Universal Description, Discovery and Integration (UDDI) project, launched by IBM, Microsoft, and
Ariba, and endorsed by nearly 50 other companies.
While such "standards" have their limits, as discussed in
Chapter 10 and elsewhere, they will ease data exchange
among enterprises. Once neutral cybermediaries, whose
goals are to attain a critical mass of buyers and sellers
rather than product differentiation, adopt standards such
as this, software agents will be able to interact with data
and work across complementary e-markets.

■ PRACTICAL STRATEGIES FOR E-AGE VISION

Keeping a clear strategic vision during a time of competitive restructuring and intensification can be facilitated by
the creation of a competitive landscape that looks at forces
not only within but also outside of an industry. The traditional strategy tool set of market analysis, competitive
analysis, globalization, and so on must be broadened to

include external "left-field" competitors and multiple outcomes. To help their companies prepare to compete against dot-coms and other companies not on their radar screen, we recommend that executives:

1. Map the competitive landscape. Prepare and maintain a topographical map of the industry. Include profiles of companies that influence the market directly or indirectly (a respected trade magazine may have indirect but powerful influence within an industry). Include major manufacturers, distributors, wholesalers, retailers, content providers, Internet cybermediaries, industry associations, credit bureaus, and so on, and map them against the market segments they influence. Profile companies at several levels: focus within the industry (industry subsegment), products and services offered, relationships with complementary companies (for example, manufacturers who own financing companies), ability to influence the direction of the industry, online initiatives, and online alliances.

Within the landscape, draw current and expected alliances: who has invested in whom, who has strategic alliances, who is selling through what distributors, and so on. Of special interest should be the investments by major players in independent e-market cybermediaries including but not limited to capital investment and/or commitment of industry behemoths to sell through the channel.

Once you have a two-dimensional picture of the competitive landscape, add the topography by anticipating the probable movements of the players over 12 to 18 months and how this movement will affect the competitive forces we have outlined in this chapter. By building and maintaining this landscape—even at a rudimentary level—you will be able to:

➤ Minimize competitive surprises by following the dynamics at play in your industry.

➤ Have at your fingertips a graphical analysis of the various business models and pricing mechanisms being played out online.

➤ Develop a gap analysis between what is being offered by traditional and by online companies.

➤ Understand, at any point in time, your competitive position relative to Internet threats and opportunities.

➤ Anticipate relationships and alignment as well as identify possible strategic partners for your own efforts.

2. Anticipate competition from outside your industry. In addition to the known players within an industry, map any outsiders such as independent e-market intermediaries (e-Steel, FastParts, and ChemConnect would be examples) that are likely to enter your industry by virtue of already being in a related industry. For example, Chemdex, already a leading cybermediary in the research chemicals and laboratory supplies industry, recently targeted the related health care industry.

3. Think outside of the existing organizational structure. We believe that companies may have to literally step outside of their current revenue models and organizational structures in order to address threats from online competitors. That is why we expect many traditional companies will either buy, spin off, or invest in a dot-com.

4. Practice stealth strategy. Some companies will not be able to envision, much less implement, long-term strategic e-visions. This may be due to company culture, organizational barriers, or lack of executive support. If so, a much more tactical approach makes sense. Plan for short-term (12 to 18 months) tactical advancements. Aim toward the iterative rather than the disruptive change and assume that extraordinary strategic shifts will occur only under direct threat of cataclysmic change—such as disintermediation or significant loss of market share to Internet upstarts or cybersavvy traditional competitors.

5. Mitigate the rise of software avatars by increasingly presenting information in a knowledge context rather than just a data context. The presentation of product context must include nonprice attributes such as quality, availability, client testimonials, and customer service. Seek intermediaries that allow for the presentation of nonprice information during the buying process.

6. Offer problem support and resolution early in the decision cycle. Business avatars will tend to be used late in the buying cycle, after clients have determined what they need. Structure contextual sites that are relationship based rather than product based and that attract buyers as early as possible in their decision process, so as to create one-to-one relationships. Suppliers who help solve a problem or provide expert help rather than just a product will be perceived as having greater value.

General-purpose avatars will be used primarily against directory listings and within cybermediary-controlled e-markets, which tend toward commoditization and multiple supplier listings. However, the technology could have its most effective use within an industry or supply chain among known participants. If used in a strategic fashion, avatar technology could be used to competitive advantage by tightening supply chains and increasing productivity.

7. Protect your expert knowledge. Highly personalized content and knowledge, whether it is targeted to individuals or to corporations and industries, will tend to ameliorate the impact of avatars by increasing the strategic value of support. Truly expert knowledge or information should be protected rather than shared with cybermediaries. Insist that links from cybermediaries back to individual suppliers be activated after a certain level of inquiry (by software agents or humans) is reached. Even if presented on an e-market in conjunction with competitive information, your data should be clearly branded.

■ CONCLUSION

In times of disruptive change, our basic suggestion is simple: You must remain flexible in order to take advantage of e-business opportunities and respond to new, and perhaps unfamiliar, challenges. But don't panic. Most Internet challengers will, at their core, simply be increasing operational efficiencies around an existing business process rather than fundamentally changing client relationships. This doesn't mean that we are suggesting the adoption of a wholesale wait-and-see attitude. On the contrary, we believe it is imperative to formulate strategy and tactics within the framework of a thorough understanding of the long-term effect of Internet commerce.

In order to do that, executives and managers must develop a vision for their company's role as an e-business. Having a big-picture strategy will allow management to remain flexible throughout tactical e-business initiatives while providing a sense of structure and purpose. This approach to planning—think big, act small—allows iterative change within a disruptive environment. The suggestions we have made in this chapter may seem obvious, but few companies are following them. Executives can create a planning atmosphere that is proactive, forward thinking, and exciting. The result is that the company will be able to anticipate market conditions, plan and execute highly beneficial competitive strategies, and use to the best advantage the unsettling and disruptive technological revolution that is e-business.

Chapter

7

Web Channel Conflict

At the beginning of the e-age, there were cries that we had embarked on a vast period of disintermediation. Like the great cataclysmic event that wiped out the dinosaurs, Internet commerce would eliminate the need for sales intermediaries. Doomed to obsolescence, vast armies of out-of-work salespeople, out-of-business distributors, and surplus sales agents would be wandering aimlessly through vast, half-empty retail bookselling establishments (the few that remained, post-Amazon), piteously trying to update their marketable skills by reading *Internet for Dummies*. Anyone defending the value of middlemen in the new economy was viewed as hopelessly behind the technology curve.

The sentiment has reversed. The popular belief now, especially with the demise of so many dot-coms and the continued low commerce transaction volumes on even the best-known B2B sites, is that the traditional intermediary is not as threatened as once thought. The sales agent, broker, and distributor would retain their undisputed position in the supply chain: the true keepers of customer access. As the president of one midsize electrical contracting distributor told us, "We know our customers' businesses first-hand. We talk to them every day. We help them through the job. We are there for them around the clock. We provide a valuable service that our suppliers cannot easily replicate. Besides, most of our customers are too small to even hit the radar screens of the manufacturers we represent. I'm not worried about the Web."

Just because few cybermediaries have gotten it right so far, doesn't mean that the premise for disintermediation is completely flawed. Few illusions should be held about the attraction of chipping away at the 30 percent to 60 percent of product revenue traditionally absorbed by channels. After decades of a yin-and-yang codependence, manufacturers have begun to reassess their position in the overall commerce value chain. Middlemen must do the same.

■ THE VALUE CHAIN IN CRISIS

To sell direct or not to sell direct, that is the question. The enormity of this question has paralyzed many brick-and-mortar companies. For some, failure to act begins a death spiral that only extraordinary measures can correct. For others, failure to act first or follow quickly has resulted in slower growth, market share erosion, lost opportunity, executive shake-ups, or corporate restructuring.

The ability to eliminate or substantially reduce the cost of sales while gaining invaluable direct access to customers would seem too attractive to ignore. Selling direct—in one form or another—is a competitive imperative. If you don't do it, someone else in your industry will. Even after the dot-com shakeout, this statement is still true.

➤ The CEO Dilemma

CEOs are trying to find a way to compete with traditional distribution channels without jeopardizing current revenue. It isn't easy. And in some cases it isn't even legal. Contractual obligations to indirect channel partners may block an easy transition to direct selling. On the other hand, you may be able to invest in an online channel, fund a new online subsidiary, or simply sit down and talk to your channels about a partnership that enhances everyone's position and makes sense for the customer.

SIDESTEPPING CONFLICT, MISSING OPPORTUNITIES

In early 1999, the CEO of a large chemical manufacturer was concerned about the possible effects of unaffiliated, venture-capital-funded exchanges establishing themselves in his industry. He was also concerned that the leaders of his company's business units, all men with 20 to 30 years of experience, did not understand the potential benefits or threats of the Internet. He assigned IT and product marketing staff to study the issue, evaluate the potential effect of Internet exchanges on the industry, educate senior executives, and recommend how the company might respond to this threat.

Working nearly full-time for three months, the committee held monthly educational meetings for senior leaders, painstakingly plotted the competitive landscape, mapped potential allies and outside threats, and finally recommended that the company form a consortium of noncompetitive manufacturers that would offer complementary products to customers direct over the Internet. The senior executives were interested. All but the CEO who, in the end, would not risk the ire of the company's major distributors, people he had done business with for 30 years. Who is the dinosaur in this picture?

The result? By mid-2000 the chemicals industry had become one of the prime target exchanges, with over 70 formed so far, including e-Chemicals, CheMatch, and ChemConnect. The committee was right: Direct sales to chemical customers did happen regardless of distributor pushback or manufacturer ambiguity.

Channel conflict has caused some companies to appear to act schizophrenically, as they constantly change their e-business strategies. Levi Strauss's business strategy is a study in opposites: first creating its own web sites and forbidding retail channels to sell the Levi's brand online, then announcing that it will stop selling through its own sites and sell only through the sites of its retail partners, ostensibly because of the expense of direct sales. General Motors pulled back from its plan to buy at least 10 percent of its dealer networks and sell direct when its announcement caused a hailstorm of denunciations and threatened lawsuits from dealers.

One thing is certain, however: Companies should not be asking whether to compete with traditional channels. They should be asking when and how. How much time do traditional companies have before cybermediaries and more aggressive competitors gain the edge by mastering the new online sales channel? How can they sell direct without triggering a massive distributor, reseller, or retailer backlash? Above all, how can they convince Wall Street that their companies are not being left behind in the wake of an Internet-driven information revolution? Unfortunately, in an age of fundamental industrial change, established wisdom does not necessarily point the way to reasonable decisions.

E-Vision: Fear of channel backlash will continue to be the primary reason CEOs hold back on establishing an aggressive online e-commerce presence. By the end of 2001 we expect tier-one manufacturers (greater than $1 billion in revenue) to derive less than 10 percent of their revenue from online orders directly from customers.

■ THE METAMORPHOSIS OF THE VALUE CHAIN

We are in the midst of an extended period of value chain metamorphosis. E-business is enabling the simultaneous deconstruction and reconstruction of channels to the customer. Ultimately, we believe that the customer, the manufacturer, and the provider of services will benefit from the dynamic direct relationship that can be set up between them.

Pure distributor-controlled channels are giving way to new intermediary models such as those discussed in Chapter 9. And while many will not last, they will forever change the role of traditional sales channels. Buyers themselves are exerting more and more control over the value chain. And while this metamorphosis is not purely linear, its permutations are squarely focused on the customer. Commerce power is moving undeniably toward the buyer and away from distributor-controlled channels.

Though most product makers, service providers, and intermediaries acknowledge this trend, few can see its eventual outcome. In customer-driven marketing, selling, manufacturing, and distribution lie the seeds for the ultimate destruction of intermediaries. After all, who better understands the buyer than the buyer? And who is better equipped to manufacture a custom product, negotiate the lowest price, and provide the most extensive information about the product than the maker?

➤ The Fewer Layers, the Better

As the product development process changes from market research controlled to customer controlled, as shown in Figure 7.1, buyers will no longer be semipassive recipients; independent of salespeople, distributors, or retailers, buyers will fashion manufacturing and service labor into forms that are as close to their view of personal perfection as possible. They will demand custom-produced products,

Value Chain Continuum

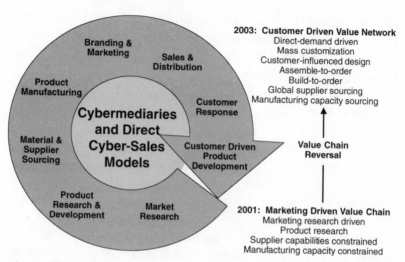

Figure 7.1 E-businesses are moving from linear value chains driven by market research to more customer-driven value networks over the next few years.

from computers to bathing suits. To fill the demand for mass-customized products, manufacturers will need direct input from customers. Any layer between the buyer and the maker will not only add cost and complexity but also create an attractive void for producers less encumbered by existing channel relationships.

The ability to provide at least the *perception* of mass customization will differentiate the victors from the victims of e-business. Manufacturers that understand this and position their channel strategies for direct customer access will be the only ones in a good position to enhance brand, price, and market share in the face of increasing customer reliance on exchanges and other e-markets.

E-Vision: Manufacturers that are in the vanguard of customer-direct interactions *today* will be the only ones truly equipped to understand how best to reengineer their shop floors, laboratories, and marketing apparatus for the coming mass customization revolution among consumers and, to a lesser degree, business buyers.

■ DRIVERS OF CHANNEL CONFLICT

As difficult as it may be to deal with, channel conflict will not disappear. The battle to control the customer gateway is becoming even more heated as the Internet expands to nearly ubiquitous buyer access. Technology has made it much easier to take up a position in the middle of a value chain, and everyone wants to be the gatekeeper to the customer. And to those who choose their distributors over their customers, who don't fashion some form of customer-direct selling strategy, this explosion of online channels is a clear and present danger.

➤ How Much Is a Channel Worth?

To determine how much a channel is worth, a company must estimate its customer acquisition, retention, and service costs as well as its distribution costs through each of its channels. The unfortunate truth, however, is that many companies cannot attribute these costs to particular channels . . . if they know them at all. Just as the estimates of processing a paper purchase order vary widely—from as low as $50 to as high as $250—so do other costs of doing business. For example, we have seen customer acquisition figures vary from as low as $1.50 for an established storefront retailer to $26 for Web retailers such as Amazon. Consider the results shown in Table 7.1 of a study conducted by the Boston Consulting Group.

TABLE 7.1   Spending per Customer, Traditional Retailer versus Dot-Com

	Bricks and Mortar	Pure-Play
Customer acquisition cost	$22	$42
Customer retention spending	16% of marketing	3% of marketing
Marketing spending	13% of revenues	76% of revenues

Source: The Boston Consulting Group.

On the surface, it would seem that it costs dot-com companies more to acquire customers than it does traditional companies. But this conclusion ignores the fact that online customer acquisition costs are *incremental* for brick-and-mortar companies. The perception is that the cost to do business online is considerably lower for established brands. Presumably, much of this cost reduction could be passed on to manufacturers and buyers if the middleman's role was eliminated or reduced. And they have a powerful incentive: a fatter profit margin and a lower purchase price.

We don't mean to minimize the risks of eliminating traditional intermediaries. Channel conflict fostered by the Web is nearly impossible to control. Geographies break down, and e-markets and technology breakthroughs can suddenly change underlying assumptions about a market. Consider the music industry's reaction to the digital music standard MP3 and cybermediaries who use it to bypass traditional sales channels. To quote Chuck D of the rap group Public Enemy, "It's the wild wild west, and everybody's got a gun."* Even without Napster, the digital download and sharing of copyrighted music will be impossible to corral.

---

* "Channel Conflict and the Net: Everybody's Got a Gun" Gary A. Bolles, *Sm@rt Reseller.*

Artists and entertainment companies will need to rewrite their contracts and revenue models if they are going to survive in a world where traditional methods of selling their music, photographs, poems, and so forth, are increasingly obsolete.

In such a world, it is important to understand the costs and revenue associated with all channels. Such measurement will help determine which can be deemphasized in favor of more efficient channels. Figure 7.2 offers one type of approach to the measurement of channel value.

Evaluating Channels

Quantitative Values	Channel 1	Channel 2	Channel 3
Percentage of customers managed by channel			
Percentage of total revenue			
Sales cost of channel			
Cost of fulfillment without channel			
Cost of fulfillment through channel			
Quantitative value of channel			
Qualitative Values			
Type of customer managed through channel			
Channel brand equity			
Value of product knowledge			
Value of customer knowledge			
Customer dependence on channel			
Qualitative value of channel			

Figure 7.2   Channels should be measured periodically on both the quantitative and qualitative value they bring to manufacturers, service providers, and the customers they service. Channels can first be grouped by type—cybermediaries as well as traditional channels—then individual channels within the group evaluated.

➤ The Lure of Operational Efficiency

A well-executed Internet-based approach to sales, customer support, and the exchange of information will enhance profitability. Companies, especially the Global 2000, have seen how automation can save extraordinary amounts of money through electronic data interchange (EDI) implementations.

By eliminating human intervention, EDI can save time, improve productivity, and enhance customer satisfaction. EDI is great for repetitive, high-volume transactions between large, known business partners. But it does not scale easily beyond a limited number of fairly sophisticated technology users. Ultimately, e-business via the Internet has the ability to deliver on the EDI promise: cheap, efficient, ubiquitous application-to-application interaction with little or no human intervention. EDI helped large companies enhance business process and profitability; the Web can deliver these benefits to any Internet-enabled business.

➤ Cost Savings Are Not the Only Attraction

The rise of traditional intermediaries can be related to the transaction cost theory,* which holds that sales and distribution will be moved inside only when the transaction costs of managing external channels outweigh the production efficiencies that come with outsourcing to specialized firms. Now, with Internet access, Internet technology, and enterprise resource planning back-end systems, companies believe that they can bring inside many activities traditionally performed by external channels.

But there's more to it. In addition to savings due to operational efficiency, selling direct gives manufacturers the ability to understand customer demand and preferences at a

---

* Mitra Barum Sarkar, Charles Steinfield, and Brian Butler, *Intermediaries and Cybermediaries: A Continuing Role for Mediating Players in the Electronic Marketplace*, white paper published by Michigan State and Carnegie Mellon Universities.

detailed level. The value of direct and immediate customer information is incalculable. The producer who understands and, more important, anticipates what the buyer values, will be well armed to win any competitive challenge. As a low-cost sales channel that allows immediate interaction with customers and ever more granular collection of sales data, the Web is too close to a perfect market to be bypassed for long—no matter how much angst it creates.

➤ Alternate Channels in All Industries Are Inevitable

Boston Consulting Group puts 2003 B2B spending at $2.8 trillion, and that is low compared to projections by some others. Forrester Research puts the number at $2.7 trillion by 2004 and Gartner Group projects that worldwide B2B spending will reach $7.3 trillion by that same year. Combine these numbers with a relatively low entry cost and the still-attractive IPO or buy-out option, and you have an explosion of alternative channels for the buying and selling of everything from vitamins to steel. And many of the new cybermediaries are not tied to traditional producers or their distribution channels. This heralds the shift of power to the buyer and away from the seller. Alternate Web channels also refocus process competition from the internal to the external. E-markets are changing the way business is done. And that, more than any other factor, will ensure that channel conflict continues.

➤ Fear of Being Left Behind

Fear of strong competitors is not all that drives channel conflict. Traditional companies, seeing the market valuations of the more successful cybermediaries, realize that as we move toward an information economy, companies that do not change will be left behind. Mergers such as the acquisition of media giant Time Warner by Internet upstart America Online add fuel to the already hyperactive speculation about the shift from industrial behemoths—to media and entertainment behemoths—to information behemoths.

This transition to "content as value" forever changes the boundaries and tools of commerce and threatens to bankrupt those companies that are left behind. And this fear will cause companies to invest in online commerce openly or through more circumspect methods, even at the expense of traditional intermediaries.

■ COMPETITION FROM ALL THE ANGLES

Channel conflict is unavoidable, and it has profound implications. Ignore the Internet as a sales channel and you risk the fate of Eckerd Pfeifer, the ex-president of Compaq. His loyalty to Compaq's dealer network in the face of Dell's extraordinary success cost him his job. Err on the other side and you risk channel backlash that could erode revenue.

➤ Intermediaries Wake Up

But while executives worry about exactly when and how they should shake up their sales channels, those self-same channels are figuring out ways to reduce costs and tie customers even closer to them using Web technology. Companies that sit on the sidelines not only risk the invasion of the new e-competitors but also risk losing the online initiative to wholesalers, distributors, and retailers that are motivated by the fear of disintermediation. Traditional intermediaries can take advantage of the Internet to reduce their order management and distribution costs without necessarily passing those savings to either the consumer, the business buyer, or the product or service provider. In fact, the transition from traditional intermediary to cyberintermediary is more of a step than a leap.

Visionary middlemen like Grainger certainly didn't ignore the opportunities. Taking a lesson from dot-com start-ups, Grainger developed Grainger.com, one of the first distributor sites outside the high-tech realm to offer online ordering to business customers. Grainger.com was followed by grander plans to build a vast, B2B horizontal portal empire focused on blue-collar* MRO commodities. Grainger's multiple cybermediation efforts include Order-Zone (which was merged with Works.com, a purchasing service for small and midsize businesses), Find.MRO, and TotalMRO.com. Grainger as a cybermediary combines the sizzle of the Web with all the muscle of a well-established back-end logistics and distribution empire—a strong combination.

Grainger recognized two important Internet axioms: (1) Information will continue to flow to the middle of a value chain, in the form of experience with both manufacturer's products and customer requirements. (2) This causes changes in distribution to be more iterative than discontinuous. Both of these truths work in favor of middlemen, not against them. Middlemen will gain strength from the information flow during the first phase of Internet commerce, a phase that will last roughly two years. After that, middlemen must plan to reinvent their revenue model and their role in the value chain.

➤ Rogue Channels

What happens when a producer doesn't want its products sold online . . . period? Mont Blanc, Piaget, Cartier, and other high-end brands have maintained a hands-off-the-Web attitude for sales and have extended that attitude to their retailers. These manufacturers believe that the Web

---

* Blue-collar maintenance, repair, and operations (MRO) products are commodity industrial products generally needed to keep a factory running. Included are replacement parts for machines, uniforms, safety equipment, and so forth. In contrast, white-collar MRO products are commodity items needed to keep all companies running, such as computer equipment, paper and office supplies, and so forth.

does not foster the sense of exclusivity essential to their luxury brands and ban their authorized dealers from selling their products over the Internet. Nor do they, themselves, sell online. To quote a Mont Blanc marketing executive, "Luxury, by its very nature, is not ubiquitous."

This would seem to alleviate the most obvious channel conflict issues. And yet problems continue, especially in the unauthorized channels that are proliferating on the Web. Even the most luxurious products can end up on the bargain basement floor of the gray market, where manufacturers have no control over the placement, portrayal, or pricing of their products. It turns out that whether manufacturers want their items sold online or not, Web channels will emerge. It is extremely unlikely that companies like the aforementioned will be able to continue to ignore the Web as a direct or even indirect sales method.

ROGUE CHANNELS: A CASE FOR CONSTANT VIGILANCE

The vice president of marketing for a major manufacturer of power tools decided to investigate potential online competition. Using a search engine, he discovered a web site that offered to sell his company's products online. This was a surprise since the company had a policy not to sell its high-end products online, either through its own web site or through the sites of its authorized retailers. He used his credit card to order one of their drills anyway—at a substantial discount over retail. Sure enough, several days later he received the real thing: a drill that had, in fact, been manufactured by his company.

Adding insult to injury, when he called the customer service number listed on the rogue web site, the person who answered presented herself as a representative of his company. This, of course, was completely untrue. After an investigation, it was found that the site had purchased overstock items from an authorized dealer. The dealer was chastised, the stock was removed from the rogue channel, and the case was closed—at least until next time.

Rogue channels endanger legitimate resellers, retailers, distributors, and the manufacturers themselves by chipping away at margins and undermining brand. But like any gray market, they will always exist. And, besides, they are one way to gauge the desire of the public to buy goods online. The bottom line: Online channels are inevitable, whether you want them or not. The trick is to judge how much control you can exert on the flow of product through all channels, even rogue channels.

> **E-Vision:** Rogue channels will be impossible to control. By mid 2002, loss of revenue due to rogue Web channels will be significant enough that companies will implement internal cyberdetectives to ferret out and shut down these gray-market channels.

■ CHANNEL CONFLICT 101

What do the reversal of the value chain, competition from neutral cybermediaries, and the proliferation of rogue channels mean to the makers of products and services and their physical intermediaries? How will brick-and-mortar companies, trying to take advantage of the digital age, deal with the channel conflict they are sure to encounter?

For many, the immediate question is how to use a new sales channel—the Internet—without jeopardizing revenue from existing channels. Is this even possible? Probably not. *There is no such thing as stealth disintermediation.* Once you offer to sell products directly to consumers or business customers and go around your traditional sales channels, you foster channel backlash—both visible and behind-the-scenes. The trick is to disintermediate selectively and in as nonthreatening a way as possible. Here are some approaches that brick-and-mortar companies can take that may help minimize the wrath of existing channels.

➤ **Use the web site as a lead generation engine only.** Direct all site visitors to traditional channels. While companies can begin to establish a direct relationship to their customers in this way, little actual sales information can be gleaned without extensive follow-up with the channels. Were leads acted upon? What was the close ratio? Were the customers sold other products or up-sold to more expensive products?

➤ **Complete the order online but fulfill through regular channels.** Several companies simply use their web site to sell online and then route the actual fulfillment through a distributor or retailer. Salespeople call these "bluebird" orders because little or no sales effort was required. This increases sales through traditional channels while establishing a direct customer relationship. But this model doesn't necessarily lower the cost of sales (COS); in fact, it will probably increase COS unless distributors can be convinced to take a lower commission for sales made through the site, or increased sales volume due to online activity offsets the cost of the Web channel.

➤ **Boldly go where no channels have gone before.** In other words, open up new markets where no sales presence currently exists. This entails building support partnerships to perform customer-facing activities normally executed by indirect channels, such as warehousing and logistics, customer service, and return management. Of course, any online activity may raise the red flag with existing channels, but this approach is less of a direct threat.

➤ **Cherry-pick your clients.** Simpson-Lawrence, a major distributor in the marine leisure industry, found that its top 150 customers generated 90 percent of its revenue. It broke off these clients and retargeted its direct sales force exclusively at these 150 firms. At the same time, it redirected the other 950 clients exclusively to its distribution network. This approach can work in the virtual world, too. Your largest (and probably most sophisticated) clients will expect traditional sales and service augmented by customized Web-based service and support. Even on the Web, your best clients need special treatment. If you don't cherry-pick your clients, someone else will.

➤ **Tiptoe through the channels.** Use online channels to sell only items that are not offered through existing channels or in which the channels have little interest: selected new products, discontinued products, high- or low-end products, low-margin/low-volume products. Generic products and excess inventory are good fodder for online e-markets, for example. This option, however, presents a greater threat to existing channels. They will recognize it as a low level of competition. And depending on the product and industry, commodities sometimes carry the best margins for channels. This can be offset, however, if combined with the activities already listed, as well as offering to host auctions for excess inventory warehoused at distribution centers or other online activities on behalf of your channels.

➤ **Use creative channel partnerships.** Web-enabled channels are effective with both business and consumer buyers. Greater access to information enhances both the customer and the channel experience. Learn from wholesalers such as MicroAge and Merisel, who found it was very cost effective to set up distributor-focused order management systems using the Web.

➤ **Do undercover selling.** A highly publicized online market promises anonymity; another promises prospective sellers that it will keep their participation confidential. These pledges are not aimed at contributors to the lucrative online pornography market or down-and-out aristocrats hoping to sell off family heirlooms surreptitiously. Rather, they are aimed squarely at the B2B market, targeted at manufacturers who urgently want to get in on the margin-enhancing direct-sales model but don't want to upset their other sales channels. These e-markets can be used effectively to sell excess material or commodities without setting up a competitive channel. But be warned: Maintaining real anonymity is probably impossible to attain. Eventually traditional channels will discover the ruse.

➤ **Appeal to self-interest.** Take advantage of channel self-interest by creating portals that offer direct sales of products, such as cars, combined with ancillary services like car insurance, automotive repair, and detailing. These portals can be targeted geographically and even franchised. The site itself can be spun off as a dot-com and channels can be offered the opportunity to get in on the ground floor of a potentially lucrative sales and market expansion tool.

But even when the effort is truly cooperative, it can be an uphill battle. Home Depot has encroached on the hometown hardware store with devastating results. In response, Ace Hardware, a cooperative of 5,100 independent hardware stores, home centers, and building material retailers, decided it needed to implement Web selling on behalf of its members. Not all the members were pleased. Some groused about being too small to support the new selling channel, being forced to have someone online at the stores, and sales cannibalization. This thinking, exhibited by some of the store managers, is an example of distribution baggage that Internet cybermediaries don't have to deal with.

➤ **Take off the Gloves.** Companies that worry more about competition than they do about channel conflict may find that the head-on approach is more palatable, especially in industries where distribution is highly fragmented—that is, where one channel does not own more than 5 percent of the market. After all, your future competition will likely come not just from the usual suspects but also from your own distributors and outside interlopers.

➤ **Practice selective disintermediation.** Understand which channel partners offer the most value and sell around the rest. Low-profit or no-profit intermediaries will eventually bog down your e-commerce efforts. Form partnerships with high-value intermediaries and use the Web to enhance their profit margins . . . then negotiate their discounts.

➤ **Buy a cybermediary.** This has been especially successful for retail companies. CVS bought Soma.com, for example. This creates an instant click-and-brick play. And don't forget the synergy between online and offline. Bain & Co. found that more than 40 percent of the visitors to a site came because of an offline affiliation. Customers feel more comfortable knowing that a company with a physical presence is behind the Web screen. And the synergy works both ways. Sears found that its online site reached an upscale audience that did not typically shop at Sears and drove new traffic to the stores.

➤ **Invest in a cybermediary.** For large companies that want to understand the new online intermediary, an investment strategy may offer the best opportunity to view operations from the inside out without necessarily creating an exclusive Web channel.

➤ **Spin it off.** Barnes & Noble, General Motors, Wal-Mart, Banc One, Whirlpool, and others have created separate Internet companies to address the Web channel. This offers many benefits beyond the potential IPO. Traditional companies can avoid the lethargy of big bureaucracy, attract and keep top talent, and even milk the venture capital cash cow, if need be.

THE ENLIGHTENED CEO

Whirlpool's biggest customer is Sears, which spends $2 billion with the manufacturer annually. While Whirlpool itself isn't going to sell to consumers in competition with Sears, its spin-off, Brandwise.com, will. In response, Sears is signed on as a Brandwise retailer. According to Sears CEO Arthur Martinez, "It's another way to compete. To not be on Brandwise would deny us a chance to reach customers. We went through tortured conversations about it. Would this hurt the appliance portion of Sears.com? But I think the artificial walls, over time, will come down."

Not all CEOs are as enlightened as Arthur Martinez. The fear of channel conflict must be balanced with the fear of customer loss to adventurous cybermediaries and less hesitant traditional competitors. As shown in Figure 7.3, the right mix will likely be a combination of relatively low- and relatively high-threat initiatives determined by careful consideration of the value of each channel.

Balancing Channel Conflict

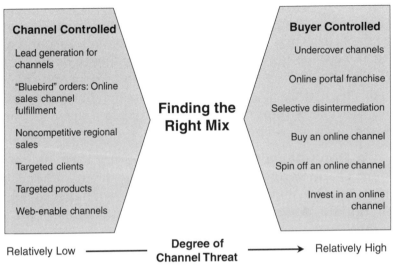

Figure 7.3 The line between alienating customers and alienating sales channels can be a thin one. While implementing low-threat Web initiatives may safeguard revenue from existing sales channels, it may also brand your company as Web-challenged and drive customers to competitors that offer compelling value via their Web channels.

■ PRACTICAL STRATEGIES FOR CHANNEL CONFLICT PREPAREDNESS

Like death and taxes, channel conflict is inevitable. Web selling is not going to just go away. Like dominoes, once one producer sells direct, others will follow. If your company doesn't have the stomach to take advantage of first-mover status and disintermediate selected channels, you must at least prepare for the moment when your board wants an immediate online channel strategy. In addition to the tactical recommendations already listed, here are several steps that can be taken to prepare for channel conflict.

1. Open the dialog.   Your sales channels see the writing on the wall. They understand that in some cases customers will demand direct access. And you can bet that they are having regular meetings trying to decide what their Web strategy should be, how they should respond to online competitors, and what you are going to do to keep customers happy. Sit down with both customers and channels and openly discuss options. It is much better to partner with important channels than to foster suspicion or, worse yet, total surprise.

2. Don't be naïve.   You will at the very least alienate some channels and at the very worst put them out of business. But that should and can be a last resort. Better to help marginal channels become more efficient and more profitable.

3. Be ready for the inevitable.   Segment customers and channels according to sales volume, profitability, and—in the case of channels—competitive advantage. Use best estimates if accurate data are not available. This will help you target the channels and customers that would benefit most and offer the best return on your Web investment. It will also highlight those customers who must be reached immediately with a Web strategy—preferably before they come to you, as they most likely will.

4. Know the online and traditional competitive landscape.   Identify alternative Web channels in your industry and assess whether they represent competitive threats or channel opportunities (see Chapter 6). You may very well wish to invest in a couple of neutral first movers or niche e-markets as a way to keep tabs on the impact online channels have within your industry. Also invest in a little channel intelligence gathering. Make sure you understand who's in bed with whom. Which of your competitors are involved in, invested in, or partnering with online channels—it may not be obvious that they have a seat on the board or a small ownership position.

5. Know thyself and know thy channels. Assess current e-capabilities for each of your significant sales and distribution channels. Map necessary integration points in a circular fashion, from the internal systems (product database, inventory, order management, financial, distribution and warehouse management, sourcing, and manufacturing) to the external (suppliers, business partners, customers). For each potential integration point, specify what (if any) electronic means of communication is available currently. This will help you understand who can be brought into an online environment and the scope of the work to be done, as well as the potential expense and likely ROI.

6. Choose any business process gaps. Map current business processes that exist between you, your channels, and your customers and channels. What changes, if any, will be required to support that process online. This will help you rate the processes that are most appropriate for the Web. Even the obvious—order processing, customer service, sales, and so forth—should be explored for next-generation process management.

7. Get ready for the Web. Web-enable applications within the enterprise, beginning with those that support customer and channel interaction including order management, customer support, product and inventory systems, and warranty and promotion management.

■ CONCLUSION

At the end of the day, it is the customers who determine which channel they use—not you, not your channels. Web commerce is not going away. It is firmly entrenched in buyers' psyches. And while virtual companies may satisfy some levels of online buyer expectations today, we firmly believe that, as use of the Web intensifies and technology becomes more sophisticated and easier to use, customers will demand direct access to the wealth of detailed information, ability to negotiate, and product customization capacity that resides only with the maker of a product. The current crop of cybermediaries, whether they are click-and-brick physical distributors or e-market makers, will satisfy only a small portion of tomorrow's Web-sensitized buyers. The only reasonable course of action is to make each of your channels compelling in its own competitive environment. And if you can't make that happen, then move beyond them—as quickly as you can.

The End of Fixed Pricing

■ PERFECTING SUPPLY AND DEMAND

In a *perfect* market, price is determined exclusively by supply and demand, rather than fixed at what could be artificial levels. Finite amounts of goods and services are allocated to the buyers who value them the most. In an e-market, as opposed to a physical market, the gap between supply and demand can be theoretically closed: Information about all potential products is made available instantaneously to all potential buyers. Response to online product concept tests can be measured in hours or days, rather than months and the product built or service offered that exactly matches the online demand. Build-to-order manufacturing value chains are possible. Service-to-demand virtual communities can be formed, in minutes or hours.

The yield management models used by airlines are the precursors to today's online marketplaces, except that the information about supply is known only to the sellers.

Is the Internet capable of creating the perfect market? Probably not, but it will come as close as anything we have imagined. Theoretically, when quantities demanded and quantities supplied reach equilibrium, price is also perfectly balanced and fair to both sides. If buyers cannot be found for products or services, prices drop. If too many buyers are found, prices rise.

➤ Information as the Great Equalizer

Perfect markets result from perfect information. This is the ultimate promise held by the Internet: that it will enable perfect information to be exchanged between buyers and sellers—information that is ubiquitous and not constrained by either time or distance. This goal *seems* possible because of the Internet's ability to globally disseminate data once it has been disconnected from its source. Facts about products, manufacturers, distributors, service provider, and buyers are thus freed from physical barriers and used to drive sales, marketing, development, manufacturing, and, of course, price.

The availability of information is spilling over to the physical world as consumers and business buyers shop for the lowest price on the Web and then use that information to negotiate better deals with their real-world suppliers. Nearly 40 percent of new car buyers gather price and availability information on the Web before they go to their dealers to buy a car.

The vision looming just over the horizon is that e-business will achieve this near-perfect equilibrium between supply and demand through the exchange of information. But the transparency of information amplifies both the risk and the reward for companies. The fluid movement of information and its disconnection from physical companies increase margin pressure on sellers. E-business will further disconnect product price from product manufacturers and their physical channels. The result will be dynamic pricing on a much greater scale than we have seen before.

■ CYBERAGGREGATION AND ITS EFFECT ON PRICE

What quickly became apparent to savvy Web-preneurs in the consumer space was that cyber selling was much more like running an entertainment company than running a department store. Search engines like Yahoo!, media sites like ESPN SportsZone, and even more recent entries like MP3.com found that if they could attract consumers they, in turn, could attract advertisers.* In fact, the success of these consumer sites has had less to do with potential shopping extravaganzas than with easy communication and information exchange.

They were able to leverage the power of community to attract first people, then advertisers, then online merchants. Once a community is formed, whether its impetus is to efficiently navigate the vast resources of the Internet, find comfort in the collective chat of teenage girls, or use humor to deal with male angst, the buying power of the club can be leveraged.

➤ Follow the Money

And while early B2B cybermediaries initially focused on supplier aggregation (Industry.net and TPNRegister are two examples), it didn't take long for B2B vendors to internalize the lesson of B2C: Follow the money! The rush to aggregate buyers was on!

But what is the ultimate outcome of aggregating buyers? Unlike their real-world supplier aggregators—wholesaler, distributors, and retailers—B2B cybermediaries

---

* MP3.com offers thousands of songs to download—but they're free. The company makes most of its money by selling ads on its site. To put this in perspective, Good-Noise, a public company that offers downloadable songs from more recognizable bands and actually charges for its MP3 files, pulled in only $20,465 in revenues in 1998. ("A Few Truths about MP3.com," *The Standard,* March 16, 2000.)

are free from physical constraints; they can concentrate on information management. Everything else can be outsourced. Theoretically, then, they have infinite capacity to represent any supplier capable of describing products electronically. Once buyers are aggregated and suppliers can be easily compared online, many suppliers will be forced to compete on price. The result is a reduction in profit margins for all but the most specialized suppliers. And that will only get worse as pricing becomes more dynamic.

> **E-Vision:** Suppliers of commodity products that participate in online e-markets will likely experience a 5 percent to 10 percent reduction in margins from that channel.

Business-to-business market makers such as Ariba, Commerce One, and Clarus have concentrated almost exclusively on, first, selling e-procurement software applications to Fortune 500 companies and then linking those buyers with their suppliers via an e-market. The stated objective is to have a significant portion of *all* buyers and suppliers within a vertical industry connected within a few interoperable e-market hubs. By concentrating on large buyers, these vendors will likely gain critical mass because of their clients' dominant status within a supply chain—smart move for them.

➤ When Supplier Aggregation Makes Sense

There are times, however, when supplier aggregation makes sense. During the early formation of online markets and the concentration of their resources, cybermediaries must make a decision as to which group to concentrate on—suppliers or buyers. This decision should be based on the market itself. Extremely fragmented markets, where the buying process is tedious and suppliers are hard to identify and differentiate, or where highly specialized suppliers need to be sourced, will benefit from supplier aggregation. In less fragmented markets, it is better to follow the money and aggregate buyers. Either way, the result is an intensification of price competition as suppliers fend off the threat of product substitution and loss of market share.

■ PRICE TRANSFORMATION IN THE E-AGE

Consumer e-commerce offers a road map for the evolution of B2B pricing devices. While Amazon.com uses a straightforward discount approach to selling, Priceline.com uses its Demand Collection System, a patented form of demand aggregation to facilitate flexible pricing on its site. Meanwhile, auctions are an integral part of many B2C sites such as Yahoo! and are the entire point of eBay. The majority of B2B selling still uses catalogs with fixed or contract prices. But this will change.

➤ Fixed and Dynamic Pricing Methods

How will pricing methods change? As information itself becomes the currency by which value is set, as makers are further removed from their products, as cybermediaries and their automated software agents replace physical intermediaries, price will be transformed. We think that price will metamorphose from being relatively stable and fixed, as represented by catalog-type selling, toward being dynamic, as represented by auctions, reverse auctions, barter, and other such pricing mechanisms. As this transformation occurs, e-markets will take on the characteristics of financial market exchanges and yield management systems, where price changes second by second, based on real-time measures of demand and real-time information about available supply. Our hypothesis (shown in Figure 8.1)—that fixed prices will become a thing of the past for nearly everything we buy over the Internet—will come

B2B Pricing Dynamics

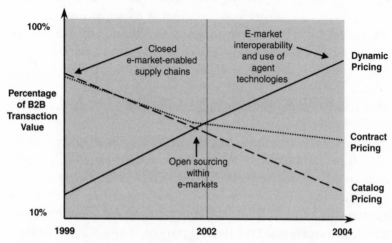

Figure 8.1 Over time the pressure to participate in multiple e-markets will drive suppliers to make their data content electronically available in XML formats. This will move product pricing away from being predominantly fixed toward being predominantly dynamic.

about as e-market technology becomes more sophisticated, so that both supply and demand can be measured up to the second and used to generate real-time price.

Fixed Pricing Models. Fixed pricing models refer primarily to catalog and contract pricing and they are the primary way B2B commerce is transacted today. In fact, according to Keenan Vision, Inc., less than 16 percent of the B2B electronic commerce transactions in 1999 employed dynamic pricing techniques. Instead, most B2B transactions rely on fixed price, either publicly represented in a catalog or on a price sheet, or as a contract price privately negotiated between a specific buyer and a specific seller. Business buyers, more so than consumers, will expect greater levels of negotiation power as a result of global sourcing. In order to understand these and other factors that will cause the migration to dynamic pricing, let's look at how most B2B buying is done today.

The electronic equivalent of the catalog sale has not changed much. Buyers look at pictures and descriptions of products, select items, order them, and pay for them. In fact, some of the most successful online retailers are those that come from the direct-sales catalog environment, including L.L. Bean, J. Crew, and Dell. Catalog selling works best when the market is fairly stable and prices are fixed. On a small one-to-one scale, fixed price is a convenient and hassle-free way for people to buy products and will always be a part of online e-commerce. But for several reasons, we see it use decreasing over time.

While a fixed catalog price works well when buyers and sellers are fragmented, the purchase process is inefficient and where the value/price relationship is fairly well established—such as in retail items, commodity products, and replacement parts—those same attributes, however, will cause its decline. Once multiple catalogs are aggregated in e-markets, many of the participating suppliers' products will be commoditized. Automated software agents will browse and retrieve items, sorted by a variety of attributes and presented by price, making fixed price a liability. Online buying will evolve, by necessity, to the point where price is not fixed but rather is a starting point for other types of bargaining, such as contract pricing.

At that point, more information will be offered in order to influence the willingness to pay for an item: Features, availability, level of individual customization, and so on, will be associated with a product. Product and attribute detail, often exchanged during verbal negotiations, will become much more automated on the Internet and will be applied to even the most mundane articles. So we believe that the way products are priced and the purchasing process itself will evolve from being relatively static to using transformational pricing mechanisms more frequently.

Dynamic Pricing Models.   Dynamic pricing mechanisms employed in B2B commerce include auction, bid response, demand aggregation, and barter.

Auction.   Online auctions in all their various flavors have proven to be successful in B2B, B2C, and C2C commerce. Excess material, often difficult to dispose of through traditional channels, is perfect fodder for an Internet auction that might reach thousands of hitherto unknown buyers. Auctions also offer sellers a way to protect margins (even for commodities) by offering their products in a bidding environment. Besides, auctions have an excitement factor that is hard to replicate.

Auctions generally fall into four categories: ascending, descending, Dutch, and Vickery. Ascending auctions, where the price moves upward, as the name implies, are the most common found today in B2B and are becoming a staple in many e-markets. In ascending auctions, many buyers bid on items from one seller, such as surplus inventory.

Descending auctions resemble traditional bid/response activity, with the purpose generally being to find the least-cost items. Essentially, many suppliers seek t o win a buyer's business by bidding against others. The auction may be formatted in a number of different ways: open to all bidders or only to invited bidders, with information about other bids being open or restricted. FreeMarkets offers an example of a B2B descending auction.

Two of the most interesting developments in B2B are the use of Dutch auctions and Vickery auctions. In Dutch auctions, a seller posts products at a particular (usually high) price and the price goes down until one of many buyers decides to purchase the items at the last posted price.

A Vickery auction is one seller and many buyers, where the items are sold to the highest bidder at a price equal to the second-highest bid. A reverse form of Vickery auction is used in B2C, where buyer demand is aggregated in an ad hoc cooperative and used to bid for products. The more buyers, the lower the price—at least that is the theory. Several sites offer this for B2C, including Mercata.com, Mobshop.com, and Accompany.com. We expect to see more demand aggregation and dynamic pricing in B2B e-markets within the next 6 to 12 months, as more exchanges seek to differentiate themselves.

Auctions work especially well in markets where the value/price relationship has not been well established. These include markets for one-of-a-kind products, antiques, excess supply, time-sensitive products, and specialty items.

Auctions are also an excellent way to gauge the value of highly targeted goods and services in emerging markets. We worked with a dot-com start-up that wanted to create an online market for technology used in the deregulated utility industry. This company had identified thousands of R&D labs that had developed salesworthy technology and thousands of potential buyers—other utilities that would benefit from the technology. The problem, however, was that the technologies had been developed by the labs, often wholly owned subsidiaries of utilities, for use in-house. Since the technologies had not been offered on the open market, there had been no opportunity for the industry to set an established value—or price—for most of them. What better way to begin to establish value in a case like this than an auction or even a reverse auction?

Bid/Response. In the absence of a fixed price or in an effort to arrive at the best price, request-for-quotation/response from vendors or bid/response models work well. Bid/response also works well where spending is regulated (as in the lowest-responsible-bidder laws that apply to government procurement), in markets where custom or specialty products or services are being sourced, and where buyers and sellers may be unknown to each other.

But we are beginning to see the use of what is essentially a bid/response pricing model in consumer commerce.

Priceline.com pioneered this approach with its name-your-own-price selling model for airline tickets and it has been extended to other categories, including groceries. Over time, we believe auctions and bid/response will be the dominant pricing mechanisms used on the Internet.

Barter Is Back. During the middle ages, barter was the dominant means of exchange. Value was set by need. Unfortunately, barter in the physical world was often inconvenient. The needs of those bartering had to match, each with a reciprocal value. If oxen were valued by the farmer and grain by the herder, the exchange was transacted. If no such match existed, barter could not take place. Also, participants had to be in fairly close proximity or had to transport their goods over some distance in order to trade. To overcome these obstacles, preferred items were selected that had universal appeal, such as gold and precious metals, as a medium of exchange. The idea of money evolved from these standards of economic exchange.

Today, goods are paid for by using either money, pure barter, or barter within a trade exchange. In the United States it is estimated that 250,000 companies are involved in barter and that 65 percent of Fortune 500 corporations use some type of barter mechanism. It is estimated that the Asian barter system is worth about $90 billion per year, even though formal records are not kept.

PRICE THAT NAME

Michael Jordan signed a 10-year contract with SportsLine USA, a three-year-old sports and information service. In return for the contract to create and manage Jordan's official web site, SportsLine will give Jordan equity plus a split of ad and merchandise revenue from the web site. For this potentially lucrative trade, Jordan is required to answer five e-mails per week and conduct one online interview per month. Michael Jordan is bartering the tremendous value of his name and a small amount of time in return for a percentage of an online venture.

The Web has reinvigorated the idea of barter. While the Internet can facilitate the transaction itself, setting exchange values for bartered goods, services, or capacity is difficult. In fact, we expect to see barter participants looking to a neutral third party in the form of an association or trusted cybermediary to oversee such bartering.

> **E-Vision:** By 2002, the relative position of fixed pricing versus dynamic pricing in e-commerce transactions will begin to reverse. We believe that by the end of 2004, online pricing will have moved from predominantly fixed forms to predominantly dynamic structures—auctions, reverse auctions, and forms of bid/response.

■ SHOPPING BOTS AND THEIR EFFECT ON PRICING

From Fido the Shopping Doggie, which provides consumers the ability to compare prices across a database containing hundreds of thousands of consumer products from hundreds of vendors, to GreaterGood.com, which shops e-commerce sites for the best price and allows consumers to feel even better about their bargain by allocating a percentage of their purchase to a charitable cause, merchants and suppliers are facing the specter of the end of fixed pricing as we know it. Shopping robots, or *bots*, will further the shift toward dynamic pricing.

> **E-Vision:** Longer-term pricing changes—from three to five years—will see the augmentation of dynamic pricing by search-and-negotiate intelligent software agents, especially among a small number of tightly integrated B2B trading e-markets.

But the value of shopping bots is based on a contradiction: Bots undermine fixed price while at the same time being dependent on it. In fact, in the absence of a fixed price, today's crop of rather simple shopping bots does not work. How can you compare prices across many sellers if the seller does not list a price? So it is not that bots will end fixed pricing; rather, bots will make pricing information transparent not only to the buyers using them, but also to competitors within an industry. It will be easier to compete on price in the absence of other differentiating factors. Bots will leverage access to price information in such a way as to lower margins across whole classes of products, such as we are seeing in automobiles and PCs.

► Shopping Bots in Consumer Commerce

How threatened are merchants by shopping agents such as mySimon and comparison sites such as Shopping.com? Andersen Consulting, when testing its BarganFinder bot, found that one-third of the merchants accessed blocked the price comparison software. However, they also found that an equal percentage of smaller merchants wanted to be involved, viewing the opportunity to be listed in the results of a search more compelling than the fear of being compared based on price alone.

To further confuse merchants, some shopping bots make it look as though the request is coming directly from the consumer's Web browser rather than a central site, thus thwarting possible bot-blocking activity. Bot technology is advancing beyond limited price comparison. MIT's Tete-a-Tete is capable of negotiating beyond simply price. Buyer agents and seller agents negotiate with each other based on a myriad of terms including return policies, warranties, delivery times, service contracts, and other factors that may influence a purchase decision.

➤ Just-in-Time Pricing

Perhaps the biggest development in business over the past 20 years is the ability to facilitate just-in-time (JIT) manufacturing, inventory, warehousing, and logistics management systems. The ability to electronically send and receive information about each step within the supplier-facing value chain has allowed companies to save billions in manufacturing and inventory carrying costs. The Internet extends this concept of JIT to the customer-facing value chain. Dell has been able to use its Internet sales channel to respond to customer demand in a more efficient way, cutting its inventory carrying time in half.

While we clearly see ever more sophisticated software agents on the horizon, most companies have taken a wait-and-see attitude. Few have incorporated the potential use of sophisticated software agents into their Internet strategy. Rather, they simply react to today's rather simple shopping bots by either allowing them or blocking them.

But as we inexorably move toward making information about products more accessible to Web access, first by humans browsing an electronic catalog and then by computer programs browsing an aggregated supplier product database, we inevitably enable a just-in-time pricing scenario. What happens when the idea of immediate knowledge through direct access to the human buyer is extended to the nonhuman buyer or software agent? Price negotiation, until now the province of human interaction, will be put in the hands of software programs that act as agents for their human counterparts either at a corporate level or at a consumer level.

■ COUNTERBALANCING PRICE EROSION

Not all the news about buyer empowerment and shopping bots is bad news for sellers. Web technology and e-markets not only will enable consumers and business buyers to have access to a wider selection of goods and services at an overall lower price, but can work to protect price and margin as well. Personalization, customization, and access to a nearly infinite number of micromarkets can help protect against brand and price erosion and help keep product margins healthy. In fact, the idea of perfect information is as important to the cost of manufacturing, the supply side of the equation, as it is to the customer or demand side. After all, cost is the primary factor determining profit margin. Manufacturers who use e-commerce not just as a means to reduce the cost of raw materials, inventory, and distribution but most especially as a sourcing tool will be able to counterbalance price erosion. E-markets have the potential to help source innovative suppliers who can provide price protection by supplying unique product components and technologies. The complete demise of fixed pricing faces other obstacles.

➤ The Need for Predictability and Its Effect on Pricing

Millions of Americans budget their household money, especially in times of economic downturn, and corporations live by the annual budget cycle. Good monetary planning is the cornerstone of achieving financial goals and is possible at the personal or corporate level only when we can predict our costs. So while the combination of supplier commoditization with shopping bots, auctions, and sophisticated negotiation-capable software agents will diminish the use of fixed pricing, the fixed price model will not completely die. Counterbalancing the trend toward dynamic pricing is the need for predictability in financial outlay. People want to know what things are going to cost. Businesses need to budget for expenditures and, while companies strive to be under budget rather than over budget, the operative word is *budget*. At some point the negotiations come to an end and a price is locked in place for a period of time, however short.

➤ "Made-for-You" Price Protection

The concept of one-to-one marketing is based on the theory that a company can find the exact target market for a product. Coupled with that is the ideal of assemble-to-order and, eventually, manufacture-to-order. Companies will build only the products that are already sold and at some point, as market knowledge becomes more perfect, will only manufacture the components for the products that have already been sold. The vision is to make each product—from raw materials to production—to an individual customer's specification. An example of this trend is the investment Ford has made in Microsoft's CarPoint site. The idea is to customize car buying and eventually develop a build-to-order relationship with the customer.

A MORE EFFICIENT MARKET

Steve Ballmer, Microsoft's president, was quoted in the press as saying, "The ways customers, dealers, and the manufacturer relate, and the suppliers to the automotive manufactures relate, are deeply changed by the Internet. Potentially, 25 percent to 30 percent of a cost of a car has to do with inefficiencies in the way the supply chain works in getting a car manufactured and delivered to the customer. The key here is creating an electronic marketplace that's very efficient."

Microsoft and Ford hope eventually to develop an assemble-to-order supply chain for cars, much like what Dell has done with computers. They envision that a customer would contact Ford directly and relay his or her specifications; then Ford would manufacture the car or, more likely, do minor modifications on the assembly line. Although legal issues in the car industry abound,* the fundamental model is sound. Ford gains several advantages: The company begins a direct dialog with customers, builds a knowledge base of customer preferences, further wrests power from its dealer channel, lowers operations and channel costs, and markets the idea of a custom-made car—at a higher profit.

Several safeguards against price and margin erosion have been mentioned: the appearance of product customization, the ability to target products to ever more granular customer niches, and the need for predictability in business procurement. Geographic proximity to clients will continue to be a great advantage for those suppliers who support JIT manufacturing, for example, but it will diminish as a safeguard as 3PLs (third-party logistics companies) gain traction in e-business and form alliances with e-markets.

In addition to these customer-facing strategies, supply chain efficiencies continue to be essential in keeping the cost of manufacturing and distribution as low as possible. Strategic sourcing is also important as a way to create distinguished products and manage costs. In this, e-markets play a dual role. While they accelerate the tendency of products toward commodity status, they can also be used to source unique or more cost-effective suppliers by procurement professionals.

Finally, as shown in Figure 8.2, the best protection against commoditization over the long term is the ability

---

* In July of 2000, a district judge, citing state laws that prohibit Ford from selling cars direct to consumers, upheld the shutdown of the automaker's used car site, Preowned.com.

Counterbalancing Price Erosion

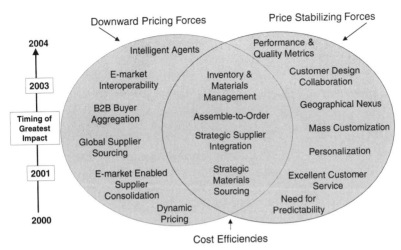

Figure 8.2 Excellent customer service (including personalization of the buying experience), mass customization, and assemble-to-order processes give companies the most protection against price erosion over the next two years.

to compete on performance metrics and unique product attributes, rather than price. Customers will always pay for quality or something that is "different."

➤ Cybermediaries Weaken over Time

Much of the focus of today's cybermediary is on industry-specific supply chain e-procurement markets underwritten by channel masters. One of the most important functions that the cybermediary performs is the rationalization of product content from multiple suppliers, the difficulties of doing this are detailed in Chapter 10. Each cybermediary provides taxonomy—commonly built around XML—that allows suppliers to present product information using a Web catalog paradigm. This enables electronic transactions, which are the foundation upon which their business models are dependent.

But the pursuit of standardization—necessary to drive greater levels of transactions through their e-exchanges—ultimately weakens both cybermediaries and their e-exchanges, as shown in Figure 8.3. Companies will work to make their product data XML compatible so that they can address the needs of their largest customers. They will employ various software products that are capable of translating their internal product schema so as to interact with multiple e-markets. Also, the number of vendors offering hosted translation services for smaller suppliers will increase. However, as e-markets consolidate, as powerful buyer consortia take shape, and as companies recognize the value of standards-setting organizations for XML—either at the industry level, such as RosettaNet, or at the standards-setting organizational level, such as the

Technology Influence on Channels

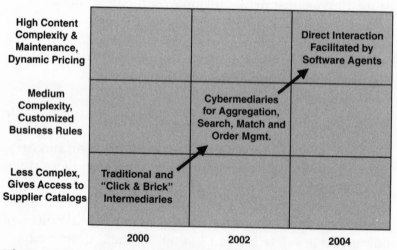

Figure 8.3 Over time, direct online channels will gain favor as technology and standardization lower the barriers to global sourcing and enable greater levels of application-to-application data integration between companies.

Oasis, UN/CEFACT* ebXML standard—standardization will start to weaken the business models of all but the strongest cybermediaries.

Buyers will want access to multiple layers of product information electronically—details about quality, availability, manufacturing capacity, and so on. Only the seller can provide this level of detail and will begin to do so—directly and under pressure from buyers.

> **E-Vision:** The aggregation services of cybermediaries will become less important as manufacturers and service providers become more sophisticated in the use of e-commerce software, as they increasingly make their internal data available to external software agents, and as these agents become more commonplace in the purchasing lexicon. By the end of 2004, the combination of technological advances and buyer demand will foster greater adoption of direct sales models.

■ ADVERSE PRICING: THE DARK SIDE

Not all customers are created equal. There are instances where detailed knowledge of customer profitability can be used against the customers. We call that *adverse pricing.*

Consider what happens when the old 80/20 rule runs amok—for example, in the banking industry. Some banks have found through analysis that 5 percent of their depositors account for one-third of teller and telephone transactions. Typically this 5 percent is, in fact, high-transaction/low-value customers. In retail banking it is not unusual that as much as 60 percent of the checking

---

* The United Nations body for Trade Facilitation and Electronic Business (UN/CEFACT) and the Organization for the Advancement of Structured Information Standards (OASIS).

and savings accounts are unprofitable, sometimes neutralizing as much as 70 percent of the total profits generated by all checking and savings accounts.

One of the contributions of the Internet is to enable companies to selectively price services based on customer profitability. Insurance companies have made a science out of rating analysis in order to do just that. Banks, however, have discovered that unprofitable customers can be found in every age and income bracket and in every product category. This makes it difficult, if not impossible, to apply adverse pricing categorically. What would be needed, then, is a way for banks to analyze all customer behavior in detail, cherry-picking the most profitable. Such an activity was nearly impossible—until Web commerce.

But with over 200 banks offering banking online and over half of all banks saying that they will offer home or Web-based banking in the future, not only will transactions become less costly for banks, but a wealth of highly personal information and behavior will be available for mining. With data collected from the general ledger of a bank and from online customer relationship management systems, banks will be able to view customers in terms of their profitability relative to other customers, balance information, and how they are trending.

Online customers (in banking as elsewhere) are commonly profiled as younger, wealthier, educated, and computer-savvy—characteristics that match banks' profiles of some of their best customers. Wells Fargo bank has over 700,000 Web banking customers who tend to have higher balances and more accounts and are more likely to view the bank as their primary financial services provider than their non-Web customers. And, by definition, online customers cost less to service. According to a Booz, Allen & Hamilton study, a typical transaction over the Internet costs about a penny, compared with $1.07 at a full-service teller window and $0.27 at an ATM. But identifying and targeting high-profit customers has a flip side: What about the less profitable customers? They can just as easily be targeted for reverse pricing—pricing that drives them away. With precision data analysis, those least able to afford quality service will be uncovered and charged a premium for it. As we said, this is the dark side of dynamic pricing. But is is a very likely result as more businesses develop customer information, thanks to the Internet.

■ PRACTICAL STRATEGIES FOR PRICING

1. Touch points throughout the customer-facing and supplier-facing value chain must be leveraged in order to retain product and price differentiation. Manufacturers and service providers that aggressively use the Internet in two fundamental ways—customer facing and supplier facing—will be more likely to retain product differentiation and control costs as the trend toward product commoditization accelerates.

Each path represents multiple opportunities to offer differentiated value. Enhanced supplier communication and integration promote speed to market and help control costs to offset the eventual lower margins of online channels. Global e-commerce allows for unique and/or specialized product components to be sourced more easily. Direct buyer interaction—even when the sale is concluded through traditional offline channels—provides the opportunity to build brand awareness, offer varying levels of customer support, and gain invaluable customer preference data.

2. Flexible direct-to-customer selling efforts must be initiated regardless of potential channel conflict. The threat of channel conflict, though real, must not be allowed to retard direct customer access. Although suppliers of commodity products will be the first to feel the effect of margin erosion, all suppliers, manufacturers, and service providers will be subject to the increase in sourcing and price comparison activity made possible by online commerce and aggregated e-markets. Companies that rely solely on intermediaries—cyber or otherwise—to initiate Web selling efforts will be less prepared to withstand the impact of the continuing shift toward buyer-favored pricing. Carefully crafted simultaneous channels should be used to establish online access to customers, as we have suggested in this chapter.

3. In order to facilitate intricate customer-facing interactions, businesses will need to make their product data accessible. Therefore, immediate investment should be made in sophisticated data warehouse, data mining, and XML translation technologies, as well as other technologies, as discussed in this book. The technology surrounding intelligent software agents should also become familiar to information technology professionals, in order to prepare for online activity such as non-price-only attribute searches, dynamic pricing negotiation, supply chain interoperability, and customer profitability studies.

4. Companies must prepare to accommodate nonhuman interaction with their internal data. The movement from fixed to dynamically negotiated pricing will require highly sophisticated product and company attribute searches. This will give the advantage to manufacturers and service providers in several ways: First, as automated software agents begin to interact directly with each other, distributors and third-party e-market makers' contributions to the value chain will begin to weaken. Catalog aggregation, data rationalization, and matching services will become less important. Second, real companies—the companies that actually make the product or provide the service—will be the most capable of providing real-time information about their capabilities.

■ CONCLUSION

Companies must begin to prepare for the shift away from the catalog metaphor and fixed price in B2B procurement. The trend toward dynamic pricing in B2B will take multiple forms, including all types of auctions, requests for quotes, and demand aggregation, as well as the use of sophisticated software agents to ferret out specific products or services and then negotiate price. As we move beyond white-collar MRO purchasing into more complex sourcing and procurement—direct materials, make-to-order custom products, excess manufacturing capacity, and professional services, to name a few—the buying process will necessitate incorporating ever more granular levels of visibility into product attributes, company qualifications, distribution capabilities, and value-added services. Only by providing heightened buyer support will companies be able to alleviate the natural trend toward downward price pressure.

Chapter

Emerging E-Commerce Business Models

Every now and then, new business models appear to spring full-blown from the imagination of scientists, college students, and entrepreneurs. The ideas of people like Marc Andreessen of Netscape Communications, Shawn Fanning of Napster, and Jay Walker of Priceline can change the business landscape overnight, weakening—perhaps even destroying—traditional business models. Why? Because there is a contextual shift in the *how* of business: how materials are bought and sold, how clients are serviced, how money is made, and, most important, how buyers expect to do commerce. We are in the early stages of e-commerce and its big brother, e-business, but already the Internet is enabling new business models to grow up around the delivery of information and human communication. These changes will be the great legacy of the e-age.

■ THE CHAOS FACTOR

Contextual shifts create chaos, and chaos creates opportunity. For example, the basic human needs for light and heat have always existed. But the fulfillment of those needs, indeed the shaping of them, changed forever when power for heat and light, in the form of electricity, could be delivered hundreds of miles from its source. New industries grew up and others descended into oblivion.

In today's chaotic environment, changes seem to happen so fast that they give the appearance of being purely discontinuous and thoroughly disruptive. This confounds an organization's ability to plan for, respond to, or even recognize changes that will affect their ability to compete. Reactions vary from the obtuse—the reaction of *Encyclopaedia Britannica* to CD-ROMs (as detailed by Philip Evans and Thomas Wurster in *Blown to Bits,* published by Harvard Business School Press, 1999)—to the brilliant—Charles Schwab's and Dell Computer's quick adoption of the Internet for direct sales and customer service.

It helps to separate the hype about new e-commerce paradigms from the reality. In order to understand these new models for buying and selling, we thought it would be important to recognize which ones have the ability to be truly disruptive—for example, the ability to cause massive industry restructuring—versus those that are more iterative—for example, changes that are brought about by enabling existing customer and supplier relationships with Internet technologies. The latter is less threatening. It is a stepped progression that allows you to participate in e-commerce with less disruption to your organization. So regardless of the hype, the reality is that as chaotic as the new e-commerce environment seems, its foundations are well grounded in business models that are familiar to all of us.

➤ A Rose by Any Other Name

We define a business model as a description of how a business works: its value chain, process interactions, cost structure, revenue sources. The common perception is that e-commerce has so altered the structure of doing business that conventional models are doomed. Well . . . not quite yet.

However, the introduction of cybermediaries into the commerce process has decidedly altered the way companies view their options for selling their products and buying the direct materials and operational resources they need to run their business.

These new cybermediaries have been labeled with an astounding range of euphemisms: butterfly markets, vortexes, vortals, e-hubs. By any name, they rely on the Internet to defy traditional barriers of distance and time. They mean to broker commerce transactions, either on the horizontal axis across industries (MRO commodities or industrial goods) or along the vertical axis within an industry (life science research, chemicals, or steel)—or perhaps along both.

Certainly the idea of an intermediary is not new. We are all familiar with distributors, retailers, and agents as the intermediaries between the makers and the buyers of goods and services. Traditional intermediaries relied primarily on the department store model—aggregating suppliers. By offering the ability to source goods and services from a broad base of sellers, they were able to attract buyers.

But traditional intermediaries faced practical restrictions. They were bound by geography, the need to hold inventory, the physical constraints of delivery, and the need to provide industry and product expertise, among other things. So their business models were also limited. These intermediaries acted on behalf of a finite group of manufacturers or service providers along well-defined horizontal or vertical bars within specific industries. They targeted business buyers or consumers and seldom mixed the two.

Cybermediaries are not landlocked—and, therefore, are capable of more easily altering business models used for buying and selling. They do not rely simply on aggregating sellers, but rather they employ a number of commerce mechanisms already familiar from the physical world, often within the same business model. They aggregate buyers (similar to traditional buying cooperatives), aggregate demand (similar to yield management, which has been used for decades by the airline industry), and broker exchanges (like the stock market model).

But here is where the similarity ends. The cyber-mediaries' business models are no longer bound by the traditional constraints of geography and, in the case of digital products, inventory management, or logistics. Further, these first-generation models are not yet as encumbered by issues of reliability, end-to-end process support, product liability, and trust as they will be when e-commerce matures. Traditional business models—brick and mortar based—will never disappear. But the Web has changed the speed and degree of interaction between buyers and sellers, enabling a fundamental shift toward unconstrained product sourcing. The commerce process is being destructured a piece at a time.

■ ONLINE E-COMMERCE MODELS

By "e-commerce business model," we mean the online process by which buyers and sellers find each other, negotiate the deal, and manage the payment transaction—the end-to-end cycle. We collectively refer to these as *e-markets* and the way in which they work separately and together as *cybermediation*. In Chapter 10 we discuss how we expect e-markets to evolve over time. But in this chapter we outline the major business and revenue models that exist today, which we have grouped and identified based on their significant characteristics. Then we offer practical strategies for dealing with a commerce paradigm still in flux.

➤ Lots of Hype, Little Real Change

We have identified six types of e-commerce models, as shown in Figure 9.1. Four are used predominantly in B2B commerce; two are found primarily in B2C commerce. We

E-Commerce Business Models

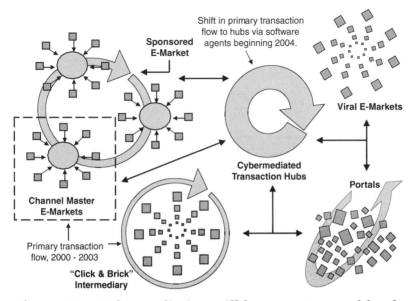

Figure 9.1 Cybermediation will happen at several levels in e-commerce: one to one, in the case of channel master extranets to neutral cybermediaries acting as transaction hubs. The most successful early e-commerce models will be those based on the more traditional supply and demand management: channel master and "click and brick."

include the latter two because we believe they have significant implications for B2B e-market evolution.

While they all use the Internet as a vehicle for communications throughout the value chain, the underlying process of buying and selling has not changed overly much—yet. In fact, among large manufacturing corporations in the United States, little real progress has been documented in the online revolution. PricewaterhouseCoopers, in a recent study of 78 industrial companies, found that only 40 percent of large companies could receive orders online and only 28 percent could accept payments online. Lots of hype, little substance.

These same companies, however, believe that the portion of their revenue from e-commerce will jump from less than 5 percent today to at least 20 percent by 2003. Either they are reading too many analysts' reports or they have an underlying belief that Internet technology will forever alter the fundamental relationship between buyer and seller. We think it is the latter.

E-Vision: The fundamental commerce models will remain fairly constant for the next two years, even though the technology enabling them will add much greater speed, efficiency, and information visibility to the process. This will lend a veneer of originality to what are essentially traditional buyer/seller relationships.

Ultimately, these new models will fundamentally affect five components of commerce: (1) the ability to easily source materials outside of known trading partners, (2) the way price is established, (3) the effect on cost and margins, (4) the relationship companies have with their customers and suppliers, and (5) the ability to operate on a global basis.

While we certainly don't maintain that the following e-commerce models constitute the only examples, we believe that they illustrate valid studies in change.

1. The Channel Master. Many procurement e-markets have the structure of a channel master* model in two important respects: They are typically many-to-one (in this case

---

* *Channel master* refers to a dominant member of the supply chain that can essentially force others to do business in a certain way. GM and Ford, for example, have created a marketplace using software and services from Commerce One and Oracle, which they encourage their suppliers to use in order to do business with them. The clear message is one of coercion. If suppliers are not willing or are unable to use the e-market, then their business with GM and Ford is likely in jeopardy.

many suppliers to a small group of dominant buyers) and the dominant buyer is willing to exert coercive influence over the subservient players in the supply chain. It is a classic hub/spoke typology, to borrow the nomenclature assigned to its earlier incarnation, EDI.

Channel masters are found at several points within a supply chain. They can be mega-retailers, like Wal-Mart, which are only one step removed from the consumer. They can be wholesalers that distribute manufactured goods across multiple channels. Or, like Motorola or General Electric, they can be manufacturers that control billions of procurement dollars spent on direct material providers. Regardless of their position in the chain, the channel masters' primary objective is to reduce cost through operational efficiency.

Channel masters may also try to leverage their procurement e-market by aggregating clusters of smaller buyers—like a price club. If successful, this builds vital liquidity or buying volume within the channel. It also helps suppliers who sell to multiple channel masters within the same industry by giving them one point of interface, the e-market. However, most channel masters do not need this liquidity to justify their e-procurement efforts.

In today's lexicon of the channel master, however, the Internet has replaced value-added networks (VANs) and point-to-point leased lines as the primary networking infrastructure. Extensible Markup Language (XML), in its various permutations, will eventually replace EDI as the primary mechanism for most document exchange.

Perhaps most important, the browser-enabled human has replaced technology as the main trigger to an application. This last point—human interaction with applications and systems—is both a step forward and a step backward in the process (see the discussions on software agents included in Chapter 6). Humans' interacting with systems is not efficient for high-volume, repetitious activity. EDI, now viewed as a somewhat arcane data interchange standard, has saved companies billions of dollars by bypassing human interaction in favor of application-to-application integration. It is still the most efficient enabler for many business processes, such as just-in-time manufacturing and vendor-managed inventory.

"IT'S MY WAY OR THE HIGHWAY"

Consider General Electric's August 1998 announcement of its e-procurement extranet. Note the use of coercion.

> GE, the largest diversified industrial company in the United States, plans to launch trading extranets for each of its 12 operating units. The systems could serve as many as 40,000 trading partners by 2002, a GE executive confirmed, all of which would have to use the network in order to do business with the $91 billion company. We're looking to enable each division to manage their purchasing on extranets, with financial data funneling to a centralized platform. Catalog creation and maintenance will be outsourced to TPNRegister, an operator of Web-based trading marketplaces that is co-owned by GE.

2. The Sponsored Consortium. As traditional companies wake up to the threat and opportunity of Internet-based trading communities, some are announcing what we call sponsored consortia. These are multiple large competitors who band together to form online exchanges with their suppliers—a sort of "dance of the channel masters." Many of the consortia formed by major manufacturers in early 2000 are examples of this type of e-market model.

Regardless of several recent announcements of e-market consortia made by behemoth industrial competitors (see Figure 9.2), we do not believe these represent any measurable trend toward *true* collaboration. That would require the homogenization of business processes, applications, and standards across these markets. That is not likely to happen.

Rather, they may try and interconnect with each other. So suppliers will be pressured to connect to whichever individual exchange is being sponsored by their biggest customer. If they do significant business with multiple customers within an industry (each of the big three automakers, for example), then they will likely have to duplicate their efforts with each specific one. So, while this sounds like a sponsored e-market as we define it, the level of direct competition among the channel masters will ensure that homogenization does not happen at a level granular enough to allow interoperability across exchanges. In other words, it sounds good, but it probably won't work in the real world. (See Figure 9.2.)

The key for a truly collaborative sponsored consortium is that the participants be manufacturers or service providers that do not compete directly. Rather, they should complement each other.

3. The "Click-and-Brick" Intermediary. Traditional middlemen are physical sales channels, plain and simple. They can be individual salespeople, retailers, wholesalers, and distributors—basically any intermediaries that position themselves between the buyers and the makers of a product or a service. During the early stages of e-commerce much was written about the coming plight of middlemen. They were perceived as an artificial layer between buyer and manufacturer that did little except add cost to the product and drive down margins. Mass disintermediation or, at the very least, heavy consolidation was predicted as a result of this shift. Like relics from the ice age, middlemen were expected to go the way of the dinosaurs, with the Internet triggering a mass extinction.

The Hype Cycle of Sponsored Consortia

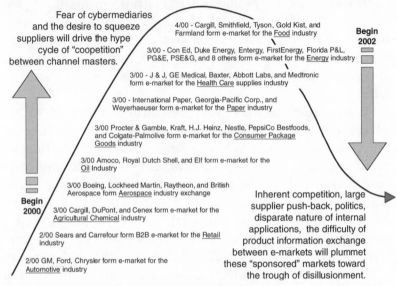

Fear of cybermediaries and the desire to squeeze suppliers will drive the hype cycle of "coopetition" between channel masters.

4/00 - Cargill, Smithfield, Tyson, Gold Kist, and Farmland form e-market for the Food industry

Begin 2002

3/00 - Con Ed, Duke Energy, Entergy, FirstEnergy, Florida P&L, PG&E, PSE&G, and 8 others form e-market for the Energy industry

3/00 - J & J, GE Medical, Baxter, Abbott Labs, and Medtronic form e-market for the Health Care supplies industry

3/00 - International Paper, Georgia-Pacific Corp., and Weyerhaeuser form e-market for the Paper industry

3/00 Procter & Gamble, Kraft, H.J. Heinz, Nestle, PepsiCo Bestfoods, and Colgate-Palmolive form e-market for the Consumer Package Goods industry

3/00 Amoco, Royal Dutch Shell, and Elf form e-market for the Oil Industry

3/00 Boeing, Lockheed Martin, Raytheon, and British Aerospace form Aerospace industry exchange

Begin 2000

3/00 Cargill, DuPont, and Cenex form e-market for the Agricultural Chemical industry

2/00 Sears and Carrefour form B2B e-market for the Retail industry

2/00 GM, Ford, Chrysler form e-market for the Automotive industry

Inherent competition, large supplier push-back, politics, disparate nature of internal applications, the difficulty of product information exchange between e-markets will plummet these "sponsored" markets toward the trough of disillusionment.

Figure 9.2 Channel masters in numerous industries are announcing consortia aimed at e-procurement, e-fulfillment, and a range of shared e-business problems. Competitive pressure and channel conflict will reduce their use and value to the members by 2002.

Instead, many middlemen have fashioned the Internet into a formidable competitive weapon. They have combined the strength of their physical infrastructure with the reach of the Internet in a click-and-brick model. They understand that customer information is the key to value and they have been able to leverage an enviable position in the middle of the value chain. If you already know, through years of service, what customers want, when they want it, what they are willing to pay for it, and what they perceive as intrinsic value, you hold the key to customer relationships.

Anyone who visits a mega-dealer to look at automobiles or buys insurance through a broker is familiar with the concept of the middleman as product and information aggregator. The Internet, however, makes it possible to aggregate products and information on a much broader scale. In fact, the middleman business model is one of the fastest-growing segments of Web e-commerce. So the model itself is not in danger of disappearing yet. Traditional players, however, must rethink their value and position or they will be disintermediated by other types of cybermediaries.

> **E-Vision:** Channel master and click-and-brick middleman e-markets will facilitate the majority of e-commerce spending over the next two years.

4. Cybermediaries. Just as brokers act as intermediaries between buyers and sellers in the physical world, the model is carried over by cybermediaries. Like any broker, they work well in situations where buyers and sellers have difficulty finding each other. In the physical world, brokers also may take some measure of responsibility on behalf of the buyer or seller. For example, a trusted insurance agent may very well intercede on behalf of his client when a problem arises with the insurance carrier. This is because he has an interest in creating a relationship that may span many insurance providers over time. Conversely, he will be successful only if he consistently brings responsible clients to the insurance companies that he represents. This continuum of service and responsibility is the value the agent brings to the transaction.

Cybermediaries that are able to translate this customer-centered value to the Internet channel will gain traction within the value chain, especially in industries where there is great distrust or confusion between buyers and sellers. So cybermediaries that can provide trusted services online—most likely by developing sites that are highly interactive and offer cyber- as well as real-person expert advice—will successfully challenge their traditional counterparts.

To date, cybermediaries have tended to focus predominantly on the matching of buyers and sellers rather than on the full-service continuum. Those who provide sell-side application software and services allow suppliers to create online catalogs and host those catalogs for them. Buy-side cybermediaries offer applications to buyers that allow them to more efficiently manage the procurement process by managing the electronic catalogs of selected suppliers. Those applications can either be hosted by the cybermediary or installed at the buyer site. Either way, the cybermediary concentrates on enabling the selling process on behalf of suppliers, the buying process on behalf of buyers, or both through a hosted environment. While this has worked well in the early stages of e-commerce, it will not survive the entry of full-service broker relationships—those that offer more than just a matching service. Eventually, as we discuss in Chapter 10, these agents will need to assume greater responsibility for the various stages of end-to-end e-commerce.

This will not only ensure their survival, it will also allow them to maximize the inherent value gained by established relationships with buyers. Once cybermediaries assume responsibilities for more of the customer "touch points" along a value chain, they can more effectively value their services beyond the "matching" phase of commerce.

Cybermediaries as Transaction Hubs.   Some of the more established cybermediaries are trying to morph into transaction hubs in order to gain liquidity. Underneath the media and market hype, however, transaction hubs look very much like old-fashioned EDI value-added networks (VANs). And many operate in decidedly extranet-like situations: first by acting as a cybermediary at the behest of a channel master and then by hoping to link across multiple exchanges. They offer data transformation services, transaction management, and e-market interconnection, just as the VANs did for 25 years. But if this is all they end up doing, they will simply be substituting the Internet for proprietary networks. Necessary but not terribly exciting, and open to commoditization because they deal at the transaction level.

What they hope to do, however, is to provide horizontal interaction across disparate business processes and multiple e-markets, building tremendous transaction flow. If successful, this will provide some level of business process standardization and will differentiate them from their spiritual father—the VAN. But, first, participants must accept a certain level of business process standardization. Then, data attributes and content in and between a multitude of e-markets must be rationalized. Competitive obstacles aside (such as we discussed in conjunction with sponsored e-markets), this is a tall order—one that is extremely difficult and that has not been accomplished before.

We are skeptical of any cybermediary's ability to accomplish this "network-of-networks" goal. First, the resources and authority to determine business process does not vest with the cybermediary; rather, it resides in the participating companies, many of them channel masters. In order to effect change across an *entire* industry, they must achieve a level of cooperation that is unlikely. In addition, as we can see in Figure 9.3, the transaction hub must enlist a number of strategic partners as they manage the life cycle of a transaction. It is more likely that cybermediaries will enable supply chains on a limited (though quite valuable) basis, within the channel master model.

5. Portals. The term *portal* is generally applied to consumer Web sites like Yahoo! Yet it describes perfectly the business model that is built around the confluence of the three C's: content, community, and commerce. Although the best-known consumer portals generally began by offering content and community, most are now including commerce capabilities in order to round out their services—and

The Challenge of Transaction Hubs

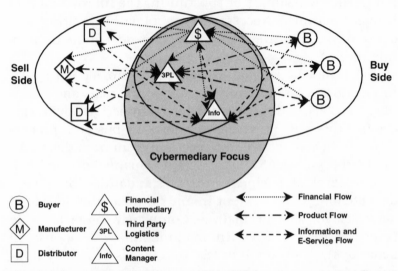

Figure 9.3 The complexity of transaction management and flow will limit the ability of all but a few cybermediaries to scale to the level of transaction hub.

expand their revenue opportunities. Significant amounts of commerce can be facilitated on or from B2C portals. But how much B2B commerce will the portal model generate?

Since it is not likely that businesses will want to pay for content and community, and will bristle at too much advertising, it will be commerce and supporting management service fees that will pay the freight for operating a B2B portal. But by their nature, portals are not, taken alone, conducive to B2B commerce. By definition, they must be broad based in order to attract a critical mass of visitors. B2B commerce, on the other hand, tends to be very specialized, done more at a micro level, and focused within a very specific supply chain. So while content and a sense of community should be part of every B2B commerce site, they will not be the primary attractions. But while B2B portals are off to a slow start in achieving profitability, their supplier-facing focus and broad base will make them attractive destinations for cybermediaries and transaction hubs by early 2004.

OFF TO A SLOW START

VerticalNet, one of the earliest and best-known B2B portals, calls itself a creator and operator of vertical trade communities. VerticalNet includes content, community resources, and commerce (storefront and auction) in its list of services. But commerce has been slow to take off: As of November 1999, the company had sold less than $1 million in products, even though it had been online for about five months and had $30 million in inventory posted on its sites in industries from agriculture to construction.

Business-to-business portals will begin to gain favor as e-commerce models evolve and technology—especially the use of intelligent software agents, discussed in Chapter 9—begin to impact product sourcing. Portal gatekeepers, by hosting large numbers of (typically) medium-size and small suppliers within a vertical industry, will increasingly offer tools to ease the difficulty of finding specialty suppliers, doing spot buys, and even bartering goods and services.

The emergence of portals as a sustainable e-commerce business model will be driven by a backlash to the layer upon layer of cybermediation that will build up over the 2000-to-2003 timeframe. Channel masters, click-and-brick intermediaries, cybermediaries and, by extension, transaction hubs will begin to overlap—adding cost, time, and confusion to the relatively simple process of buying and selling. By late 2003, the desire of buyers to go direct to suppliers without too many layers in between will make the vertical portals an attractive alternative to other overhead-bloated e-commerce models.

6. Viral Business Models: E-commerce Meets Tupperware. Remember Tupperware parties? Tupperware's original selling model depended on friends and neighbors to market products. Even though it was definitely a sales situation, buyers generally knew the people involved (or had an opportunity to extend their circle of friends) and showrooms were equipped with doilies and family pictures. A great deal of trust was embedded in the extended friendship and the close proximity of the channel. This low-cost direct sales channel used word of mouth to build brand and demand. Now it has been recreated on the Web with a really cool name: *viral marketing.*

The Internet provides the perfect opportunity to turn simple chat and e-mail into marketing tools, as buyers compare notes on products or share free samples of content. Part of Amazon.com's appeal is the online book review by readers, eBay relies on real buyers to rate sellers' trustworthiness, Hotmail was an early example of the power of viral marketing. It attracted 12 million users in 1.5 years. Napster has gone Hotmail one better. It passed the 25 million user mark in less than a year.

The underlying concept of viral marketing is sound; after all, studies have shown that any two web sites are separated by less than 19 clicks. But the commercial success of sites hoping to use viral marketing as their main asset will be limited by several factors, including these: (1) Free services in the absence of a highly specialized community context will be difficult to differentiate; (2) free Web-based functionality that simply duplicates PC-based functionality (such as calendaring and e-mail) will not attract and retain users; and (3) viral marketing by its nature is transient and difficult to structure and, therefore, difficult to develop into a sustainable business model.

For this last reason, it is unlikely that viral e-markets will be widely used in B2B. But they have had a profound effect on B2C and C2C. They work best in unstructured, highly niche-oriented underground communities where participants are bound together by common, often esoteric, interests. Here they will constantly form and disperse, creating niche-selling opportunities for equally flexible cybermediaries.

There are elements of viral marketing that will affect B2B in two areas: performance monitoring and market expansion. As e-markets evolve, the ability for individuals to rate the quality of a product or performance level of customer service and share that information publicly will increase. This will become an important factor in determining which companies and products are able to demand higher prices in the market.

In addition, the person-to-person neural network will become a vital, if somewhat underground, method of expanding market share. Valuable digitized content can be given away for the purpose of viral sharing. New customers and whole new markets can be uncovered in this way. While it may be a challenge to deal with these unstructured markets, they could easily account for a significant amount of e-commerce.

■ MAKING MONEY: ONLINE REVENUE MODELS

The differences that exist between physical companies and their virtual counterparts are striking when it comes to discussions of return on investment (ROI), value, and revenue generation. In interviews with hundreds of e-commerce vendors, cybermediaries, and traditional companies, we learned that the only aspect of e-commerce that was more volatile than the business model itself was the method by which companies expected to make money online.

Until March of 2000, profit motive did not seem to exist for the virtual players, especially those that had venture capital funding or high stock valuations. Instead, their overwhelming focus was to drive site visitors and/or transaction volume. In stark contrast, brick-and-mortar companies viewed the Internet as a low-cost channel to source and sell products. Their executives expected online expenditures to return increased profits, higher margins, and greater market penetration, and many were not inclined to fund online expeditions just for the sake of experimentation.

➤ Any Which Way That Works

Purely virtual companies were willing to try any revenue model that looked promising. They were also willing to change it abruptly if it fails. Actually, the freedom to constantly rework business plans is an advantage—if only a temporary one. Real companies with brand to protect and stockholders to pacify find it more difficult to turn on a dime.

Consumer portal sites like Excite make money by selling advertising space and getting fees for linking visitors to affiliate sites. Portals are also adding on transaction fees when sales or auctions are conducted. eBay takes a small fee for each transaction, for example. Many of the B2B business models look very similar to traditional distributors and retailers, making money on the spread between the wholesale and retail price.

B2B Internet revenue models are an odd combination of money-making techniques. So it is not unusual that revenue is derived from a variety of sources, and the mix changes constantly. Companies should build a matrix of revenue opportunities into their business plan, giving them the freedom to employ several at any one point in their evolution. It is best, however, to use a flexible revenue model from the beginning so that the market perception is one of a menu of service options rather than arbitrary changes in the pricing structure. (See Figure 9.4.)

E-Commerce Revenue Models

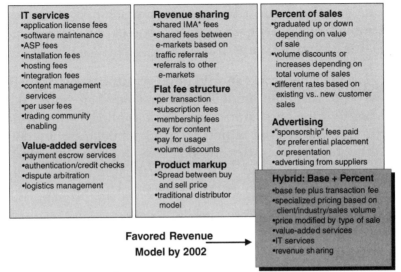

IT services
- application license fees
- software maintenance
- ASP fees
- installation fees
- hosting fees
- integration fees
- content management services
- per user fees
- trading community enabling

Value-added services
- payment escrow services
- authentication/credit checks
- dispute arbitration
- logistics management

Revenue sharing
- shared IMA* fees
- shared fees between e-markets based on traffic referrals
- referrals to other e-markets

Flat fee structure
- per transaction
- subscription fees
- membership fees
- pay for content
- pay for usage
- volume discounts

Product markup
- Spread between buy and sell price
- traditional distributor model

Percent of sales
- graduated up or down depending on value of sale
- volume discounts or increases depending on total volume of sales
- different rates based on existing vs.. new customer sales

Advertising
- "sponsorship" fees paid for preferential placement or presentation
- advertising from suppliers

Hybrid: Base + Percent
- base fee plus transaction fee
- specialized pricing based on client/industry/sales volume
- price modified by type of sale
- value-added services
- IT services
- revenue sharing

Favored Revenue Model by 2002 ➝

* Internet Merchant Account

Figure 9.4 E-markets are struggling with revenue models, many in an effort to become profitable before their funding runs out. As a result, pricing for their services is in a state of flux and is confusing to their clients. However, we believe that over time a hybrid pricing model will emerge that is tailored to the industry, client, and value of sales enabled by the e-market.

■ PRACTICAL STRATEGIES FOR WEB-SPEED BUSINESS MODEL ADAPTATION

1. Companies that use cybermediaries should remain flexible when dealing with them and expect relationships to be somewhat chaotic until models begin to stabilize in the 2002 time frame. Companies will need to be highly flexible to take advantage of the new opportunities and competitive challenges offered by e-commerce business models. Change will be the norm. Online businesses will not have the luxury of a yearly or even quarterly fine-tuning. That simply won't be fast enough. Therefore, companies that do a portion of their business online must be prepared to deconstruct and reconstruct their processes, customer relationships, revenue sources, alliances, and organizational makeup.

2. Cybermediaries should employ multielement business and revenue models. Easier said than done. But there are some basic rules that, when applied, will provide a framework around which warp-speed business models can be developed. A flexible business model will include key elements from all of the major business models described in this chapter. For example:

➤ The middleman model recognizes the value of information. As power shifts more and more to the buyer, devise models and back-end applications that gather and leverage buyer information.

➤ The ability to leverage the neural network—one of the key elements of the viral business model—can be used effectively to build brand, aggregate demand, and broaden market opportunities.

➤ Matching buyers and sellers is a basic service of every business model. Problems will arise, however, if it remains the only service offered by a cybermediary. Over time, matching buyers and sellers (as complicated as the infrastructure and applications necessary to accomplish it) will simply be the entry price for e-markets. Added-value services centered around product flow, money management, and trust must be included in the cybermediary's portfolio, as Chapter 10 discusses.

➤ Portals exhibit the most effective use of content and basic Web services to drive traffic to sites. While content and community may not be the primary business drivers of B2B commerce, they can certainly enhance commerce. Determine how your business applies these same concepts to B2B, but make them secondary to the facilitation of commerce and supply chain integration.

3. Companies should limit their use of cybermediaries for any type of strategic procurement to those who aggregate large buyers at least through 2003. E-businesses shift power to buyers. Therefore, cybermediaries that adopt commerce models that favor buyer needs, expectations, and perceptions will ultimately gain more online traction than those using traditional seller-oriented models.

4. Cybermediaries should act quickly over the next 12 months to strengthen their online brands. At least for the next 12 months, information will continue to flow through the middle of the value chain. So in most industries, indirect rather than direct sales channels will be the early beneficiaries of e-commerce. Rather than mass disintermediation, e-markets created by click-and-brick distributors and channel masters (versus those created by cybermediaries) will manage the majority of online e-commerce spending.

5. Manufacturers should build a portfolio of e-business initiatives to ensure direct-to-customer relationships. Over the next 12 to 18 months, while information continues to pool in the center of the value chain, manufacturers will be further disconnected from their customers. Strong cybermediaries will appear and traditional channels will build online order processing and customer service sites. To survive this period, traditional companies must take care not to completely surrender brand and detailed product information to disconnected intermediaries. They should build a portfolio of channel strategies: direct, indirect, and online.

6. The need for complex product information and buyers' desire for dynamic pricing will drive cybermediaries as well as click-and-brick intermediaries to seek

close integration with technology-savvy manufacturers.
Manufacturers will exercise greater control over their
online channels as the need for ever more granular levels
of information increases. The desire to negotiate directly
and the ability to offer the lowest price/value ratio will
begin to drive commerce to the extremes of the value
chain—the buyer and the manufacturer.

**7. The days of transactions as the sole base for rev-
enue generation are numbered.**   Online commerce will
tend to commoditize low-value, transaction-oriented
cybermediaries. Therefore, only a few of the most successful will prosper (by "most successful," we mean those
that have the greatest volume or highest value of transactions).

■ CONCLUSION

E-commerce business models define the structure of electronic relationships among customers, manufacturers,
suppliers, and intermediaries. As we traverse the e-age,
agility will be the key to transformation and success. The
opportunity is to participate in multiple e-commerce
models, thus providing maximum flexibility. Companies
should build, invest, and participate in a portfolio of
online channels, recognizing that e-commerce is not a
destination but an unfolding process, full of false starts
and hidden obstacles. But when has business been this
much fun?

The Evolution of B2B E-Markets

■ THE FUTURE OF ELECTRONIC MARKETS

Perhaps the greatest change that e-markets have brought about is the way B2B buyers of any ilk—whether they are purchasing managers, lab technicians, chemists, or shop floor maintenance engineers—approach procurement. The linear value chain has disappeared and in its place is a constantly revolving exchange that has forever altered the relationship between buyers, sellers, and those who inhabit the space between. How so? At any point in time, each may play all roles: as buyer, as seller, and as intermediary. The roles are interchangeable, sometime simultaneous, and always dynamic.

➤ Power to the People

The Internet has transformed the consumer into a power buyer. No longer bound by geography, consumers can literally search the world for products. The bookstore, broker, retailer, and travel agent are available through a keyboard, Palm Pilot, cell phone, television—indeed, any electronic device. And if you don't like the price, the next seller is only a click or a call away. What has suffered, of course, is loyalty. A study published by the Bristol Group in early 2000 found some interesting results on loyalty: Of nearly 1,600 adult residents of Canada and the United States, 60 percent of offline customers said they were very likely to continue to buy from particular retailers, but only 43 percent of online customers said they were very likely to buy from particular retailers. As power continues to shift to the consumer, competition, margin erosion, and product substitution within the customer-facing supply chain will increase.

The growth of consumer power increases pressure on retailers, who pressure their distributors, who pressure their manufacturers to compress supply chain processes in order to reduce costs, increase inventory turns, and present ever more customized products to ever more granular customer niches. How will this be done? Through the rise of Internet e-markets in every industry and every client sector. These markets will be formed around a number of business models, such as the ones we describe in Chapter 9—from classic channel master models like the GM, Ford, and DaimlerChrysler Covisint consortium announced in early 2000, to neutral cyber-mediaries like Altra Energy, Arbinet, and FastParts. Eventually, however, the models for B2B e-procurement will coalesce around two business objectives: sourcing and supply chain management.

➤ The Great Divide: Different Views

Sourcing e-markets will operate vertically within an industry and horizontally across industries, depending on the commodity—sometimes simultaneously. The most successful will be operated by cybermediaries that take on several roles: application provider, business process enabler, information aggregator, content manager, matchmaker, transaction manager, network provider, and exchange guarantor. One of their chief attributes will be the *percep-*

tion of neutrality—not owned or too closely associated with any one manufacturer or distributor.

Industry-specific *supply chain management* e-markets will complement the sourcing models. Wal-Mart's manipulation of its supplier network is perhaps the most well known of these types of supply chain management schemas. Wal-Mart, as a dominant retailer within the chain, dictates the business process, applications, and network its suppliers use to communicate. It even dictates the data standards used. In this way, Wal-Mart has been able to lower inventory carrying costs, decrease the processing cost of purchase orders, increase the efficiency of forecasting, and so forth. Wal-Mart benefits by pushing costs further down the supply chain—essentially getting its suppliers to carry more of the operational burden. In the online world, Dell is one of the best examples of using new technologies to increase customer satisfaction while lowering operational costs. The competitive advantage is gained at both ends of the supply chain.

➤ Sourcing Power

The rise in consumer buying power along the customer-facing value chain is increasingly being mirrored along the supplier-facing value chain. In other words, the already powerful business buyers are using the Internet to gain even more power and use the e-procurement cybermediaries and the e-marketplaces they create to facilitate more efficient sourcing of both direct and indirect goods. In fact, we have already seen nearly 30 percent of the Fortune 500 in the process of implementing an e-procurement market for their indirect goods—focused primarily on white-collar MRO commodities like office supplies and computer equipment. The second wave of e-procurement is blue-collar MRO—industrial goods, replacement machine parts, and so on. A convincing argument can be made that these classes of commodity items are the easiest, and therefore the most obvious, procurement activities to automate.

That is not to say that the return on investment does not justify the cost. Indeed, high-volume, low-cost operations material can amount to hundreds of millions in largely unmonitored spending for large corporations, especially in service industries like insurance and finance. But much opportunity exists for the cybermediary that begins to bring higher levels of efficiency to other classes of purchasing, including travel and entertainment, direct materials, and especially services—perhaps the most difficult for which to create standardized taxonomy.

The early e-procurement vendors are fast expanding their offerings beyond just matching buyers and sellers. In a move that we see as a harbinger of the future, Ariba and Citibank have announced an e-market for Citibank's corporate customers, where Citibank will be offering money and payment management services.

The Citibank-Ariba deal points to a shift we believe is important to the future trending of e-markets and the procurement processes they enable: the need for software and infrastructure vendors to team up with partners that can elevate the marketplace services to a higher level. It will not be enough for e-markets to simply match buyers and sellers and automate the purchase order/invoice transaction. E-markets of the future will also need to facilitate the movement of products and the movement of money, and be viewed as trusted intermediaries. These last two points will be especially important in B2B markets. In fact, they will become an essential part of the successful cybermediary's portfolio of services.

Therefore, we will concentrate on this B2B e-market paradigm shift as it affects sourcing rather than how e-markets will assist in tightening known supply chains, which we discuss in more detail in Chapter 11. To better understand these changes in B2B sourcing and plot its likely evolution, it is worthwhile to first analyze business-to-consumer trends.

■ B2C AND B2B COMMERCE MYTHS AND REALITIES

Business-to-consumer (B2C) buying and selling has a head start on B2B. Therefore, B2C buying patterns are important to follow because they illustrate important trends that we think will be mirrored as the B2B market matures. And while there are many points of difference, there is enough similarity to justify drawing the analogy. In fact, the significant differences between B2C and B2B e-commerce will not be in areas such as purchasing processes, personalization, loyalty, or buyer expectations. Rather, these areas will actually grow more similar over time. Instead, we believe the truly significant differences will be found in three areas: the physical movement of products, the complexity of money transactions, and the infusion of trust.

These are but some of the myths surrounding the differences between selling to consumers and selling to businesses that we explore in the following discussion.

➤ Myths about B2C and B2B Differences

Business buyers know exactly what they want to buy, so they don't want to browse a catalog like a consumer. The user interface for B2B, therefore, is much different. Guess what, consumers don't particularly like to browse an online catalog either. The reality is that most consumers know exactly what they want to buy before they shop on the Internet: a particular book, airline tickets, a specific CD, computer equipment, even a familiar article of clothing. They are not strolling through a mall, browsing. They are looking for very specific items. At this point, they are using search engines or first-generation software agents like mySimon to find products. Or they are visiting well-known (and trusted) sites like Amazon and Dell. But their exploration is not random. In that way, they are very similar to business buyers and the user interface will, over time, look more like B2B interfaces.

As the Internet matures, all buyers will expect an ever more personalized experience, whether a portal, a community site, individual micro-marketplaces, or intelligent software agents present it. So while the actual data presented will be very different—the latest release from your favorite jazz artist versus replacement parts for a milling machine—it will be targeted at the specific viewer.

Relationships between business buyers are more stable than those with consumers. The switching costs are too high to easily change from one supplier to the next. The reality is that B2B switching costs will decrease as the number of online suppliers increases. We maintain that the length of supplier contracts will decrease even for strategic suppliers—and the likelihood of supplier switching will increase as companies can more easily source through electronic marketplaces.

After all, the revenue model for e-markets depends not on the length of time a contract is in place between two companies, but on the amount of traffic and or liquidity placed through the market, which is a result of the number of players in the market. It is, therefore, in their best interests to provide open sourcing by making as many buyers and sellers available to each other as possible. If their revenue model also has an annual baseline fee to participate, some professional services, and software components, then size definitely matters.

The only real barrier to switching is the integration of business processes and systems between sellers and buyers. So if my supply chain *is* truly integrated at all points— with visibility into inventory levels and automated forecasting—then switching costs throughout the supply chain increase. But like dominos, one out-of-sync player can dramatically reduce the efficiency of the whole chain. The reality is that very few supply chains are integrated today beyond the largest suppliers. The majority of small and mid-tier suppliers still transact business via phone, fax, and e-mail—not exactly a barrier to supplier substitution. As shown in Figure 10.1, traditional relationships decrease over time in favor of short-duration "as-needed" relationships.

Users do not bring the same level of expectations to B2B Web commerce interactions as do consumers. In fact, business buyers' behavior and expectations will be influenced by their experience as consumers on the Web. It is likely that business buyers will actually have heightened user expectations. They will expect companies in their industry and circle of suppliers to have detailed information about their buying patterns, requirements, and negotiated contracts. They will expect helpful suggestions on alternative products and appropriate content. Unlike con-

Spectrum of Supply Chain Relationships

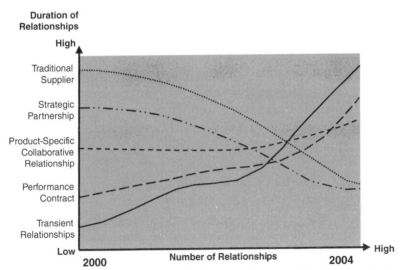

Figure 10.1 By 2004, global-sourcing-enabled e-markets will greatly increase the number of transient—or one-time—transactions between buyers and sellers while decreasing the number of traditional static relationships within a supply chain.

sumers, who are somewhat used to poor customer service, because they started buying online in the early days of the Web, business buyers will not tolerate poor service for long, especially from suppliers that offer commodity products and services. So in order to anticipate how buyers will want to interact with B2B sites, it is important to study the trends in B2C web site development: live chat, mobile access, streaming media, and so on.

When we look at B2C expectations, we see consumers have four major needs: (1) the need for simplicity, (2) the need for immediacy, (3) the need for transparency, and (4) the need for relevancy. It is unwise to assume that B2B buyers will want anything less from their online experiences when they go to work. They will expect Web commerce to be simple, response to be immediate, and information to be transparent throughout the supply chain, and for the data that are presented to be relevant to the task at hand. In the B2B space, this means that the online experience of procurement managers and other business buyers will be only as good as the extent to which the supply chain is integrated.

B2B pricing is not as dynamic as consumer pricing. The bulk of traditional purchasing between companies has been conducted primarily through negotiated fixed price, list price, or discounts off of list price. But as the Web becomes a more common infrastructure for B2B commerce, pricing between companies will follow the B2C models—favoring dynamic pricing over fixed pricing. The closed communities facilitated by proprietary network infrastructure, EDI, and fixed price are waning.

In contrast, Web commerce, facilitated by online catalogs, search engines, intelligent agents, and industry-specific community sites, is in its hyperactive growth stage. In fact, we are seeing a fragmentation along product lines within industries and niche micromarkets being launched nearly every day. The model is gaining in prominence. Web technology standards such as XML and UDDI will, over the next three years, enable thousands of small and large e-markets to interoperate within and outside industry borders. This will provide cross-industry procurement and selling opportunities to participants. Even before these standards are widely adopted, a class of vendor we call a *metamediary** will enable market-to-market interoperability.

> **E-Vision:** As e-markets expand, the traditional relationships between buyers and suppliers will weaken. E-markets will greatly increase sourcing freedom and put everyone in the value chain at risk, including the channel masters.

➤ Real B2C and B2B Differences

Up to this point, we have been discussing the perceived differences between B2C and B2B commerce. We have been exploding some of the myths around these differences, but here is where we diverge and begin to discuss the significant differences that we believe do exist.

Content management is more complex in B2B. One of the most significant differences between B2C and B2B that e-market cybermediaries must deal with is the management of product databases. While the catalog metaphor has been useful in B2B and the deployment of individual electronic catalogs is a fundamental value offered by e-markets, catalog development and aggregation is much more difficult in B2B, particularly when the products are highly customized or made to order. In a make-to-order industry, the catalog content and pricing are virtually meaningless. Extensive human interaction is needed to arrive at the final product and price, and this has yet to be satisfactorily captured in an e-market.

---

* We define technology metamediaries as technology companies that facilitate the translation and transmission of data between e-markets.

B2B content management is also more difficult because of semantic differences: at any point in the supply chain, various manufacturers and distributors often describe the same product in different ways. Even the code used to identify the same product may be different between a manufacturer and the distributor or direct buyer. Abbreviations are also a problem. "Black" becomes "blk"; "kg" could mean keg or kilogram; "HP" could mean high pressure, horsepower, or Hewlett-Packard.

So in order to search across multiple suppliers for the same product, cybermediaries must perform several tasks: They must first scrub the data so that duplicate, incomplete, and inconsistent records are reconciled, then they must normalize the data (e.g., transform the variables in all product descriptions), and then account for semantic differences (e.g., different meanings for the same word). This is a task that is complex and expensive, especially if the products represented are intricate or highly technical. Data normalization and semantic reconciliation have never been done easily or inexpensively. EDI as a standard could accommodate this only by laborious adoption of industry standards and then individual buyer-to-seller negotiated trading partner agreements and implementation guidelines. EDI doesn't work well in a many-buyers-to-many-sellers dynamic environment such as cybermediaries try to foster in e-markets. Rather, people working with specific product databases must do B2B content management. And often the people needed to perform the normalization and then semantic reconciliation of data must have industry knowledge to accomplish an accurate translation. Specialized vendors such as Requisite, Harbinger, and Aspect Development Group have emerged to deal only with this problem.

The problem is even more complex as cybermediaries try to streamline the procurement of far more complicated products than the white-collar MRO categories they have been focused on to date. A tremendous amount of data required for a purchasing decision falls below the five levels of UN/SPSC (Universal Standard Products and Services Classification) or similar taxonomies used by cybermediaries to normalize product categories today. Product attributes such as tensile strength, weight-bearing capacity, and heat absorption, normally found in a paper catalog or on a specification sheet, do not easily translate into a standard but often must be provided for a technical buyer to compare different products and make a decision.

But in order to facilitate ever wider supplier sourcing, e-markets will need to provide ever more granular content management services—either themselves or, more likely, through alliances with specialized content management services. Even the adoption of taxonomies such as UN/SPSC and languages such as XML will only ameliorate, not eliminate, the problem of semantic reconciliation in business procurement.

The movement of products is quite different in B2B than it is in B2C. So far, e-markets have essentially ignored the question of how products get physically moved. In the consumer space, companies such as UPS and FedEx have picked up the slack—at a real profit. It can be argued that the successful UPS IPO can be attributed to the company's position in the new vortex of consumer electronic commerce. But apart from a very few dot-coms such as WebVan, B2B e-markets have left it up to the buyer and seller to arrange for product distribution.

But we see a growing need for e-markets to provide distribution support as a differentiating service. Just as Amazon.com had to add "brick" to "click" and build warehouses (increasing its cost of doing business), e-markets are adding physical infrastructure to their cyber business models. Various levels of relationships exist between the cybermediaries and their logistics partners. VerticalNet bought NECX's electronics components division, the second largest distributor of excess inventory. FastParts has a business relationship with America II, the fourth largest distributor of electronic circuit boards. XSag.com uses four regional distributors to ship agricultural products from sellers to buyers. None of these cybermediaries actually takes title to the products that flow through their sites, but they all facilitate the shipment of goods.

Handling payments and the movement of money is much more complex in B2B than it is in B2C. Most consumers use a credit card or write a check to purchase goods over the Internet. Credit card purchasing used in B2B takes the form of procurement cards. Employees typically use p-cards to purchase low-value goods. The cards carry maximum amount ceilings and offer companies some ability to more closely track expenditures such as office supplies and other indirect purchases. Procurement cards are especially popular in service industries and government agencies, where the bulk of procurement dollars is spent on non-production-related materials. By capturing detailed transaction information, cybermediaries will increase the use of p-cards by offering level 3 information about transactions. (Level 3 information includes such data as quantities ordered, product codes, freight amount, and duty amount at the point of sale.)

But for the manufacturing and industrial sectors, a (relatively) simple credit card transaction does not begin to address the complexity of money management. Raw materials needed to produce goods are generally bought in bulk and delivered over the course of a production cycle. Blanket purchase orders must be drawn against and corrected in the case of partial deliveries or unacceptable shipments. Business buyers prefer direct bank transfers for large transactions, not checks or credit cards.

In B2B, the process of selecting and negotiating with a potential supplier can also take on complexities not typically seen in consumer purchasing, as seen in Figure 10.2. Buyers and sellers that work with each other constantly may very well have worked out all the details of the exchange of money. And they have established trust. But as e-markets gain prominence, buyers and sellers will increasingly do business with unknown partners, where the back-end money management has not been worked

B2B's Complex Transaction Chain

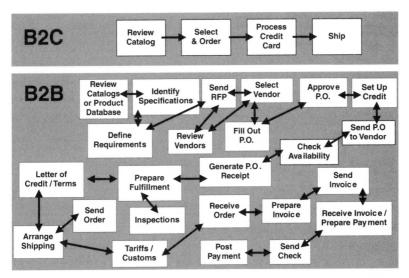

Figure 10.2 Though somewhat simplified, this figure represents a view of the differences in process complexity between a B2C and a B2B purchase.

out. They will need some mechanism to ensure that participants are real companies with good credit ratings and that money transactions are handled in a secure and reasonable fashion.

Most B2B e-markets today do not address this issue, leaving it up to the individual participants to manage terms of credit, payment, and settlement interactions among themselves. We believe that e-market makers will need to offer money transfer and payment management services if they are to be successful e-commerce players over the long term. The more advanced B2B e-markets, such as AttraEnergy, E-Chemicals, Ventro, and FastParts, have already created relationships with banks to fill this hole in their service offerings.

As purchasing becomes more dynamic and buyers begin to deal with suppliers where no formal relationship exists, money interactions become less structured. This, of course, will require more expert intermediation than most e-market makers are capable of handling themselves. Temporary escrow accounts will be extremely beneficial as one-time buyers pay one-time sellers for goods that they have not seen beforehand. Corporations may want to set up central cyber bank accounts to deal with multiple auction markets enabled by the Internet. The way money is handled will change as e-commerce expands its hold throughout the world. E-market makers will need partners that understand and can handle the movement of money for their participants.

Security, trust, and the branding of e-markets will emerge as the key to e-commerce success. Perhaps the least understood and most overlooked opportunity in e-commerce is the development of trust. In both B2C and B2B, trust is generally invested in brand. Brand is built over time by essentially delivering on both explicit and implicit promises made to buyers. Sears's money-back guarantee is a promise to stand behind all of the items purchased through its stores. Nordstrom is known for personalized customer service, and Amazon.com built its brand through offering an excellent online shopping experience and exemplary customer service.

Today, businesses that buy from other businesses, especially direct materials that are crucial to product manufacturing, depend on a known circle of suppliers. But the Internet is changing the dynamics of procurement. E-markets offer a much greater ability to source goods and services from unknown suppliers than at any time in the past. By shrinking the boundaries of time and distance and making the sourcing process easier, e-markets increase the likelihood of supplier substitution. By linking with financial institutions, the e-market cybermediary also allows for the management of money between unknown buyers and sellers. The last, but perhaps most important, ingredient for a full-service e-market is trust.

Most of the e-procurement markets being set up today are still channel master markets, in which a dominant buyer encourages all of its suppliers to use a particular e-market. The automotive industry's recent procurement network announcements are examples of this dynamic. But as buyers and suppliers begin to participate in greater numbers of e-markets and the e-markets improve their interoperability, familiarity and structured business relationships decrease. Buyers and sellers may have never done business together before. They may not know each other—indeed, they may not have even heard of each other. In this type of transaction, a trusted third party vouches for the participants. A bank, government entity, accounting firm, or trade association are logical candidates to play the role of trusted third party.

The services that this trusted third party could offer are numerous. Even on spot buys within an e-market, buyers may want to have some indication of the supplier's ability to fulfill an order on time. It may be desirable to maintain anonymity throughout a particular transaction, yet each player may want to be assured that all participants conform to a predetermined revenue or quality threshold. The seller may very well want to understand a buyer's credit rating. Buyers and sellers will want to be assured that they are who they represent themselves to be. Therefore, digital certificates and authentication services could be provided by the e-market as part of a higher-level (and more expensive) offering. The investment of trust will be essential to e-markets that want to operate at the highest levels of B2B commerce. Yet cybermediaries will not necessarily have the luxury of time in which to gain trust. And as the threat of hackers and cybercrime increases, e-market cybermediaries will turn more readily to third parties that may be able to add a real veneer of security and trust to their services.

E-Vision: Within the next 8 to 24 months, consolidation of e-markets will begin. One-dimensional e-markets, meaning those that facilitate transactions only, will fail. Multidimensional competitors will absorb their trading exchange customers.

Fundamentally, most B2B cybermediaries have, to date, been concerned with the management of fairly simple transactions—matching buyers and sellers, creating purchase orders and invoices, and so forth. They provide tools for the visibility of some product information, typically in some form of electronic catalog or through some type of information and transaction exchange, similar to the stock market. Pretty much everything else is left up to the individual participants. But this is changing. E-commerce of the future will gravitate toward cybermediaries that enhance their services far beyond just publishing electronic catalogs and facilitating transactions. In fact, as Figure 10.3 proposes, cybermediaries that expect to thrive over the next two to three years will need

Evolution of B2B E-Market Services

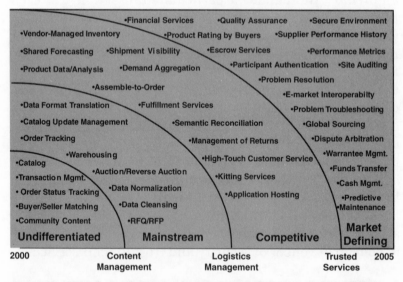

Figure 10.3 Successful cybermediaries that manage e-markets will progress along a logical line of evolution that will eventually include not just the management of complex content and transactions but also the handling of physical goods, complex financial transactions, and, finally, the engendering of trust in the e-market itself.

to provide market-defining services that establish them in the role of trusted intermediary.

■ THE E-MARKET OPPORTUNITY

Now that we have explored the myths and realities of B2B versus B2C differences, let's look at other factors that will differentiate the winners and losers in cybermediation.

➤ Size Matters

Gartner Group has published perhaps the biggest number yet for B2B e-commerce transactions, estimating that they will reach over (U.S.) $7.3 trillion worldwide by 2004. As gargantuan as that number seems, it is simply the last in a long line of gargantuan numbers proffered by a host of research firms. The probability of these numbers, however, is beside the point. There is no doubt that several things are true:

> ➤ The ways goods and services are being procured are changing and the velocity of change will only increase, not decrease, as the Internet becomes more entrenched in electronic commerce.
> ➤ E-markets, both closed industry (such as the automotive industry) and open sourced, are fast becoming not just the catalyst for change but the underlying mechanism by which a large percentage of procurement will be done.
> ➤ Whatever the final numbers are, they are big! Big enough to attract more investment and more players, even as capital markets tighten.

Given these three constants, let's look at how e-market cybermediaries are performing today and analyze what likely changes will occur.

➤ B2B Focus

While there is much to learn from B2C and many similarities between the two, B2B is compelling because it offers much more opportunity to add value than B2C. Because B2B encompasses all the companies and processes from raw materials through retail, each step offers an opportunity to create multiple e-markets that could add value. Potential B2B e-market services include transaction management, in-transit visibility, product movement, money management, and trust development.

➤ Paper Clips and Computers

Many exchanges have identified white-collar MRO materials as the target for their e-market services. (See Figure 10.4.) As a result, we expect a major consolidation of the MRO procurement market in 2001 to 2002. This is in spite of the continual high expenditures by corporations on MRO goods. According to Aberdeen Group, companies spend roughly 35 percent of their total revenues on non-production goods such as office supplies, computer equipment, and travel expenses. But that number can reach as high as 60 percent to 70 percent in service-related companies. And most of it has been pretty much uncontrolled from a corporate perspective. Unlike raw materials, indirect items are seldom inventoried or tracked through automated procurement software. Even with the relatively recent deployment of e-procurement software within the largest U.S. companies, much opportunity exists for software and services focused on gaining control of this huge expense.

With North American businesses spending $1.4 trillion on nonproduction goods and services per year, the market for e-markets focused on the procurement of indirect materials has attracted numerous vendors. Especially when the returns are so promising: Killen & Associates found that a 5 percent improvement in supply chain procurement expenses can result in a 28 percent increase in corporate profits, with no required

Procurement vs. E-Market Focus

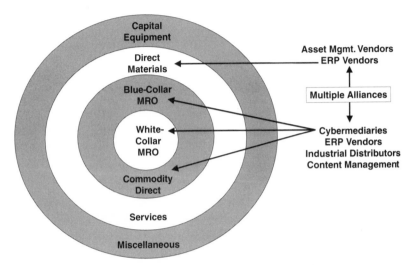

Figure 10.4 Most of the vendors that are trying to stream-line purchasing are focused on white- and blue-collar MRO—office and industrial indirect goods. These include ERP vendors such as SAP, Oracle, and PeopleSoft; cyber-mediaries such as Ariba, Commerce One, Clarus, and Es-sentialMarkets; content management vendors such as Harbinger, TPN, and Requisite; and enterprise asset man-agement vendors such as PSDI.

increase in top-line sales. Alternately, a corporation would have to increase its sales by a factor of 10 (assum-ing a 10 percent profit margin) to achieve the same level of savings.

Indirect purchasing is also a headache for procurement professionals. These types of purchases are typically high volume but low value. So lots of people are creating paper transactions with lots of vendors for things like pencils, paper, computer accessories, and other white-collar items that are simply required to keep an office going. Money is wasted with off-contract buying; procurement resources are spent dealing with large numbers of transactions, writ-ing checks, and so on; and productivity is lowered because people are looking through catalogs and filling out requisition sheets instead of doing their real jobs. In a recent survey, over 40 percent of NAPM (National Association of Purchasing Managers) respondents anticipated utilizing e-procurement markets for MRO, and between 18 percent and 26 percent for all purchases. Ninety-three percent of the companies surveyed planned to outsource in the next three years, and 90 percent of these same companies are satisfied with the outsourcing service concept. E-markets are viewed as essential to the control of these types of purchases.

The combination of purchasing inefficiency, large expenditures, and many exchanges targeting the segment focuses a lot of attention on MRO commodity procurement, even though it is only one type of purchasing for which procurement managers are responsible. As the shakeout in MRO procurement intensifies, we expect many vendors to look for less crowded markets.

■ THE CYBERMEDIARY COMPETITIVE LANDSCAPE

To say that cybermediation has attracted a large number of vendors is to make a gross understatement. All the major software vendors are trying to stake their claims on the e-market landscape. In fact, a recent spate of software vendor/cybermediary announcements brings this point home. SAP, for example, has made two rounds of investment in Commerce One. The latest was $250 million in return for a 4 percent stake and the understanding that Commerce One would provide its customers with SAP's supply chain, product life cycle, and customer relationships management software, as well as business intelligence.

Segmentation of vendors is difficult, as offerings tend to blur over time, but three major types of services can be identified: pure product, product and service, and pure application service. Again, the market is extremely volatile, so vendors are busy morphing from one type of offering to another. But, in general, most e-markets will be enabled by a coalition of vendors that offer both software and services through a hosted environment.

Pure software vendors are in a period of transition. All of the traditional EDI vendors made attempts to infiltrate the e-market space. Most failed, and a period of consolidation began, which left the top vendors either out of the business or busily trying to reposition their companies. GE Information Services (GEIS) formed a joint venture, first with Netscape and then with Thomas Register, to address the early e-procurement market. Harbinger, recognizing the end of sustained growth in EDI, first bought Premenos (the first EDI vendor to successfully build a product to transport EDI securely over the Internet) and then acquired Acquion, an e-catalog vendor. Harbinger was then acquired by Peregrin Systems, an infrastructure management company. IBM has gotten out of the active EDI market and Sterling Commerce was sold to SBC communications.

EDI vendors also tried to reposition their products in the emerging data transformation market. With the exception of Mercator, however, this also failed. They lost favor to the new XML-based data translation vendors such as WebMethods and Extricity. The EDI vendors—in fact, EDI in general—should not be regarded as having much growth potential, as companies increasingly embrace industry-specific XML standards to accomplish data integration.

The idea of paying for the use of applications rather than buying them and implementing them in-house has become much more viable for a larger number of companies with the commercialization of the Web and the ubiquity of the browser. Software vendors that offer applications over the Internet are called *application service providers* (ASPs). People who have been around the technology field for any length of time would recognize this software usage model by its former name: *timesharing*.

One difference between old application timesharing and the new ASP model is the cost associated with network computing. Rather than expensive leased lines into a computer center at the vendor's data center, applications can be accessed over the Internet via much less expensive lines. In addition, applications are being browser enabled, making the user interface much simpler.

The ASP model has several benefits: Software applications that previously helped only large companies with sophisticated IT staffs can now be used by smaller, less IT-savvy companies. Not only does this effectively broaden the market for software companies, it also gives them a recurring revenue stream, as applications are rented over time rather than licensed outright. In a broader sense, the ASP model also tends to rationalize business process across companies within an industry and therefore makes the use of de facto standards more likely. This, in turn, increases the ability for e-markets to emerge within industries that achieve critical mass. In fact, we believe that the ASP model is rapidly evolving to include a much more service-intense structure. As Figure 10.5 shows, the ASP model is essentially morphing into a BSP model: *business service provider.*

A hybrid software and services model will be the primary delivery mechanism for e-markets. Applied to the e-commerce market, an ASP model addresses only a part of the business opportunity. And e-markets, themselves, will require a layer of services wrapped around the application to effectively address the needs of buyers and sellers. So rather than a pure ASP model, we believe that e-markets will require additional services including strategic consulting, business process reengineering, data transformation, content rationalization, professional services, help desk, supply chain management, authentication, liability and risk management, logistics services, money management, legal advice, and payment and settlement services.

In other words, e-markets will facilitate a series of complex business processes within specific industries, espe-

E-Market Delivery Models

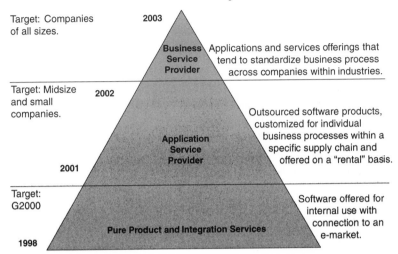

Figure 10.5 As e-market cybermediaries offer a myriad of hosted applications to smaller companies, business process for noncore services such as administration, human resources, and indirect materials procurement will tend to become standardized. Over time, companies of all sizes will selectively take advantage of these business service providers.

cially as one-to-one supplier relationships lose some ground in favor of more open supplier sourcing. In that environment, much more uniform business processes will need to be adopted and greater external control over the transactions and processes will need to be exercised. Therefore, e-markets will need to become more sophisticated in order for companies to feel comfortable making this trade-off between strategic supplier relationships and opportunistic supplier relationships developed through B2B exchanges. As these hybrid business models evolve, so will the need for third-party ASPs to manage payment settlements, content management, and issues of buyer/seller authentication and trust. Unfortunately, most purchasing managers and the CEOs that are buying into these e-procurement market visions do not understand all the complexities of these interlocking business and technology relationships.

E-Vision: Enabling the order processing transaction, as difficult at that is, will prove to be the easiest part of e-market services. Ninety percent of the e-markets in existence today will never go beyond transaction management and, therefore, will be unable to realize the objective of dynamic *open sourcing* for its participants. Rather, they will essentially be big supply chain extranets focused on exactly the same set of manufacturers and tier-one suppliers that the old EDI networks were focused on.

■ PRACTICAL STRATEGIES FOR E-MARKET MANAGEMENT

1. E-markets and the companies that use them should have dual purpose: sourcing and supply chain management. Of these, sourcing offers the most compelling business model for long-term e-market success. Over 50 percent of purchasing managers from Fortune 500 companies at a recent conference on B2B exchanges said that their primary reason for establishing or joining e-procurement exchanges was to consolidate and therefore gain negotiation power with their suppliers. While important, this is a shortsighted goal. Instead, visionary executives should look for e-markets that broaden rather than limit their sourcing capabilities. Why? Because just as powerful companies seek to squeeze cost out of their supply chain, so, too, will they be marginalized by more and more powerful customers. Companies should focus their e-market participation on maximizing their ability to do wider strategic sourcing—especially with smaller suppliers that often represent the leading edge of product and component development. After all, the supplier that can offer unique product components, industrial design, or enriched services will be the one that helps a company differentiate its product.

2. E-markets should be evaluated against a checklist of services that include the ability to scale. And by this, we don't really mean infrastructure scalability, although that is important. But the reality is that e-market cybermediaries face two obstacles that require heavy investment in human resources: (1) semantic normalization of product content and (2) small and medium-size supplier enablement. Of these, reconciling semantic differences is the most difficult. The common marketing pitch used by most e-market vendors is that they will accept product content *in any format.* The trick, though, is to make it mean the same thing to all buyers. That means the descriptions of products must be homogenized across multiple suppliers, a task that cannot be accomplished without human intervention. People—especially those with industry knowledge—are expensive and in short supply. Furthermore, small and medium-size suppliers will not typically have the technological staff or expertise to enter e-markets without help. Most cybermediaries do not have enough internal resources to accomplish both of these activities and must rely on outside partners. Companies should investigate the capabilities and references of implementation partners, review any content alliances, and make sure that regional integrators are available to help smaller participants get up and running.

3. Don't forget to ask the *how* questions. Cybermediaries should be able to answer a series of *how* questions. For example: How will they integrate into back-end order processing and financial systems? How will they support less sophisticated suppliers within their e-market? How will they authenticate participants in the e-market? How will they resolve disputes that arise between the buyers and the sellers? How will they anticipate and serve evolving buyer expectations? How will strategic as well as spot sourcing be accomplished? Each company should develop its own weighting system and its own specialized questions, but the key is to focus on both the viability and the capabilities of potential e-market partners.

4. Businesses that look to participate in e-markets should evaluate these markets on their ability (or at least their vision) to offer value-added services beyond just order management. We believe that trusted services such as credit rating, escrow account management, payment management, fraud protection, and authentication of participants will be absolutely essential to the B2B e-market maker. Other value-added services include benchmarking vendor performance against contract promises, quality rating and product comparisons, and objective customer satisfaction feedback from all buyers. Likewise, other e-market services could include auditing and payment performance of buyers.

■ CONCLUSION

The difficulties of cybermediation—the creation and management of e-markets—continue to be underestimated, even by those who are actively involved in them. The development of electronic catalogs, which form the foundation content for e-markets, is relatively straightforward—not simple and easy but at least able to be structured according to a defined taxonomy. However, the broader enabling of e-commerce presents problems that have yet to be solved and, therefore, opportunities for the astute business leader.

Chapter

11

Collaborative Business Communities

When children are little, we teach them to share—their toys, their presents, and so on. But things gradually change. By the time they reach high school, parents increasingly focus on building their competitive spirit—because that's what it takes to get into (and through) college and graduate school.

Our point is that collaboration runs contrary to our culture—and contrary to virtually everything we are taught as individuals. Business-to-business (B2B) collaboration is even more contrarian. The notion that it is good for a company to share critical business information such as pricing, production schedules, inventory levels, and design specifications with its customers and suppliers causes many executives to worry that collaboration could cost them competitive advantage. This is especially true today, with markets in turmoil due to hundreds or thousands of new dot-com start-ups and B2B exchanges. For this reason, as well as others we will explore in this chapter, the amount of B2B collaboration has been limited to relatively bounded joint projects, supported by contractual relationships, and limited to sharing very specific elements of data relative to those projects. But that will change quite a bit over the next few years, as collaborative business communities emerge. But more about that later. Let's back up and discuss the roots of business collaboration.

■ INTERPERSONAL VERSUS B2B COLLABORATION

For the last 10 years, e-business collaboration has been focused on relatively specific, hard to solve, problems like how to create tools to help teams jointly develop documents, or write software, or design new products. Mostly, these teams were made up of people working for the same company, and most of the collaboration involved individuals working together, rather than enabling business applications to share data. But now the focus of collaboration is on B2B collaboration, and on a set of processes and software that enables a select group of enterprises to share data more freely. There are limits to this sharing, in order to maintain competitive advantage. For example, B2B collaboration typically requires preexisting contracts among the participants, a relatively consistent way of defining information, and a common goal—such as being part of the same value chain.

Today, most B2B collaboration is not critical to the process of the enterprises involved and may even be little more than a marketing ploy. For example, two companies announce that they will be collaborating on a next-generation product. The key questions to ask management are

➤ How much money changed hands?

➤ By what process will the people from the two companies work together?

➤ What specific information will they be sharing?

➤ What are the specific deliverables of collaboration?

If the answers to these questions suggest that these companies are locked in a mutually dependent business relationship that will result in process changes and real deliverables, then the collaboration is critical to both companies.

■ MEASURING B2B COLLABORATION

In the last year, hundreds of large coporations have announced B2B consortia, whereby these companies will be collaborating on procurement of commodity items, sharing transportation services, and generally working together on a variety of e-business projects. But will these efforts really be critical to each of the participants? Here are four criteria for measuring the criticality of these industry consortia:

1. **The commitment on the part of all parties must be significant.** This can be measured in terms of the number of people involved, the percentage of their time that is devoted to collaborative efforts, and the frequency of interaction with individuals from other enterprises specifically related to collaboration.

2. **The quality and immediacy of the information being shared.** This may be measured in terms of whether the information shared is just as accurate (to the second) as the information available to systems and persons within the enterprise.

3. **The richness of the collaboration.** This can be measured in terms of the complexity of the information or the number of data elements, the difficulty in gathering the data, the degree to which the information itself has been standardized among the enterprises, or the extent to which it must be converted to the different formats used by the participating enterprises.

4. **The changes that result from the collaboration.** This is measured by the number of changes to systems or specific changes made to a product or service as a direct result of the collaborative process. The more immediate and extensive the alterations, the more consequential the collaboration is to the participating enterprises.

If the collaboration doesn't meet most of these criteria, it is probably not critical to the participants and may not be worth more than a few press releases.

> **E-Vision:** Over the next two to three years, more than 75 percent of Fortune 1000 businesses will be active participants in multiple B2B collaborative processes where they share and mutually act upon critical business information via an online, interactive process.

■ IMPLEMENTING B2B COLLABORATION

As the major enterprise application software vendors, including Siebel, Oracle, and SAP, add collaboration features to their enterprise-level applications, we expect to see real-time collaboration integrated with the tools that companies use to monitor their critical business performance metrics. Over the next few years, the interlinking of the production applications among a group of enterprises that are part of the same value chain will make it possible for applications to know the available-to-promise inventory levels of particular parts from dozens of different suppliers at any given time. So if data from one of these suppliers' manufacturing scheduling applications shows that the supplier will not meet its committed delivery date due to an unforeseen problem, a shipment of substitute parts can be immediately ordered, based on a preestablished agreement, and a factory shutdown can be averted. The automation of this process is possible only if the companies agree to collaborate and share information with one another in near real time.

Making this sort of integrated multienterprise collaboration structure a reality requires that the relevant applications be furnished in the participating enterprises and that they have a shared set of business rules for handling information. This is a major improvement over the situation only a few years ago, when all the enterprises involved needed to have implemented the same version of the same application. But just building collaborative capabilities into software does not eliminate the need for integration of disparate products and processes, which is still expensive. But even with leading-edge systems and data standardization, nothing makes enterprises collaborate faster than a threatening letter from a powerful customer.

■ COERCION DRIVES COLLABORATION

Critical B2B collaboration does exist today, and it does add significant value in such applications as concurrent engineering in the aerospace industry. The image of multiple enterprises actively and openly sharing critical and formerly proprietary business information in order to solve common business problems in a meeting or an interactive Web forum is more myth than reality. Certainly businesses that share customer-supplier relationships do talk to each other and do exchange data. But if one defines collaboration as the open sharing of mutually beneficial business information, the free exchange of ideas, then most e-business collaboration does not qualify. Why? Because there is precious little information that is mutually beneficial in a competitive environment, and there is very little interest on the part of management in helping support weak suppliers or nonpaying customers or any company that could be a potential competitor. Our point is that the best examples of e-business collaboration are actually built on a platform of coercion, and that without coercion, most e-business collaboration would cease to exist.

For example, *vendor managed inventory* (VMI) is a business practice whereby consumer products suppliers and distributors (a.k.a. vendors) are forced to manage the inventory of their powerful retail industry customers. In order to implement VMI and retain large customers, distributors and manufacturers had to share previously secret inventory data replenishment plans with each other and with retailers. The objective of VMI was to make sure distributors and manufacturers owned the problem of ensuring adequate inventory was in place in each retail store to meet demand. Another goal of the retailers was to reduce their carrying charges by reducing their in-store inventory levels. On the bright side, VMI did enable enterprises to lower inventories in stores and at the retailers' distribution centers (DCs). It also enabled retail chains to increase inventory turns and improve the predictability of their order frequencies. On the downside, VMI resulted in substantial build-up at third-party DCs, paid for by the manufacturers and distributors, in order to meet the relatively unpredictable demands of individual retail stores.

But even though VMI was backed by the coercive power of retailers such as Wal-Mart, Kmart, Target, and other mass merchandisers, the business practice lost favor in the consumer product goods channel because it could not coexist effectively with the heavy promotional activities that continue to dominate this industry. An example of this is "trade loading," where the goal of a manufacturer is to "load" their distributors with so much product they have no room to stock the products of other manufacturers. Retailers also discovered that many of their suppliers simply could not handle the technical problem of managing the replenishment of 10,000 to 20,000 retail outlets, as their systems were designed to manage only a few dozen or a few hundred distribution centers.

VMI has fared much better in the industrial B2B sector, since the amount of promotion, deal buying, and trade loading is lower, and the number of locations that have to be replenished is significantly lower than in retailing. Because the participants have fewer process issues to overcome and the replenishment by its nature involves high volume and repeat business, the sectors in which VMI adoption has grown are chemicals, oil and gas, industrial equipment, and building materials. Where VMI programs have succeeded, participating companies have been able to improve the timeliness of information flow, as well as the accuracy of production forecasts, transportation schedules, and product design changes.

■ REQUIRED PROCESS CHANGES

The fact is that, if collaboration is going to work on a widespread basis, a number of counterproductive business practices need to change, and these changes need to happen among all the members of a value chain. If only some members of a chain make these changes, then others will take advantage, and everyone will revert to the old ways. The problem is exacerbated as value chains become more circular and interconnected. Difficult process changes are needed, such as:

1. **Eliminate trade loading.** The practice of overshipping to distributors still persists, particularly among powerful, multiline manufacturers and distributors. The only way to reduce this practice is if manufacturers, distributors, and retailers collaborate on a forecast and a replenishment plan, and then manage by it.

2. **Eliminate deal buying.** In most value chains, significant discounting and deal making exists, and with the growing use of online marketplaces and real-time price negotiation, there is an opportunity for even more deal buying. The result has been, and will continue to be, inventory build-up of particular products at particular points in the value network, and network capacity that does not match up with demand for particular products.

3. **Eliminate data hoarding.** Because almost everyone believes that information is power, most companies and managers engage in data hoarding rather than data sharing. An example we have observed is a man-

ufacturer of small appliances that employs field sales and market analysis staff who devote significant effort toward forecasting demand. Unfortunately, these forecasts are not used to generate purchase orders to suppliers. Instead, historical purchase order data is used, and the forecasts stay in the sales department. The inherent inaccuracy of forecasts based on incomplete information and the cost of updating these forecasts and making purchase order changes over and over again are the best justifications for collaborative forecasting and other forms of collaboration.

4. **Manage conflicting demands.** All enterprises, both small and large, participate in not one but dozens or even hundreds of different value chains and markets, even within the same division or product group. As a result, there is not just one set of coercive demands and collaborative processes that must be supported, but hundreds. It is not reasonable to expect that a multiline enterprise will use the same business process, service the same set of customers, or implement the same set of business applications for all of its products or services and for all of its customers and suppliers. Each of the companies a firm interacts with makes (and will continue to make) conflicting demands on company resources and management. Any collaboration among enterprises will be limited by the need to develop solutions that are as common as possible, while still satisfying all the unique demands of powerful customers and business partners.

5. **Agree on the meaning of data and how to share it.** One of the most important ingredients for successful B2B collaboration is getting the parties to agree about how to share the information, exactly *what* information should be shared, and exactly *what* a bit of data *means* to each of the companies involved. Let's say that there are 10 major players that dominate a par-

ticular value chain, including component suppliers, manufacturers, distributors, resellers, and end customers. Each of these major players is likely to be one of the top players in its market and is accustomed to setting the terms and conditions for their partners and suppliers, while ensuring that their customers are kept happy. This includes a set of "standards" that best suit their internal systems. The management of each of these companies must be willing to compromise in defining the process and technology standards that will form the basis for their collaboration. When a standards-setting meeting becomes a political forum, little can be accomplished. In such cases, third parties may be needed to develop and manage the collaboration among a group of companies.

6. **Develop a revenue and cost-sharing framework supported by all participants.** The price that an end consumer pays is indicative of the total value the consumer places on the sum total of all activities associated with that product throughout the supply chain. Today there is significant variability in the margins among the participants in a supply chain. How should one allocate value and thus the margin that each participant makes from a single end-consumer transaction? Building a benefits structure that balances the rewards with each partner's understanding of the contribution it makes is crucial to maintaining close partnering relationships.

■ NEXT-GENERATION COLLABORATION

Over the next several years, we expect major changes to the B2B exchanges that emerged between 1998 and 2000. Of course, it is easy to predict a shakeout in this segment; indeed, this is already happening. Rather, what we are suggesting is that today's exchange market will fragment, with the addition of collaborative technologies and business practices, combined with the commoditization of exchange-building software. Specifically, many of the exchanges that sought to be industrywide but did little more than introduce buyers and sellers or broker excess inventory will have to be reinvented as micromarketplaces—focused on a single buyer or seller, or on tiny subsegments of an industry. These micromarkets will have limited capitalization (under $5 million) and only a few dozen to a few hundred participants. Managing a micromarketplace will be a practical small business opportunity, as we expect the cost of setting up these micromarkets will drop from several million to under $100,000 by 2003. That is, managing micromarketplaces may well be the McDonald's franchise opportunity of the new century!

At the high end, we are suggesting that only a few exchanges will make the leap to the high ground of collaboration. Accomplishing all of the process changes we describe here and coping with all of the politics and technology challenges of getting companies to open up their systems and procedures to others will require a level of funding that is 10 times the funding of most current exchanges, or $500 million annually. Clearly, this will require the active financial participation of all of the major (and most of the minor) players in an industry, not unlike the industry-specific consortia we mentioned earlier. This next generation of exchanges, which we call *collaborative business communities* (CBCs) will be formed from the merger of several large exchanges and/or consortia within an industry. We do not expect only a single CBC to control any industry, as there would clearly be antitrust issues that would cause the U.S. government (and other global political interests) to intervene. But we do expect that a relatively small number of CBCs will dominate industry landscapes and have a major impact on how the companies in these industries conduct business.

If every company in an industry or value chain had equal power and/or shared the same goals and processes, then these companies could come together and collaborate as equals and design a mutually beneficial process that would be owned and managed by the collective. But this is not the case in capitalist society. We (and our companies) are not equal, and we do not have the same business objectives. For effective collaboration to take place in an environment where the participants have vast differences in their responsibilities, loyalties, and amounts of power in their company and their industry, a third party is needed to manage the collaborative process. This third party must design and implement a collaborative process that enables the preservation of power relationships while simultaneously establishing a common-ground set of business rules, semantics (or the meaning of information), and processes for sharing each of a broad range of information types. We believe that managing the collaborative process among enterprises is a perfect evolutionary path for the most sophisticated of today's vertical exchanges or consortia.

We expect to see the analytical capabilities of today's supply chain management applications incorporated into some of today's industry-focused exchanges to create a next generation of exchange that we call *collaborative business communities* (CBCs). Collaborative business communities will have a core focus on enabling continuous collaboration among partners and customers of a specific trading community, rather than focusing just on buying and selling goods and services, which is what exchanges do today. CBCs must have a technical infrastructure and a set of management services specifically designed to foster collaboration among participants that are unequal in their power and that do not share common goals and business rules, or a common technical infrastructure. We recommend that enterprise executives invest their time and money in the following four different types of multienterprise collaboration, as we believe these will be the critical shapers of business strategies and industry trends over the next several years. As Figure 11.1 shows, these different types of collaboration are distinct enough that they may form the basis of separate CBCs that are focused on specific businesses (hence the four CBC circles for 2003).

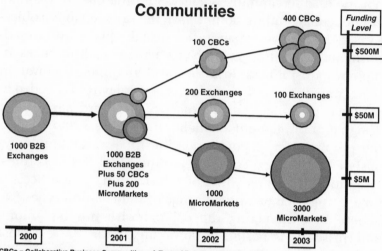

**The Future of Exchanges:
MicroMarkets and Collaborative Business
Communities**

CBCs = Collaborative Business Communities = A Type of Relationship Management
MicroMarkets = Private (one to many) exchanges +specialized many-to-many exchanges

Figure 11.1 Functionally, CBCs will have a core focus on enabling continuous collaboration among partners and customers of a specific trading community, rather than just focusing on buying and selling goods and services, which is what exchanges do today.

➤ Four Types of B2B Collaboration

We do not mean to suggest that CBCs will be an environment where companies will freely share information. Rather, we believe that CBCs must be focused on specific collaborative projects if they are to succeed.

➤ Collaborative Planning and Execution

Rapid technological change, ever shorter product life cycles, and increased supply chain complexity in many industries have all compounded the challenge of matching supply to demand. Close collaboration among supply chain partners can better align the parties and thus enhance the value of the network's combined activities. Collaborative planning and execution is a three-pronged effort, encompassing demand planning, order fulfillment, and capacity planning. It also requires the support of the latest technology. Together, these efforts send a more accurate demand signal throughout the supply chain, which minimizes waste and maximizes responsiveness.

➤ Collaborative Demand Planning

This type of collaboration is accomplished by allowing order and market information to flow upstream continuously from the point of sale, while information on product availability and inventory levels flows downstream. This continuous information loop eliminates or substantially lessens the type of incremental distortion that occurs when each participant responds to its own interpretation of supply and demand data.

➤ Collaborative Order Fulfillment

This type of collaboration goes beyond the types of collaborative planning already discussed. It is characterized by negotiated or joint decisions, such as order size and frequency, and by the transfer of management and possibly ownership of inventory from the customer to the supplier. As a result, there is even less incremental distortion of demand. The greater the synchronization, the greater the value added to the entire supply chain's performance. The most highly synchronized order fulfillment approaches let customer demand data directly drive orders, instead of basing orders on forecasts.

➤ Collaborative Design

In make-to-order industries and so-called heavy industries, where designing a new car, submarine, aircraft, or industrial machine can take years, collaborative design has been around in one form or another for decades. People from multiple companies involved in the process worked together on teams, communicating in the traditional ways. Early technology-enabled collaborative design applications used proprietary software and proprietary networks. They were implemented by firms that could afford the multi-million-dollar investment they required. Others continued to collaborate offline.

Not only is the future of collaborative design moving toward networked Internet applications, it is also moving away from being managed by a series of powerful hub manufacturers working with dedicated subcontractors. As a network-based service, collaboration can be opened up to a larger number of companies with more specialized capabilities at a reasonable cost. This trend in collaboration is appealing because design is a combination of creativity and engineering talent, both of which thrive in small companies with unique areas of expertise. (See Figure 11.2.)

➤ Managing the CBC

> **E-Vision:** The best of the new generation of B2B exchanges will become CBCs over the next three years by providing a common set of processes, a relatively consistent infrastructure, a set of relationship analytics, and the financial impetus to develop mutually beneficial relationships.

➤ CBC Governance Options

To be effective, a CBC needs a management structure that accommodates the need of each participating enterprise to differentiate itself from the other participants. It can work like a trade association or like local government, with elected leaders. On the other hand, a CBC may be driven by a subset of the membership that is willing to fund leadership positions out of its corporate budgets. This is particularly likely when a consortium of major brick and mortar firms adds CBC functionality. Under another alternative, a

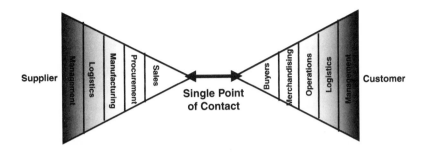

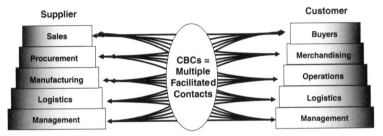

Figure 11.2 Broadening of the scope of collaboration through CBCs.

third party would fund a community manager out of the advertising, transaction fees, or other revenue generated by interactions among community members and with non-members. The CBC manager will be responsible for converting enterprise sell-side requirements to the buy side. The manager also will ensure that the multienterprise production and fulfillment processes are profitable for the CBC members—whether the demand and the orders are generated within or outside of the community.

■ PRACTICAL STRATEGIES FOR COLLABORATION

1. Implement relationship analytics. Relationship analytics are a common set of tools to help the members of a CBC understand and optimize the various aspects of their relationships with partners within the CBC and related CBCs. For example, companies need to develop a consistent set of information for each partner, which requires extracting and aggregating partner data from all existing enterprise applications and databases. Companies need to analyze and differentiate each of their partners, which requires the use of data mining technologies designed to profile and segment partners. Companies need to optimize their interaction with their partners across the various digital and physical channels by developing cross-channel management programs. Companies need to predict the flow of goods and services to and from each partner by SKU, and this requires the use of predictive modeling and personalization tools to make projections about supply and demand that are specific to each business partner.

2. Define an enabling infrastructure. Technically, CBCs will be difficult to implement. One of the reasons is that they require a relatively consistent set of technical interfaces among the members. These common-denominator interfaces include EDI (electronic data interchange), a transaction standard, XML (extensible markup language), a standard for interactive content, and common semantics (i.e., the meaning of data) for use in developing applications. All three are critical for developing truly collaborative communities in which large and small enterprises can participate.

Common semantics almost never happen when integrating preexisting applications, unless there is an agreed-upon technical infrastructure. For example, a message that explicitly associates the inventory-level data element with the value 5 is not useful until the contextual meaning of 5 can be coded and understood by the recipient application. XML as a syntax specification cannot create messages that are fully understood by heterogeneous applications with different data models, any more than the alphabet by itself generates meaningful words or phrases. Therefore, XML is not a magic-bullet technology that will solve the collaboration problem as some vendors would like us to believe.

Even if it were, we do not expect the next two years to produce a consistent implementation of XML. Rather, we expect the litany of vendor-specific (e.g., Ariba and Commerce One) versions that exist today will continue through 2002. Nor do we expect adherence to any single set of semantic standards, regardless of the coercive power behind them. This is in large part because each enterprise will be a member of multiple CBCs. For these reasons, there will continue to be a need for application integration tools and services.

3. Eliminate win/lose relationships and contracts. Enterprise management should work to purge the company of dysfunctional processes that are win/lose relationships and replace them with more agile and collaborative processes that can leverage community-level strategies and metrics. In the short term, enterprises would be well advised to carefully select a small group of partners and processes for collaborative activity rather than looking to industrywide initiatives and standards to provide the solution. The best-of-breed exchanges that CBCs will be those that solve fundamental problems for their members—such as semantic reconciliation across multiple enterprise planning applications or those with the greatest market liquidity (or critical mass of buyers and sellers).

4. Look to a new generation of services vendors to lead the collaboration charge. A wide range of new companies and products will emerge over the next few years to take advantage of the move to CBCs. Already a few leading-edge vendors have introduced Internet-based collaboration to the design phase of production—which generates nearly 80 percent of the cost of bringing a new product to market, according to research by the Aberdeen Group. One such company, Vuent, has focused its Internet-enabled 3-D modeling product, Envision, on the business need to share engineering change orders in real time, in order to detect potential problems in design or manufacturability. Their product enables design teams spread across multiple departments, enterprises, and continents to simultaneously review 3-D designs, annotate them, and get the underlying specifications on particular objects or elements simply by clicking on the objects.

5. Develop a participant formula to govern economic relationships among CBC members. Many relationships among enterprises that are aimed at collaboration fail because there is not a clearly defined formula to govern which party is responsible when various types of problems occur in the course of doing business. Such things are spelled out in a merger or acquisition, but may not be in the less formal collaboration agreements.

6. Evaluate partner support for collaboration. Talk to your most valued business partners and customers. Informally investigate what types of collaboration or other information sharing is in place or contemplated (internally or as part of other B2B collaboration efforts). Find out if they have done the types of process quantification you are undertaking, and see if they found the studies worthwhile. Look beyond initiatives that focus on functional excellence since breakthrough opportunities typically come outside the functions themselves, chiefly at interface points. Pay close attention to the timing of partner participation and do not be afraid to look outside the industry to identify improvement opportunities. Ensure that there is adequate coercion to support the collaboration. Review the list of participants. Make sure that one or two of the companies have the clout needed to force the others to collaborate in a meaningful way, and that they are willing to use their clout to bring this about.

■ CONCLUSION

CBCs offer a managed environment that will support participation in collaboration by enterprises with unequal amounts of power, and these CBCs will encourage enterprises to share data and synchronize their planning and operational activities. CBCs will in many cases require a restructuring of existing supply chain organizations and reskilling of the employees as they are implemented. Leading B2B exchanges and consortia will be key enablers and managers of CBCs over the next two to three years in order to differentiate themselves, as simple buy/sell exchanges become commodities.

Chapter

E-Business Technologies: Realizing Their Potential

Steve Day . . . was the Commander of the recently established Net Force. . . . His Virtual Global Interface Link—virgil for short—had a flashing telephone icon in the upper right corner of the small LCD screen. He touched the icon and a number blinked onto the screen. Marilyn, calling from home. He looked at the timesig. Just after eleven. . . . Virgil was not much bigger than a pack of cigarettes—he'd given *those* up twenty years ago, but he hadn't forgotten how big a pack was. . . . Virgil was a terrific toy. It was a computer, a GPS unit, phone, clock, radio, TV, modem, credit card, camera, scanner and even a little weavewire fax, all in one.

While virgil, as described by Tom Clancy in *Net Force,* sounds a bit like the next generation of Dick Tracy's two-way wrist TV, neither device is so far-fetched. But our book is about practical strategies for e-business, not about cool, slightly fantastic toys. Nevertheless, e-business is being driven by technology, and corporations and executives must adapt or get out of the way. On the other hand, over the last decade we have watched as hundreds of companies with cutting-edge technology were trounced by companies with second-rate technology, but better marketing and management. We have also seen too many companies (both vendors and users) make bad decisions because they were hung up on what was technically possible while ignoring what was practical or economically, politically, and psychologically reasonable.

There are dozens of interesting technologies that have the potential to impact e-business. But most of these technologies will never realize their potential due to resistance such as embedded older technology (e.g., ATMs that can't accept smart cards), resistance by consumers (e.g., personalization that invades privacy), or other market forces (e.g., grocery store kiosks that sit idle because their providers didn't understand how and why people shop). Our task in this chapter is to pick few technologies that are most likely to survive economic, social, psychological, and political challenges, and manage to have the greatest e-business impact on the largest number of companies over the next two to three years.

E-Vision: By 2003, over 60 percent of the world's population will have the opportunity to have at least one option for high-speed Internet access, at a price they can reasonably afford. (See Figure 12.1.)

■ COMMUNICATION TECHNOLOGIES

We believe that some of the most important technologies for e-business over the next two years are those that enable more businesses, more employees, and more consumers to immediately access all types of content, services, and resources from anywhere in the world. Satellite, broadband, and wireless technology will make Internet connectivity ubiquitous over the next several

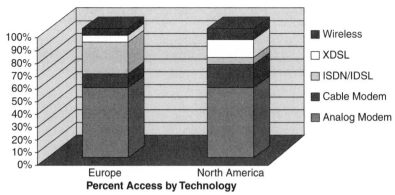

Figure 12.1 Internet access technology uses in 2004. *Source:* Gartner Group.

years, thanks to the dramatic cost reductions in manufacturing and data handling capacity improvements. This access will, in turn, create opportunities for rich content delivery technologies, such as streaming media, discussed later. Collectively, these communication technologies will be needed to deliver acceptable performance for a broad array of interactive Internet applications, as shown in Table 12.1.

Bandwidth is a drug; once you are hooked, you only want more. Currently, carriers are pursuing strategies that only incrementally sate this craving. While cable systems can theoretically deliver up to 36 megabits per second of bandwidth over the same coaxial cable that also carries video programming to television sets, they are typically delivering much lower data rates in practice. The telephone companies and some Internet service providers are using digital subscriberline (DSL) to squeeze capacities of up to several megabits per second out of ordinary copper wire. But these broadband technology solutions pale in comparison to bandwidth enabled by optical networks. For example, a single optical fiber can easily carry more than 600 Mbps to individual users. But all this bandwidth comes at a price.

TABLE 12.1   Data Rates for Selected Broadband Applications

Application	Minimum	Acceptable	Best
Complex Web pages	384 kbps	1.5 Mbps	12.5 Mbps
LAN access (today)	768 kbps	1.5 Mbps	6.0 Mbps
LAN access (future)	768 kbps	20 Mbps	60 Mbps
Entertainment video (NTSC)	1.5 Mbps	6.0 Mbps	12.0 Mbps
Entertainment (HDTV)	19.3 Mbps	19.3 Mbps	38.6 Mbps
Video catalog pages	500 kbps	1.5 Mbps	6.0 Mbps
Videoconferencing	384 kbps	384 kbps	1.5 Mbps
Video games	1.0 Mbps	5.0 Mbps	11 Mbps
Digital photography (consumer)	1.0 Mbps	6.0 Mbps	12.0 Mbps
Digital photography (professional)	3.0 Mbps	20 Mbps	120 Mbps

Source: Kim Maxwell, *Residential Broadband: An Insider's Guide to the Battle for the Last Mile* (Wiley, 1998).

➤ Resistance Factors

Despite the advantages of optical networking, access networks are virtually all copper—an investment worth well over $100 billion—and telephone and cable companies are not eager to abandon this huge sunk cost. The cost of building new fiber-optic networks is extremely high. Depending on the specific conditions under which the network is being built, the cost of building the network can exceed $45,000 per kilometer, with a large portion of that cost consisting of construction and right-of-way acquisition and management. This translates into a cost of $6,000 to $10,000 per home in many areas. Frankly, we doubt consumers will pay thousands of dollars just to merge computers with TVs. This suggests that fiber is more likely to be deployed for businesses, with homes sticking to cable, DSL, and perhaps fiberless optics over the next two years.

➤ Market Context

Some pundits have argued that access to the Internet and its global marketplace will do nothing less than shift the balance of power in e-business and global trade, as South America, China, and Africa implement massive numbers of satellite ground stations and wireless networks and devices. We disagree. Simply having access to the network will not change the rest of the manufacturing and distribution infrastructures of these continents and nations, which are still years or decades behind the so-called developed countries. However, we do see a very bright future for companies in the satellite communications industries, both the market leaders and regional and technical niche players. Major network providers (Cisco, AT&T, Worldcom) will continue to prosper, as will many of the firms focused on providing high-speed satellite and wireless services to Asia, South America, Africa, and Eastern Europe.

■ WIRELESS

Beyond the speed of communications, the other communications technology that will forever change e-business is wireless. Anyone who thinks that cell phones and other forms of wireless communications are ubiquitous in the United States need only travel to Scandinavia or South America to see a much broader range of wireless applications. For example, in Finland it is very common to trade stocks, make reservations, and even locate a restaurant via cell phone or Global Positioning System (GPS), all without talking to a human. We expect that over the next several years wireless will become even more cost effective and reliable with the widespread deployment and availability of high-bandwidth communications satellites, as already discussed.

➤ Resistance Factors

Even as the Internet continues to drive demand for wireless applications such as access to stock quotes, text messages, and other types of information, the very critical nature of this data suggests that e-businesses require even stronger security and guaranteed connectivity than is now typical of wireless communications (at least in North America). We expect that e-businesses will find wireless service to be an unacceptable transmission medium for corporate communications unless wireless providers implement security improvements and offer guarantees that provide a shared-risk environment for these businesses. Even though the reality is that wireless communications are no easier to intercept than any other Internet communications, overcoming public perceptions of risk will be essential in getting businesses to shift critical business applications to a wireless environment.

Of course, many business applications are not suitable for communication via phone. The biggest issue for many of the folks we talked to over the last year is the fact that the telephone interface is not very suitable for entering information or even receiving lengthy or complex data. For example, composing an e-mail message requires a sender hit the "2" key three times to produce a single letter "C"—how many of us have that kind of time? But the "real" wireless devices that will drive the future of e-business are not phones at all—they are computers, handheld PDAs, TV set-top boxes and other networked appliances, including microwaves and refrigerators, as we discuss later.

➤ Market Context

Emerging standards that link PCs and cell phones pose some potential security risks that must be resolved before mission-critical applications can be supported. Another piece of the wireless puzzle is the emergence of a standard protocol for sending and receiving business data via a wireless link. The Wireless Application Protocol (WAP) standard, combined with the Wireless Markup Language (WML), will be used to communicate data over wireless links, similarly to the way Extensible Markup Language (XML) is used to communicate web site content. These emerging standards will provide a relatively consistent technical environment for which companies can design new wireless business applications. While the wireless market, particularly in the United States, is still in turmoil due to a host of incompatible standards and technologies, we believe these will largely be sorted out over the next few years, if only so that the U.S. wireless market can catch up to what is happening in Europe, where a single standard, the Global System for Mobile communications (GSM) standard, has made it safer for technology vendors and users to develop critical wireless applications.

E-Vision: By the end of 2003, wireless communications users will grow by a factor of 10, thanks to new wireless data standards such as bluetooth and the wireless application protocol. New wireless messaging applications and services and the implementation of flat-rate pricing to many countries will be key enablers of the wireless proliferation. Efforts to regulate cell phone usage will become more numerous, but the growing number of other wireless devices and applications will more than compensate for limitations placed on handheld wireless phones.

■ DECENTRALIZED, PEER-TO-PEER NETWORKS

It all started with Napster. But it won't stop there. High-speed Internet access and wireless communications form

E-Vision: By the end of 2003, we expect that tens of millions of users will be active participants in multiple peer-to-peer networks such as FreeNet and Gnutella, freely exchanging information of all types, including copyrighted content. Peer-to-peer exchange hubs as Napster and Scour will be under severe legal and financial pressure, if they survive at all. We suspect blanket usage licenses will be the method through which any compromise among the artists, the entertainment industry, and Internet "distributors" will be reached.

the basis for what is essentially a new way of sharing information. The pervasiveness of cable modems, DSL, and wireless devices enables us to be always connected to the Internet. But the real e-business value goes well beyond always being able to get access to information. The real value is that being continuously connected allows virtually everyone to be a *source* of information storage and computing power to virtually anyone else.

The power of peer-to-peer (P2P) networks came to light earlier this year, thanks to the lawsuits, media coverage, and U.S. Senate Judiciary Committee hearings into the music web site Napster. Charges were filed by record labels and artists that the site allows hundreds of thousands of people to anonymously share digital music, violating copyrights and paying no royalties to the record companies or artists in the process. Lawsuits were also brought against Scour.com, which enables the exchange of digital copies of movies, as well as music. But the bigger threat/opportunity for e-business is to be found in the more general-purpose P2P technologies, such as Gnutella and FreeNet.

Gnutella was created by a team of programmers from America Online, released on a Web page in March of 2000 and pulled off as "experimental" less than 24 hours later. The program is at its core a simple way of trading files among peers, including pirated copyrighted material, without requiring participants to connect with any central computer. This means that, unlike its music-swapmeet cousin Napster, it's virtually impossible to stop.

FreeNet is very similar in structure to Gnutella, is also focused on P2P content sharing. Information is distributed throughout the FreeNet network in such a way that it is difficult to determine where information is being stored, which protects those who allow their computers to form part of FreeNet from the prying eyes of the law. Unlike the Web, where every available piece of information is stored on a particular machine (the owner of which can easily be determined), FreeNet protects those who choose to donate some of their computer's resources to FreeNet by making it extremely difficult to determine what information is being stored on a particular node (even by the owner of that node).

An interesting, related feature of Gnutella is that users can create their own virtual private networks (VPNs). These VPNs can form spontaneously and disappear without a trace. This, of course, makes them ideal for exchanging all forms of illegal or copyrighted content. Such programs threaten the very fundamentals of intellectual property, copyrights, and entrenched business models around the world. Can such technologies be stopped, or should they be stopped?

➤ Resistance Factors

The resistance to Napster, Gnutella, FreeNet, and other P2P content distribution models has been notable in that it has brought together artists, music industry executives, publishers, Christian fundamentalists, trade associations, lawyers, and politicians. All are eager to stop, control, manage, or at least understand this new phenomenon that threatens established interests in every area related to the concept of intellectual property. The best-known example is the rock band Metallica's lawsuit against Napster for copyright infringement. But there are hundreds of law-suits and hearings and a flood of press releases through which the various parties involved in creating and managing intellectual property are actively working to explain and defend their positions.

The resistance to FreeNet and Gnutella is harder to gauge. Unlike Napster, with Gnutella and FreeNet there is no single company (or companies) at the center that is clearly profiting, so there is no one to sue. One of the biggest concerns is that investigations of both Gnutella and FreeNet have uncovered extensive traffic in illegal content. For example, private Gnutella networks are announced in obscure newsgroups or shared quietly among small groups with common interests such as music, movies, stolen credit card numbers, and pirated software.

➤ Market Factors

While it is not at all obvious how the issues surrounding P2P distribution of intellectual content will be resolved, it seems certain that new business practices and agreements will have to be enacted. For example, we would expect to see music industry companies make it easier to broadly license their content for online distribution, following practices such as the blanket licenses that were granted to satellite TV providers so they could show local TV programming (in competition with broadcast and cable TV).

In addition, we expect to see more and more content producers develop subscription models for content, such as the deal offered by MusicChoice.com, or SpinRecords, which offers users exclusive access to live and unreleased music tracks, Webcasts of concerts, music festivals, and parties, all for $4.95 per month. This subscription model has generally been acceptable to artists, as the revenue from the subscriptions is divided among the artists in proportion to how many of the artists' works are downloaded. Sites that use a pay-per-view (or pay-per-track) type of model, such as emusic.com, seem likely to adopt a subscription model as well, as it requires fewer "buy/don't buy" decisions by consumers.

As for the broader P2P networks like Gnutella and FreeNet, the lack of a clearly profiting entity suggests that they will be treated much as hackers are handled today, with law enforcement agencies using undercover cops masquerading as group members, trolling suspect newsgroups and chat rooms to catch those distributing illegal content or copyrighted material via these networks. For those who use Gnutella or FreeNet for legitimate purposes, these tools could prove to be personally cost effective, as well as efficient ways to share files, services, excess storage capacity, and computing power among decentralized networks. But the technologies need to be freed of the stigma that has been attached to them before they will likely be adopted broadly by e-businesses on a large scale.

■ STREAMING MEDIA

Another component technology that will enable the next generation of e-business applications is streaming media. When combined with broadband networks and IP multicasting, streaming media will enable companies to turn virtually every web site into an interactive shopping channel. One of the best examples is sporting events. We already have race car drivers, golfers, and other individual participants with sponsor logos plastered all over them. It has come to the point where they are simply walking (or driving) advertisements who happen to be involved in a contest of some sort. It's not much of a stretch technically to have well-sponsored players, like Tiger Woods, wearing preregistered clothing, so that all a fan has to do is use his or her remote control to point, click, and buy the shirt he's wearing. Movies and TV shows already make extensive use of fee-based product placements. The integration of TV with the Internet will make it possible to buy any and all of the registered items on the set of their favorite drama or sitcom. Finding out what items are registered for sale could be accomplished by dragging a cursor across the screen, and the prices of registered items would appear in a bar across the bottom of the screen.

As of 2000, the applications for streaming media are comparatively simple. The need to inject greater humanity into EC has created demand for two-way video interfaces on online shopping sites. A number of vendors are attempting to solve this problem, including eFusion, E-Talk, Peoplesupport.com, ChatRep.com, and Neuromedia.com. These companies offer services to enable customer service representatives to talk to shoppers over the Internet in real time. The stated objective of many of the customer service applications is to reduce shopping cart abandon rates, which still run 60 percent to 70 percent in most consumer-focused e-businesses. However, both the voice quality and video quality are poor, and we expect it will take at least two to three years before high-speed communications links and compression technology enable voice or video over the Internet to become acceptable in most customer service interactions.

➤ Market Context

As of mid-2000, Macromedia and RealNetworks are the dominant players in the streaming media market, though other companies are entering the market as the number and value of the e-business applications grow. Over the next two to three years, we do expect to see consolidation of second- and third-tier players that do not develop application niches and brand-name customers. Macromedia has launched a series of extremely popular products including Dreamweaver, Flash, and Fireworks. These products are designed to provide highly interactive, multisensory experiences to Web consumers worldwide. Macromedia also supplies the Internet's most popular media players with Flash and Shockwave, now installed in over 100 million systems. Close behind is RealNetworks, which claimed more than 90 million users as of December 1999, with more than 85 percent of all streaming media Web pages on the Internet using RealNetworks' products.

Businesses outside the media and entertainment industries are beginning to employ streaming media for a variety of purposes: to train employees, broadcast executive speeches, and move closed-circuit television onto their data networks. The business value of streaming video in the business-to-business environment will be focused on highly visual, technically complex processes, such as collaborative design. For example, streaming video will shortly enable the nearly instant video collaboration of multienterprise engineering teams spread out all over the world. Such collaboration was previously possible only using proprietary applications and private high-speed networks. This will significantly expand the value of e-business collaboration beyond what has been achieved in companies where special-purpose collaborative design projects are common, such as automotive and aerospace industries. The key business impact is on the elimination of redesign resulting from poor manufacturability. The elimination of this expensive type of rework will result in as much as a 20 percent to 30 percent reduction in cycle time, according to a few of the manufacturers that have been prototyping such solutions (including GE Plastics, Boeing, Caterpillar, and other aerospace and heavy equipment manufacturers).

➤ Resistance Factors

On the other hand, the quality of the streaming video images is still poor, thanks to network congestion. Even in large corporations, where high-speed networks to most desktops are the norm, 44 percent of respondents to a survey by Perey Research (which was commissioned by Real-Networks) said that network congestion and network performance are significant barriers to broad deployment of streaming media. In addition, 32 percent specifically noted the cost of switching out embedded network solutions as a factor that would delay deployment of streaming video technology. So when the leading vendor's own research shows there are major barriers to widespread deployment of streaming media, it clearly indicates that video over the Internet will not be pervasive until a year or more after high-speed network access becomes more pervasive, near the end of the 2002–2003 timeframe. Of course, those firms that have training, design, or other e-business applications that require streaming media before that time can deploy it over semiprivate high-speed networks, such as the Real Broadcast Network (RBN), which is RealNetworks' Internet broadcast service.

E-Vision: By the end of 2003, we believe that streaming media will be a platform for over 10 percent of internal e-business applications, such as training, and will be the platform for about 5 percent of interenterprise applications, such as collaborative design and customer service.

■ COMMUNICATING DEVICES

Today, the Internet is used primarily to link individuals and the computers they use for the purpose of interpersonal communications. But by the end of 2003, we believe the role of the Internet will begin to change, as it gradually becomes a standard information bus that provides a vehicle for sharing information among a variety of Internet appliances or devices, including cars, televisions, handheld computers, and a wide range of monitoring systems and other types of passive and active devices. In short, the Internet will become a network of devices as well as a network of people and computers.

The Internet enabling of traditional appliances, such as refrigerators, microwaves, and home heating systems, will be one of the biggest areas for Internet technology and e-business growth over the next several years. According to the market research firm IDC, the market for the Internet appliances is expected to exceed 89 million units, or $17.8 billion in 2004 versus 11 million units and $2.4 billion in 1999. Many of the nontraditional Internet devices are targeted at keeping office workers continuously connected, such as wireless personal digital assistants. But over the next few years, the range of devices that will be Internet enabled will broaden significantly, with many of the applications focused on giving people constant awareness of everything that is going on at work and at home. Other applications will be focused on automating critical notification and replenishment functions, with preprogrammed devices eliminating the need for human involvement in many mundane tasks.

➤ Market Context: The Workplace

Many of the applications for communicating devices are for the automation and control of manufacturing operations. For example, the sensors that start, adjust, and stop machines, as well as those that monitor and control the work environment (e.g., temperature, humidity, air quality) will increasingly be Internet enabled. Today these sensors are either monitored directly or connected to a proprietary, high-speed factory network, so the value of connecting them to the Internet is to enable a cheap, consistent way of integrating information from all across a business—from factories, to offices, to workers on the road in their cars. Using the Internet as the vehicle for linking these various sensors and monitoring devices enables management to instantly understand the capacities, current status, and potential value of all the assets of an enterprise. In addition, by linking the monitors and sensors directly to applications that can analyze vast quantities of data, these applications can recommend actions to respond to, for example, production shortfalls, missed deliveries, test failures, and other problems with production processes.

➤ Market Context: At Home

Think for a moment about the devastation of a household fire or the tragedy of an elderly loved one, living alone, suffering a heart attack, or a loss of property and the sense of security that results from the crime of burglary. This fear-inducing pitch is one of the key types of appeals that cable, satellite, security, and appliance manufacturers will use to drive the percentage of U.S. homes continuously connected to the Internet from the current level of only about 5 percent to nearly equal the 65 percent of U.S. homes that are equipped with cable television. One of the best rationales for continuous Internet connectivity via cable modem or satellite link is not the ability to shop online without the hassle of dialing in—it is nothing less than ensuring the safety of your home and family. Over the next several years, the widespread deployment of integrated infrared sensors, bar-code readers, and other devices that will communicate household status information, household item consumption data, and other information via the Internet to utility companies, security service providers, and local merchants for the purpose of replenishing household inventories will take place. An increasingly mobile population will be able to constantly monitor the status of a wide variety of devices from anywhere in the world, making adjustments or taking other action as needed. The intelligent, communicating sensors that are being built into next-generation appliances will allow consumers to determine that, yes, they did leave the oven on! Not only that, the technology will allow them to turn it off while still basking in the sun on the beach, by using their communicating handheld computer!

➤ Resistance Factors

For Internet appliances to be widely accepted, there are several market resistance factors that must be overcome. For example, thousands of companies make a nice living today developing, installing, and providing home monitoring and other security services using proprietary technologies and networks. These companies will naturally resist Internet-driven commoditization, particularly of the monitoring service, as that is the most scalable and profitable business model—whether monitoring smoke detectors, motion detectors, or user-worn devices. Manufacturers will readily switch over to new infrared and IP communications technologies, because they can sell add-on or replacement devices to those on their existing customer list. But monitoring services companies will not fare as well, as the Internet will open up these markets to thousands of new competitors. Their resistance will delay most implementations to the end of 2003, and possibly beyond.

In the home, consumers may also resist the commercialization of their appliances. That is, any device with a display and an Internet connection is not only capable of being programmed and monitored remotely, but also capable of displaying advertisements from the manufacturer or, more likely, companies that sell services and consumables. The result, for example, will be refrigerators that can not only scan food items as they are put in or removed, but also monitor inventory levels and order replenishments as items are consumed. Articles promoting smart appliances have generally ignored the fact that appliances will become electronic tendrils, allowing corporations to reach into the home to understand consumer behavior for the purpose of highly targeted, continuous marketing.

> **E-Vision:** By the end of 2003, we believe that as much as 15 percent of the Internet communications traffic flow will be generated by devices that are not currently Internet enabled, including cars, televisions, monitoring systems, and even home appliances such as refrigerators and microwaves.

■ BIOMETRIC TECHNOLOGIES

Biometrics refers to the automatic identification of a person based on his or her physiological characteristics. This method of identification is technically far superior to current methods involving passwords and personal identification numbers (PINs) for various reasons: The person to be identified is required to be physically present at the point of identification and identification based on biometric techniques obviates the need to remember a password or carry a token. With the increased use of computers as vehicles of information technology, it is necessary to restrict access to sensitive or personal data. By replacing PINs, biometric techniques can potentially prevent unauthorized access to or fraudulent use of ATMs, cellular phones, smart cards, desktop PCs, workstations, and computer networks. PINs and passwords may have been forgotten, and token-based methods of identification like passports and driver's licenses may be forged, stolen, or lost.

➤ Market Context

As concerns about security increase, we believe biometric identification applications will become more widely deployed by large (i.e., Fortune 500) corporations to protect proprietary research and development as well as a variety of physical assets. Several different types of biometric systems are now being used for real-time identification; the most popular are based on face recognition and fingerprint matching. However, there are other biometric systems utilizing iris and retinal scan, speech, facial thermograms, and hand geometry that are deployed on a more limited basis, in applications where it is absolutely necessary to verify the true identity of an individual. Going forward, we expect to see broader implementations of biometrics in security, particularly in access control for devices such as ATMs, cellular phones, smart cards, desktop PCs, workstations, and computer networks.

➤ Resistance Factors

For some people, biometrics represents the ultimate intrusion: governments and corporations keeping a database of information about the physical characteristics of citizens, customers, and employees. Therefore, before biometrics can begin to realize its potential, the use of biometric technologies must be explained and justified to the many thousands (perhaps millions) of individuals who would prefer not to be finger printed or tracked in any manner. Any effort to apply biometric technology to e-business must address the very real moral questions regarding what will be done with the information, how it will be collected, and who will have access to it. Otherwise, biometric advocates will find themselves slapped with so many lawsuits and so much regulatory control that they won't get any products to market between court appearances and filling out forms.

> **E-Vision:** By the end of 2003, we believe that biometric technologies will be used for some (not all) identification and security applications by over 30 percent of the Fortune 500 companies, up from less than 2 percent today.

■ BUSINESS AVATARS

The term *avatar* may be considered a loaded word, as it has its origins in religion and mysticism. But since our focus is on the applications of technology and concepts of the problems of e-business, we prefer a more secular definition of the term. For example, Webster's defines *avatar* as a manifestation or embodiment of a person, concept, or philosophy. The Random House dictionary describes an avatar as an embodiment or concrete manifestation as of a principle attitude or way of life. As of early 2000, developers of intelligent software agents have already imbued these agents with (1) communication languages, (2) specific expertise, (3) instructability, (4) a simplified form of reasoning, and (5) the ability to collaborate with other agents. Therefore, our argument that agents will, over the next four or five years, become the digital embodiments of persons, including physical statistics, account balances, negotiation requirements, and color and style preferences, is not such a stretch. The bottom line is that today's shopping bots or agents are very simplistic compared to what is both technically feasible and potentially valuable to both consumers and business buyers. These avatars would enable users to store a relatively complex set of requirements in a secure software tool (i.e., the business avatar) that would have the capability to interface with other programs on servers around the world, analyze the relative closeness of match to statements of need, and potentially negotiate and close a deal.

➤ Market Context

There are many companies working on e-business agents today. For example, Artificial-Life, a Swedish company, has developed the software to give agents a clear personality, which we believe is important in getting humans to interact effectively and positively with agents. Also needed to make agent technology acceptable is a clear value proposition for the end user. We believe this value proposition will, in part, be based on the consumer's need for greater control over his or her information, in the interest of protecting privacy. For example, software agents will likely emerge as intelligent managers of a person's information. Not only will they do mundane things like fill out forms if a site is found to adhere to specific privacy standards, but they can be given enough information to negotiate on behalf of a person. Given the flexible pricing that is becoming common in almost every industry (see Chapter 8), we believe that agents that can negotiate prices, services, guarantees, and delivery dates will be particularly valuable to customers.

➤ Resistance Factors

There are a variety of forces that will work against the broad implementation of business avatars, not the least of which is the lack of standardization for this complex technology. Without some degree of standardization, both agents and business avatars can be rejected or ignored by e-businesses that cannot interface to these programs. Other sources of resistance will be a lack of user understanding of how these work and the unwillingness to entrust to a business avatar the detailed information needed to empower it to act on behalf of the human. The less information provided to the avatar, the less powerful and valuable it can be in the service of humans. Even if business avatars are standardized, some businesses could still resist (e.g., dominant merchants such as Amazon and eBay that don't want their prices or other data compared by customers). Some of these resistance factors will be addressed by education. For example, the point of avatars is to not just shop on price, like simple agents do today, so merchants should welcome the more complex decision criteria of avatars. Other resistance factors such as the lack of standardization and trust will take time and the rise of dominant players such as Microsoft, AOL, and Oracle to embrace the technology in order to break them down.

E-Vision: The current generation of intelligent software agents will be gradually imbued with the capabilities of avatars, but we do not expect them to have a major impact on e-business before 2004.

■ PRACTICAL STRATEGIES FOR EMERGING TECHNOLOGIES

There are several practical things that people can do relative to these emerging technologies: (1) They can review the technology infrastructure of their company and undertake a research program to determine whether and how each of the technologies fits with their plans to evolve this infrastructure over the next two to three years. Once this is done, they can (2) develop a technology rollout plan for their firm that plots a specific timeline for how they will implement these and a variety of other emerging technologies in their e-business. But, let's not leave out the financial angle. People can also (3) invest in some of the technology providers in these markets. We have mentioned only a few companies, but there are many more that should be researched and considered. The risk of such investments by both corporations and individuals should be obvious, particularly since we have only covered some of the resistance factors. There is no one of these emerging technologies that we believe will be significantly more important than the others, but there will be major differences in the relevance and value of particular technologies to a particular business, depending on the industry and application involved. The bottom line is, like it or not, Tom Clancy's vision of the future as dominated by technology is consistent with where we see e-business heading over the next several years.

■ CONCLUSION

Collectively, the technologies we present in this chapter will have a pervasive and relatively near-term impact on how all businesses and consumers understand and use the Internet. While some visions of the future of the Internet are more transforming and possibly profound than the ones presented here, we believe the collective vision offered by these technologies has the advantage of being realizable and actionable. Some of these technologies will prove to be market drivers, demonstrating yet again that the Internet is in its infancy in terms of both penetration and value provided. For e-businesses, some of the best advice we can give is to seek out presentations of vision from the leading technology vendors and consultants. Make every effort to directly involve senior executives at every opportunity. Where senior executives or visionaries drive the company, work to ensure that these visions take both market context and potential resistance into account, so effort and money are not wasted on pursuing unrealizable visions or far-out technologies.

Chapter

Conclusion: Top E-Business Trends and Practical Strategies

Throughout this book, we have tried to maintain a balance: We've tried to get folks excited about where we see B2C and B2B e-business headed over the next two to three years, while avoiding as much of the hype as possible. We also know that we're writing for busy executives and managers who may not have time to read the whole book, but who would like to have a concise summary of the key trends that we believe will drive e-business over the near term, and the practical strategies for profiting from these trends.

So whether you skipped directly to this last chapter or found your way here by reading the 12 chapters that preceded it, we offer you our analysis of the major trends in e-business, from 2001 to 2003, and some practical strategies to help you capitalize on these trends.

1. A shift from starting e-businesses to measuring their contribution. In 1999 and 2000, people couldn't start e-businesses fast enough. There was plenty of VC money and no shortage of entrepreneurial ideas. Many brick-and-mortar (B&M) businesses were and are spinning off dot-coms, and a number of dot-coms were buying

B&M businesses to respond to customer concerns about trust and to support the physical infrastructure needed for tasks such as order fulfillment. What all these events have in common is that they require an understanding of the value of an e-business and a recognition that traditional methods of measuring value no longer apply. This issue is not just about determining an IPO share price, or even ROI, it is about determining whether an executive of an e-business is doing a good job. How do you determine the value of establishing an online brand relative to profitability or sustainable competitive advantage? Is the usability of the company's web site only measured by quantitative statistics? How important is the volume or dollar value of goods sold over the Internet or the number of buyers and sellers participating in an exchange to its ultimate value?

A practical strategy to implement e-business metrics is to begin by making it clear how the value of having an online business will be measured. We would specifically recommend that e-business managers shift from measuring only functions to defining metrics for business processes that cross functional and enterprise boundaries, such as fully delivered cost and order fulfillment precision.

2. The rise of relationship analytics.   Companies are beginning to move beyond customer relationship management (CRM) to what we call collaborative business communities (CBCs), which have collaboration as their core value rather than transactions. Relationship analytics are key to the value of CBCs, because they provide enterprises with a common set of tools to help them understand and optimize the various aspects of their relationships with partners across all the various points of interaction. For example, companies need to develop a consistent set of information for each partner, which requires extracting and aggregating partner data from all existing enterprise applications and databases. Companies need to analyze and differentiate each of their partners, which requires the use of data mining technologies designed to profile and segment partners. Companies need to optimize their interaction with their partners across the various digital and physical channels by developing cross-channel management programs. Companies need to predict the flow of goods and services to and from each partner by SKU, and this requires the use of predictive modeling and personalization tools to make projections about supply and demand that are specific to each business partner.

Relationship analytics are the result of the integration of the analytical tools focused on customers (i.e., as part of CRM applications from companies such as ePiphany, Kana, and Siebel) with the analytical tools in today's supply chain management applications. A first generation of these analytical tools and services are offered today by I2, Oracle, SAP, and other ERP vendors. Another practical issue that must be resolved is determining who actually analyzes and manages the relationships of the enterprise, and who has access to the information about these relationships. Because a relationship is not owned by one party or another, the analysis of that relationship can be effectively owned or managed by either party. As a result, we expect that relationship analytics will be a third party service that will help the best-of-breed exchanges of 2000 and 2001 become the collaborative business communities of 2002 and 2003.

3. The rise of the business service provider (BSP). In 1999 and 2000, the rage was e-business incubators— companies that provide funding, technology, office space, a wide range of administrative services, and even the rental of executive talent to start-ups. Companies such as CMGI, Divine Interventures, and dozens of others bet that the capital markets would reward them well for nurturing e-business "bright ideas." However, with the markets flat, a more conservative approach is required. Business service providers (BSPs) will emerge over the next few years, based on the original incubators' shared services model. The shared services model reduces risk for the entrepreneurs, and it enables the BSP to better optimize demand for resources among the portfolio of companies. It also makes these BSPs the natural hubs for B2B collaboration, value chain management, and other services that must be implemented and managed above the level of the single enterprise.

Another key function of the BSP is to manage the company toward profitability—which is much easier with a shared services model, because this model won't break the bank of start-ups with limited capital.

The dominant revenue model for BSPs is likely to be subscription based, with pricing based upon the number of monitored processes or services or data elements. We see at least four distinct opportunities for BSPs. The first is monitoring the capabilities of the technical infrastructure to meet evolving demand from Web users, value chain partners, and internal users. The second opportunity is monitoring business process capabilities (e.g., the number of tasks handled, the flow of information, the number of customers satisfied). The third opportunity is to focus on quality: monitoring customer satisfaction and employee satisfaction, and integrating this information with product quality metrics. The fourth opportunity focuses on monitoring other service providers, focusing on how well these other providers comply with existing service-level agreements. In some cases, the services offered will be a rehash of existing consulting services, but with a focus beyond the enterprise using a set of Internet-based methodologies. In other cases, the services will be as innovative as the tasks and processes they are monitoring. Again, the focus will be on the relationships among enterprises, rather on the performance of a single enterprise.

4. A shift from online "shopping" to more automation of the buying process for B2B and B2C. Over the next few years, we believe that new developments in agent technology and the automation of buying, selling, and other online transactions will take us beyond the era where users have to go to one (or more) web sites in order to buy or sell something. Too many web site designers are still stuck on the concept of trying to create attractive and involving content to get human beings to visit a web site, place an order, and watch his or her e-mail for notice of the transaction's execution. Over the next one to three years, we will see the rapid emergence of agent-based solutions that monitor a company's inventory, based on preestablished criteria, and place a sell order for the excess, monitor who buys it, arrange for delivery, and record the profit or loss, all without anyone having to visit the web site of an e-market of any sort. The intelligent agents used by companies and by individuals will be programmed based on preexisting agreements or have the freedom to choose the most commercially attractive e-service to carry out the transaction. Our model for how this will work is drawn from the algorithms used by telephone switching systems and transportation management systems. Both systems determine the least expensive and most efficient route.

A practical strategy for coping with the automation of corporate interactions with business customers and consumers should focus on defining a specific process or task that an agent could be developed to handle. An example of what a sophisticated agent could do is develop a set of industry norms for service contract duration and coverage, while gathering pricing data relative to the products covered by these agreements. The goal would be to give potential buyers a sense of the relative value of service contracts compared to the price of the products. Agents could also be used to keep track of changes in any set of data being monitored (e.g., inventory levels), relative to preestablished norms, and execute a given action on the basis of the delta between the norms and the current levels, considering the rate of change in the data over time. In short, the faster something is selling, the larger the reorder should be.

5. The shakeout of the B2B exchanges continues.
One of the reasons we expect the shakeout to continue is
that there are only so many exchanges that can live up to
their hype of being the one global place to meet all your
needs. Another reason for a major shakeout is that since
the market collapse, corporations no longer believe there is
any urgency to join an exchange, which means little or no
liquidity on 90 percent of the exchanges. The third reason
that we expect the B2B exchange shakeout to continue is
that most of these exchanges are shockingly inadequate in
meeting the basic technical requirements of businesses.
For example, of the 600 exchanges being tracked by AMR
Research, only 10 provide application integration with the
members' own systems. This means that an order or
request or update entered into one of these exchanges must
be entered again (or manually converted) to the requirements of each member's applications. If the exchange
member uses Oracle, SAP, or other packaged applications
vendors, solving this problem is easier. Many companies
require custom applications integration, which they had
expected to find in the exchange but did not. Our point is
that many of these exchanges were designed around the
model of customers going to a web site and manually entering orders. This simplistic, consumer-oriented model is the
very thing that will doom most of the exchanges that have
spent all of their money on marketing and have none left
to provide applications integration. The shakeout will force
perhaps 70 percent of the B2B exchanges to more narrowly
define their focus—becoming micromarkets or private
exchanges for a single buyer or seller. These micromarkets
will give second- and third-tier exchanges a new lease on
life and/or the opportunity to build defensible niches. On
the other hand, perhaps 10 percent of the best-of-breed
exchanges will add the necessary applications integration
and collaboration functionality to become collaborative
business communities (CBCs), as described in Chapter 11.

A practical strategy to prepare for the shakeout among
the B2B exchanges is to avoid joining any exchange that

does not have a lot of liquidity—active buying and selling—particularly by major industry players. The management team should also be able to demonstrate to your
satisfaction how it has maintained buyer and seller loyalty
in the face of challenges from direct competitor exchanges.
In general there is little value to starting or joining yet
another exchange in industry X. Even getting a substantial
piece of equity in an exchange may not be enough to justify participating in a me-too project. Look for transaction
volume and revenue numbers from management, rather
than lots of hand waving and talk about getting to market
first.

   **6. E-fulfillment or logistics becomes less of a differ-
entiator for enterprises.**   Over the last several years, companies such as Wal-Mart in the physical world and Amazon
in the online world stood out from the crowd in part due to
their ability to move goods faster and more reliably than
their competitors. Despite high-demand volumes and the
difficulty of managing tens of thousands of SKUs, their ability to fulfill orders faster and keep goods in stock proved to
be a major competitive advantage in the marketplace. But
this is changing, as more companies begin to understand
the importance of e-fulfillment and logistics management;
some are attempting to hire better e-fulfillment management, while other companies outsource this to professionals (i.e., third-party logistics and e-fulfillment companies).
But from 2001 to 2003, we believe the trend will be toward
logistics aggregation—where multiple enterprises in an
industry or a value chain form a consortium to share an
e-fulfillment infrastructure along the lines of the General
Mills-led consortium announced in early 2000. While this
will level the playing field for e-fulfillment among the
members of the exchange or among the participants in a
particular value chain, we expect it to set the stage for a
global battle for logistics optimization among exchanges.
   A practical strategy to help companies take advantage
of this trend is to speak with the persons in charge of

sourcing (i.e., inbound logistics) and distribution (i.e., outbound logistics) at your company. Learn what efforts are under way to move toward an e-fulfillment model and what relationships the company already has with third parties and exchanges that provide inbound or outbound logistics management. The objective is to figure out the best way to improve the efficiency of e-fulfillment, while getting the support of those managers already involved. It would also be worthwhile to speak with the CEOs of any exchanges already focused on your industry or on those value chains of which your company is a participant. The purpose is to determine what e-fulfillment capabilities these exchanges can offer already, and what services (e.g., automated replenishment) they are planning to implement. If one or more third parties offer services that could improve the operations or reduce costs versus current in-house capabilities, outsourcing e-fulfillment should be seriously considered.

7. E-business expansion will continue. Again, this is easy to say, but it is much more difficult and risky to have a clear e-vision regarding the dimensions along which this expansion will occur. Figure 13.1 shows that the next generation (Gen2) of e-business will have the following characteristics:

➤ Gen2 will be driven by Europe, Asia, and South America, rather than the United States, with the pattern of B2C followed by B2B growth that the United States experienced being repeated in other regions.

➤ Gen2 in the United States will be driven by many of the undifferentiated exchanges refocusing on micromarkets for single buyers or sellers, or aimed at narrow industry-specific and process-specific segments.

➤ Gen2 will be driven by a shift from an emphasis on attracting casual browsers to an emphasis on automating necessary Web-based tasks, as using the Internet becomes a necessity.

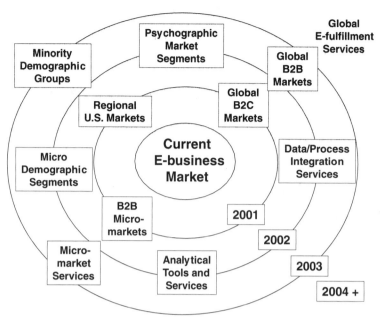

Figure 13.1 Dimensions and timing of Gen2 e-business. *Source:* eMarket Holdings.

➤ Gen2 will also be driven by corporate expenditures aimed at integrating the channel and process complexity of doing business over the Internet with traditional sales channels and business practices.

The most important aspect of a practical strategy to get the jump on the move to Gen2 of e-business is to design business plans, financial models, and technical architectures around the elements of e-business that will coalesce in the 2001 time frame. Specifically, we suggest that any emerging e-businesses steer clear of trying to develop broad-based B2B exchanges as most vertical segments are already too crowded. Further, we suggest avoiding most B2C plays, unless they have a strong international revenue component. But these crowded markets do create other opportunities. For example, there are many vertical and horizontal opportunities to help companies manage the confusing array of online channels for sourcing and sell-ing. Last, we suggest that companies invest in technolo-gies, applications, and services that will add personality and attitude to e-businesses, as these will generate both emotional involvement and customer loyalty, particularly in the B2C market segments.

8. First-mover advantage becomes a history lesson, and execution is all that matters. Before the Internet changed the rules, people used to talk about the risks of being first into a market. Being a pioneer meant opening up a market—for someone else. Today, dozens of articles have been written about the value of first-mover advan-tage. Over the last few years, the uncharted territory of the Internet provided a new world of opportunity for those firms that won the land rush to be the first to define a par-ticular B2B or B2C segment, or were the first to implement a particular business model. Of course, these firms also had to stake their claims with multi-million-dollar adver-tising campaigns. But, let's face it: Whether we're talking about coal mining or e-business, all but one of us is some-thing other than first. The question is: How can compa-nies that are not first movers (and who don't have Amazon's $50 million annual advertising budget) manage to survive and thrive as e-businesses? The answer sounds incredibly cliché: It's all in the execution. Many first movers rushed into the e-business market with a clever idea, a veteran CEO, a few talented developers, a two- to three-page business plan and, of course, $20 to $30 million in venture capital. Over the next few years we see a differ-ent scenario. The steep decline in the B2C market will be followed by a comparable decline in the B2B market, which will force more companies to actually prove their business can work before they get either customers or funding. In short, we see a shift from bravado to capability, and from marketing to execution. Beyond executions, we believe that differentiation will be based on who does the best job of implementing "e-relationships"—the relationships between the human and the web site, as well as the electronic enablement of the relationship between a company and its trading partners.

In conclusion, after analyzing the e-commerce and e-business markets for nearly 15 years, we have learned that e-business is all about trying to get people and organizations to change how they do things—how they spend their free time, how they buy things, how they manage information, how they provide goods, services, and how they participate in their marketplace and community. We have also observed that oftentimes those who want to instigate change have a vision—an e-vision, if you will—of how things will work better if only certain changes would occur. We believe the biggest failures in e-commerce and e-business result when the instigators of change do not make the effort to understand the perspective and the motivations of the other people and organizations that they are trying to change. The results are projects that never get funded, marketing campaigns that fall on deaf ears, exchanges that never attract enough buyers and sellers to be viable, and standards that are not implemented.

On the other hand, the biggest successes in e-business will be experienced by those managers and organizations that take the time and effort to define exactly who and what they want to change, exactly what changes they want to bring about, and exactly how they are going to measure the changes and the value created by these changes. We believe that every business plan, every mission statement, and every policy and procedure of an e-business should reflect a fundamental understanding of the changes that the company seeks to bring about, the incentives it will use to cause these changes, and the methodology that management will use to measure their progress in implementing the changes. Without this focus on change, an e-business is just a business with an "e" in front of it.

Appendix

Selected Web Sites Used or Referenced in Our Research

■ CHAPTER 1: E-CONSUMERS: POWER TO THE PEOPLE

www.fool.com	The Motley Fool, an excellent, relatively objective source of information for individual investors.
www.forrester.com	Forrester Research, one of the leading market research companies focused on the Internet.
www.alladvantage.com	All Advantage, one of the leaders in the "pay you to surf the Web" marketing companies.
www.epinions.com	ePinions, a leader in paying users to provide content based on the number of people who view that content.
www.sfgate.com/cgi-bin/article.cgi?file=/chronicle/archive/2000/01/22/BU40556.DTL	*San Francisco Chronicle* article comparing various web sites that pay users to write their opinions.

■ CHAPTER 2: BUILDING E-MOTIONALLY INVOLVING E-BUSINESSES

emotion.salk.edu/emotion.html	Contains a nice overview of research on emotion.
www.cc.gatech.edu/gvu/reports/index.html	Georgia Tech University's Graphics, Visualization and Usability center has lots of free, useful research on the Internet and how people use it, among many other subjects.
http://eratings.com	Nielsen//NetRatings has lots of useful information on Internet statistics, but it's for subscribers. Some useful free data is in their press releases.

www.marketingandsales.com/MS/111/ Achieving_Customer_Delight _Organization.htm	Web site for the book we cite *Achieving Customer Delight in Your Organization* (Paul).
www.rheingold.com/howard	Web site for the author of *Virtual Community* (Rheingold). An entertaining and eclectic site.
www.theonion.com	A newspaper parody site that is one of the best sources of sophisticated humor on the Internet.
netaddiction.com/bio/bio.htm	The Center for Online Addiction, started by Dr. Kimberly Young, author of *Caught in the Net.*
www.press/uchicago.edu/cgi-bin/hfs.cgi/ 00/13841.ctl	Site for Jack Katz's book, *How Emotions Work.*

■ CHAPTER 3: FROM E-TAILING TO CONSUMER AUTOMATION

www.nrf.com	The National Retail Federation's web site, which is useful mainly if you're a member of the NRF.
www.ecommerce.gov	The U.S. government's joint e-commerce initiative web site, with lots of useful information and statistics.
www.botspot.com/dailybot	The Bot Spot, which includes a very useful description of bots or agents, and analysis of some of the uses of this technology for e-tailing, etc.
www.agorics.com/new.html	A very useful site for understanding the different types of auctions.

■ CHAPTER 4: BUILDING AND MANAGING MICROBRANDS

www.adbusters.org	*Adbusters*, an online magazine, with a lot of critical—and funny—things to say about the advertising industry.
www.creativegood.com/survival	Creative Good is one of the best sources of research on online customer satisfaction. They offer a free *Dotcom Survival Guide.*
www.engage.com	Engage is one of the more comprehensive Web marketing companies we encountered.
www.viralmarketer.com	Some case studies on viral marketing, courtesy of Reach Online, a marketing company.

■ CHAPTER 5: CAN CUSTOMER LOYALTY SURVIVE THE WEB?

www.hbsp.harvard.edu/products/hbr/julaug00/R00410.html	Recent and very interesting *Harvard Business Review* article, called "E-Loyalty: Your Secret Weapon on the Web," by Frederick F. Reichheld and Phil Schefter.
www.freeperfectnow.com/book/book_frameset.html	Web site for Robert Rodin's book, *Free, Perfect and Now.*
www.bristolgroup.ca/main.html	Web site of the Bristol Group, authors of the study on loyalty, that we cite.
www.aicpa.org	Site of the American Institute of Certified Public Accountants and home of the WebTrust program.

www.thestandard.com/research/metrics/ display/0,2799,17375,00.html

A recent article on Web loyalty, called "Wanted: Loyal E-Shoppers," by David Lake in TheStandard.com.

■ CHAPTER 6: HOW TO COMPETE WITH THE UNKNOWN

www.prenhall.com/stratplus/html/ porter.html

Brief description of Michael Porter's five competitive forces.

http://spuds.cpsc.ucalgary.ca/ articles/WN96/WN96HF/WN96HF.html

A study published by Brian R. Gaines, Mildred L. G. Shaw, and Lee Li-Jen Chen at the Knowledge Science Institute of the University of Calgary on the effect of building communities on the Web.

http://bprc.warwick.ac.uk/bp-site .html#SEC4

List of research sites on business process reengineering and technology.

http://agents.umbc.edu

University of Maryland Baltimore County resource for education on avatars and intelligent software agents.

http://ecommerce.media.mit.edu/ tete-a-tete/mas.html

Chart showing one view of how agent technology matches buying behavior.

■ CHAPTER 7: WEB CHANNEL CONFLICT

http://mckinseyquarterly.com/home.htm

Articles on a variety of electronic commerce subjects, including channel conflict, from *The McKinsey Quarterly*.

www.sidley.com/cyberlaw/features/ selling.asp#A. Channel Conflict	Paper discussing the implications of selling directly over the Internet by Ron Ben-Yehuda, a partner at Sidley & Austin.
http://cwis.livjm.ac.uk/bus/busndere/ ae3037/MAIN3037.HTM	Series of lectures by I. Noyan Dereli, Liverpool Business School, Liverpool John Moores University.

■ CHAPTER 8: THE END OF FIXED PRICING

http://cism.bus.utexas.edu/works/ articles.html	Research papers available from the University of Texas at Austin.
http://appell.crmproject.com	White paper written by Moai Technology and Andersen Consulting on the effect of dynamic pricing.
www.ibm.com/iac	Technology papers on a wide range of electronic commerce subjects including pricing methodologies available from the IBM Institute for Advanced Commerce.
www.research.ibm.com	Research topics, technology papers, and electronic commerce links from IBM.
www.ebreviate.com/education/ whitepapers.htm	White papers on auctions and e-procurement.

■ CHAPTER 9: EMERGING E-COMMERCE BUSINESS MODELS

www.brint.com/Systems.htm	List of research for the study of complex technology adoption theories.

http://ecommerce.ncsu.edu/topics/ intro/intro.html	An online guide to the graduate-level management course taught at North Carolina State University by Professor Michael Rappa. Link to several interesting discussions of business models and electronic commerce.
www.electronicmarkets.org/ electronicmarkets/electronicmarkets .nsf/pages/archive.html	Archive of articles on electronic commerce subjects available for purchase from the University of St. Gallen, Switzerland.
www.marshall.usc.edu/main/magazine/ index.html	Magazine of the Marshall School of Business University of Southern California. Includes articles on emerging business models and new intermediaries.

■ CHAPTER 10: THE EVOLUTION OF B2B E-MARKETS

www.unspsc.org	Site for the Universal Standard Products and Services Classification (UNSPSC) Code organization, an excellent source for understanding the complexities of product presentation taxonomy.
www.netmarketmakers.com/reports/ index.asp	List of research report on B2B e-commerce.
www.unspsc.org	Standards body made up of the United Nations body for Trade Facilitation and Electronic Business (UN/CEFACT) and the Organization for the Advancement of Structured Information Standards (OASIS). They have initiated a worldwide project to standardize XML business specifications.

www.b2business.net/eCommerce_Info/
B2B_Articles

Links to research and articles
on B2B e-markets.

www.superfactory.com

A useful web site on
manufacturers, including
research on supply chain and
online selling.

■ CHAPTER 11: COLLABORATIVE BUSINESS COMMUNITIES

www2.metagroup.com/cgi-bin/reFrame
.pl?http://domino.metagroup.com/
CollabCoeff.nsf/CollaborativeSurvey

Meta Group, a market
research company, has
developed a survey to
measure the readiness to
collaborate. This is the site
where the survey can be
found.

www.vendormanagedinventory.com

This is a simple site with
answers to some frequently
asked questions about VMI.

www.probe.net/neubauer/sp1999/
ism6026/assign3/robosc3.htm

A nice summary description
of network loading, a.k.a.
trade loading.

http://collaborate.com/publications/
intranet.html

A web site with a number of
publications and case studies
on collaboration.

■ CHAPTER 12: E-BUSINESS TECHNOLOGIES: REALIZING THEIR POTENTIAL

www.gartner.com

Gartner Group is the leading
IT market research firm. It
also includes Dataquest. It
conducts extensive research
on the impact of IT on
e-business, for its subscribers.

http://webbooks.net/books/_Wiley2/
Maxwell.html

The reference site for Kim
Maxwell's book, *Residential
Broadband.*

www.zdnet.com/intweek/stories/news/ 0,4164,2555816,00.html	An interesting article in *Interactive Week* entitled "Fiberless Optics."
www.wirelessdata.org/index/ read.asp?id=178	A web site that offers a compendium of research studies on the wireless technology market.
www.bluetooth.com	An extremely comprehensive web site devoted to the bluetooth standard for wireless communications.
www.zeropaid.com/gnutella	One of the best sites with information on Napster, Gnutella, Freenet, and other decentralized (peer-to-peer) file-sharing programs (though sites on this subject tend to change frequently).
http://freenet.sourceforge.net/index .php?page=front	A site specifically devoted to the Freenet distributed computing project.
www.streamingmediaworld.com	A useful online magazine devoted to streaming media.
http://netappliances.about.com/gadgets/ netappliances/library/weekly/aa050300a .htm	A section in About.com (a valuable research tool) devoted to Internet appliances.
http://freenet.sourceforge.net/index .php?page=front	A site specifically devoted to the Freenet distributed computing project.
www.afb.org.uk	A rather academic site devoted to biometric technology, with lots oflinks to other biometric technology sites.
www.kdnuggets.com	A portal-like site devoted to data-mining technology, with lots of links.
www.ai.mit.edu/pubs.html	The web site of the artificial intelligence lab at MIT, with a searchable database of AI research publications.

www.agentlink.org

A Europe-focused research site devoted to agent technology and agent-based computing.

www.artificiallife.com

Artificial Life, a software vendor that builds agents.

■ CHAPTER 13: CONCLUSION: TOP E-BUSINESS TRENDS AND PRACTICAL STRATEGIES

www.bcr.com/bcrmag/2000/05/p08.asp

An article from *Business Communications Review*, which discusses the concept of the management service provider, or what we refer to as the "business service provider."

Index